WITS, FLAKES, AND CLOWNS

WITS, FLAKES, AND CLOWNS

The Colorful Characters of Baseball

Wayne Stewart

ROWMAN & LITTLEFIELD
Lanham • Boulder • New York • London

Published by Rowman & Littlefield
An imprint of The Rowman & Littlefield Publishing Group, Inc.
4501 Forbes Boulevard, Suite 200, Lanham, Maryland 20706
www.rowman.com

6 Tinworth Street, London SE11 5AL

British Library Cataloguing in Publication Information Available

Library of Congress Cataloging-in-Publication Data Available

ISBN 978-1-5381-2521-2 (cloth : alk. paper)
ISBN 978-1-5381-2522-9 (electronic)

♾ ™ The paper used in this publication meets the minimum requirements of American National Standard for Information Sciences Permanence of Paper for Printed Library Materials, ANSI/NISO Z39.48-1992.

CONTENTS

ACKNOWLEDGMENTS

A huge thank-you goes out to all members of the media, players, coaches, and managers (more than 140 helpful people) who granted me interviews over many years. There would be no book without them. Thanks also to my editor, Christen Karniski, who has provided great input for this book.

INTRODUCTION

This book is the result of on-again, off-again research and exclusive interviews with more than 140 former and active players, coaches, managers, broadcasters, and other baseball people over nearly 30 years. From players who were just a wee bit "off," to those who were off the wall, to the ones who were completely off their rocker, humor is the common denominator for the subjects of this book. Further, the lines often blur—a baseball flake may have also been quite witty, and not all clowns were flakes—but labels don't matter. Funny is funny.

This book will cover many, but not *all* of the men who fall into at least one of our groups. In fact, more than 135 characters are included here. Nor is every funny line or great tale about these men included. That's especially true of the most widely chronicled characters such as Casey Stengel, Yogi Berra, and Dizzy Dean. For such men, the book provides a sort of ample Whitman's Sampler of some of their most famous quotes and escapades while trying to focus more on new, exclusive commentary and lesser-known anecdotes.

Limiting a bit of coverage of those men also freed up room for some lesser-known stories and quotes about players such as the wonderfully zany Moe Drabowsky, the refreshingly wild Joe Charboneau, and the witty Andy Van Slyke. Casual baseball fans will be introduced to colorful men such as Doug Rader, Jerry Reuss, and Turk Wendell. Today's players are represented by men like Bryce Harper, Yasiel Puig, and Francisco Lindor.

The quotes used in this book are primarily taken from exclusive interviews conducted by the author, while some quotes have been published in multiple sources. When material came from one specific, outside source, an endnote is provided. All statistics in the book are through the 2018 season.

The dates inside the parentheses next to each player's name indicate the range of years he spent in the major leagues, even when there was an interruption in his big league career. If that player was also a manager, the *span* of years running from his first managerial job through his final year is also given. The order of the players presented in each chapter is chronological.

1

BACKGROUND

To paraphrase writer George Plimpton, in the world of sports, the smaller the size of the ball, the richer that sport is in its interesting and humorous quotes and anecdotes. He observed that there are tons of great golf and baseball stories and some, but considerably less, from football and basketball. Then he whimsically noted that there are certainly no good stories about beachballs.

Aside from the fact that there are absolutely no funny tales from the sport of ping-pong, Plimpton was correct. Without a doubt, baseball is the richest source of humor. Furthermore, a disproportionate percentage of the laughs that baseball provides comes from a cadre of colorful characters.

One point about today's players—they are much more educated than those from long ago, frequently coming to the pros from college campuses, not straight off the farm like a Bob Feller or out of an inferno of a factory or emerging from a dungeon of a gloomy mine, blackened by coal dust. Current players are also much more sophisticated—no player nowadays sports a nickname such as Rube, Babe, Dizzy, or Daffy.

Many critics contend that what now passes for a nickname is frequently simply a shortening of a surname such as calling Jeff Bagwell "Bags." In a 2007 interview, Cleveland coach Joel Skinner went a step further when he said, "I think the characters of the game back in the '50s and '60s are gone."

In 2009, Andy Van Slyke said he felt that perhaps "one of the things that's missing is a little more fun in the game." He mourned the demise of bench jockeying: "When I first came up [in 1983] players would rag on the other players, and it wasn't that you were disrespectful, it was just part of the chatter. Again, you weren't really being derogatory, it was just part of the language—and that chatter is basically gone. It's a part of the game that I miss, but the game changes in a lot of ways and that's one way the game has changed." He seems to feel that players today are, by and large, much more professional, but that approach is somewhat clinical, eliminating much of the bench jockeying and the color of the game.

All-Star Mark Teixeira added, "It's a friendlier game now. Guys play [for several teams] so often nowadays that you could be on four or five different teams within five years. It's definitely changed. It's always nice to see former teammates. Playing against guys kind of makes the big leagues one big happy family."

Award-winning reporter Gus Garcia-Roberts said, "Players these days are more professional in every way. For example, they work out, where they used to think the gym was bad luck. You might be less inclined to do [pranks] to your colleague who's making $25 million and takes himself very seriously than you might have in the past when it was somewhat more of a Beer League atmosphere."

Some feel that baseball has gone from the days of vicious bench jockeying by colorful characters, when venom and vulgarities were spewed between dugouts during games, to today's mannerly ways where one would almost expect to see a library-like "Silence, please" sign in both dugouts. But wait a minute—maybe every generation contends colorful characters are missing from the game. Just as Teixeira and Van Slyke expressed such thoughts rather recently, a 1972 *Baseball Digest* article stated the same beliefs, citing a player from the 1950s who echoed that lament.

Joel Skinner qualified his stance a bit, saying that Casey Candaele "was a guy who definitely kept the clubhouse loose, and you look at guys like [5-feet, 10-inch, 214-pound] John Kruk who had some quotes out there like, 'I'm not an athlete, I'm a baseball player.' So, the colorful guys are still out there."

In 2007, Atlanta pitcher Buddy Carlyle also argued that flakes and colorful characters still abound. "They're all over the place. It doesn't take too long to look around and find guys that'll make you laugh in the clubhouse."

Therefore, while today's game *may* have a somewhat diluted pool of characters, every era has had its share of flakes, wild men, and colorful characters. The bulk of this book focuses on men who played, coached, or managed in at least one season from around 1950 through 2019.

Stretching the time frame here to provide some background, a look at some flakes from long ago is in order. Start with country bumpkin Rube Waddell, who broke into the majors in 1897. His 349 strikeouts in 1904 established a record that lasted 61 years until Sandy Koufax broke it, and Waddell, who owned a 2.16 earned run average (ERA), led his league in K's six straight years. Through 2018, only two lefties—Koufax and Randy Johnson—ever fanned more batters than Waddell, and just one righty, Nolan Ryan. Waddell once won a 21-inning game (that featured just 19 total players) in which he strung zeroes on the scoreboard for 20 consecutive innings.

This was a free spirit who loved racing to the scenes of fires, often chasing right behind firetrucks. On one occasion, wearing a fireman's hat, he actually helped put out a blaze and once reportedly rescued a woman from a fire. He waded into a Florida lake to wrestle alligators. Years after he defeated Cy Young in a marathon contest, he exchanged the ball he claimed he had used in that game to a bartender for drinks—and he repeated that scam on numerous other barkeeps for years to come. One publication called him the "Sousepaw." After some wins, he departed the mound by turning cartwheels, and he poured ice water over his arm before pitching, boasting that if he didn't, his fastball would scorch the catcher's mitt.

"Connie Mack told me that Waddell was the greatest pitcher he ever managed," recalled Hall of Fame broadcaster Ernie Harwell. "He said he had more stuff than anybody, but he had a 10-cent head." Mack felt Waddell, who had a short attention span and may actually have been slow, lacked any intention to be a responsible baseball player. Teammates saw him as a big kid, and Waddell even joined young kids on sandlots to play pickup games. Once after warming up to start a game, he disappeared, found later in full uniform playing marbles with a group of kids outside the ballpark.

One story, probably made up, has it that one night after imbibing, Waddell told his roommate Ossee Schreckengost he could fly. To prove his point, he jumped out of the window. The next day, from his hospital

bed, he asked his roomie why he hadn't prevented his dive. Schreckengost replied, "Heck, I bet you could do it."

Once when Waddell went missing, two teammates were standing outside their hotel. They heard music coming from nearby, then saw Waddell leading a marching band down a street, tossing a baton high in the air
and twirling it with a flourish. Baseball executive Branch Rickey stated,
"When Waddell had control—and some sleep—he was unbeatable."

Once when a manager fined him for a disgraceful hotel episode in
Detroit, Waddell is said to have fired back, "You're a liar. There ain't no
Hotel Episode in Detroit." This story is probably apocryphal, as it's also
been attributed to Casey Stengel.

A contemporary of Waddell's, Jimmy Austin, said his team tried to
keep Waddell in a good mood because when riled, he would bear down.
So, as if to amuse a child, Tigers manager Hugh Jennings purchased toys
such as a jack-in-the-box. Then, from his location in the coach's box,
he'd get Waddell's attention as jack popped out of his box. Waddell's
face would split into a slow grin and, in a happy mood, he pitched without
laser intensity. They also say opponents sometimes held up shiny objects
to distract him. Coincidentally, Waddell died on April Fool's Day in 1914
at the age of 37.

One of the next big links in the chain of flakes was Herman "Germany" Schaefer, a clown prince of baseball who made his major league
debut in 1901. He was known for hijinks such as eating popcorn while in
the coach's box and batting with a fake mustache placed above his lips.
Once Schaffer tried to influence an umpire to stop a game due to heavy
rain by taking the field while wearing rubber boots and a raincoat while
toting an umbrella.

But the topper came in the late innings of a 1908 tie game between his
Tigers and the Indians when he pulled off a "Ripley's Believe-It-or-Not"
play. Schaefer was on first as Davy Jones took his lead off third. Schaefer
flashed the double steal sign to Jones and took off for second. Cleveland
catcher Nig Clarke thwarted the plan, making no throw. On the next
pitch, Schaefer inconceivably broke back *toward* first base, once more
trying to draw a throw from Clarke. Schaefer made it, blatantly defying
basic strategy by "stealing" first base and refuting the ancient baseball
axiom that you *can't* steal first.

After that, he *again* took off for second, drew a throw and made it
easily, sliding into an uncovered bag. Not only that, but this time Jones

did score on the back end of a most unusual double (triple?) steal. It was almost enough to cause a new entry to be added to the record books: "Most times stealing the same base during one at bat, two, by Germany Schaefer, 1908."

Ernie Harwell shared another tale about Schaefer. "Have you heard the story about Jack Sheridan and Schaefer?" he began. "Sheridan was an old umpire who lived in Chicago and he drank a lot. There was a tavern they went to in the wintertime and Sheridan was sleeping in the back of the tavern by a pipe that came down from upstairs. And Schaefer got up there and scared him to death by saying through the pipe, 'Your time has came [*sic*]. Your time has came.' Sheridan got so flustered he got up and ran out of the tavern. Then, the next summer, Sheridan calls Schaffer out on a called third strike and, of course, he didn't know who had done it [the prank] before. So Germany turns to him and says, 'Your time has came.' Sheridan shouts, 'You're outta here.'" Harwell chuckled, recalling one of the game's most bizarre ejections.

Shoeless Joe Jackson couldn't read or write, but he could hit and one day he produced a great put-down line. A heckler repeatedly peppered Jackson with the insult, "Hey, Jackson, how do you spell illiterate?" Later in the game he destroyed a pitch for a triple. Standing on third, he shouted to the obnoxious fan, "Hey, loudmouth, how do you spell triple?"

Bugs Raymond got his nickname for his buggy, crazy behavior. He was also a heavy drinker, so his manager, John McGraw, hired a detective to keep track of him. The detective's assignment came to a halt when McGraw caught him out on the town drinking with Raymond. One story has it that the detective was named Fuller and he and Raymond once showed up at the ballpark drunk. Raymond supposedly slurred this pun to McGraw: "I'm full, but he's Fuller."

McGraw told Raymond he would protect him from drinking so much by sending his paycheck directly to his wife. Raymond's comeback was, "If she gets the money, let her pitch." And make no mistake, Bugs was a valuable pitcher. One year he went 15–25, but his wins were almost one-third of his weak team's victory total, and his ERA was 2.03. Plus, in the minors he once worked both ends of a doubleheader and threw no-hitters in each game.

Author Barry Sparks remembered that when colorful Ping Brodie was traded from the Phillies, he said that there were two attractions in Philadelphia—the Liberty Bell and himself—but after the trade, he complained that there was only one attraction now. "So he goes to New York and was roomed with Babe Ruth who had quite a night life. Bodie seldom ever saw the Babe in his room. When the reporters asked him about rooming with Ruth, he said, 'Well, I don't room with him, I room with his suitcase.'

"Ping had a great fondness for pasta. They held a spaghetti eating contest between him and an ostrich. Supposedly, on the eleventh plate, the ostrich stopped eating and Ping won. So Ping Bodie was the spaghetti eating champion."

Another pip of a player came along in 1923, Hack Wilson. Standing 5 feet, 6 inches, weighing at least 190 pounds, and wearing size 6 spikes, he was described as being "built along the lines of a beer keg and not unfamiliar with its contents." This fireplug of a slugger held the National League record for the most round trippers in a season (56) for an eon, he won the home run crown four times over a five-year period, and still holds the mark for the most runs batted in (RBI) for a season (191).

Over one four-year span he *averaged* 150 RBI, a number so high it has been reached only 48 times in baseball history through 2018. He even drove in 55 runs in one month. He remains the only man under 5 feet, 9 inches to lead the majors in homers. He also led the majors in lighting fire to people's newspapers in hotel lobbies.

A classic Wilson anecdote took place when his Chicago Cubs manager Joe McCarthy was trying to preach to him the folly of drinking whiskey. In order to demonstrate the point that whiskey would damage both Wilson and his career, McCarthy dropped a worm into a glass of water. He then extracted the not-too-happy but still alive worm and then dropped it into a glass of whiskey. The worm quickly died, McCarthy broke into a smug little smile, and asked Wilson if he had learned something from this experiment. Wilson replied, yes, "It means that if I keep on drinking liquor, I ain't going to have no worms."

Wilson once said, "I've never played drunk. Hung over, yes, but never drunk." And Al Drooz wrote, "Hack Wilson batted right-handed and threw right-handed, but he drank equally well from either side."[1]

While most people no longer consider excessive drinking to be amusing, men such as Wilson and King Kelly (from the pre-1900s) did. Kelly was asked if he drank while playing and he replied, "It depends on the length of the game." And Jim Pagliaroni joked that when he had to show up for morning batting practice, he said, "Ten-thirty? I'm not even done throwing up at that hour."[2]

The long line of fun-loving guys continued with Lefty Gomez who spent 1930–1943 in the majors and who owned an unblemished 6–0 record in World Series play. Years later, in his 60s, he was asked if he thought his undefeated record would stand forever. He responded, "Well, I don't think I'm gonna lose any."[3]

One time Gomez, who earned the nickname Goofy, was on the hill with bases loaded, a tight situation. Shortstop Frank Crosetti came over to encourage Gomez: "C'mon, Lefty, bear down, the bases are loaded." Gomez snapped sarcastically, "I know they're loaded. I didn't think they gave me a second infield."

Gomez managed Whitey Ford in the minors, and once set him up for a curfew violation. Ford went to a carnival and decided to take a final ride on a Ferris wheel before hustling to the hotel to make curfew. Oddly, the operator of the ride let it go on and on, beyond curfew time and despite Ford's pleas to stop. Ford returned to the hotel where Gomez, who was in cahoots with the Ferris wheel operator, was waiting; he slapped Ford with a $5 fine.

Years later, Ford overheard Gomez recounting his prank so he confronted him and demanded his *$10 fine* be returned. Gomez forked over the money. Ford grinned, "We're even now. You only fined me $5."[4]

There was a time when Yankees second baseman Tony Lazzeri was getting a great deal of media attention about how savvy he was. Gomez took the mound not long after reading about that, and was spinning a shutout into the eighth inning. With a runner on first and one out, Hank Greenberg hit a tailor-made double play ball back to the box. A Gomez throw to Frank Crosetti, who was near the bag at second, was in order. Gomez threw instead to Lazzeri who, positioned about 10 feet away from second, naturally thought he was a spectator on this play.

A stunned Lazzeri caught the ball, but both runners were safe. He trotted over to Gomez to ask why he had made such a crazy play. Gomez smiled and said, "I keep hearing about what a smart player you are. I just wanted to see what you would do with that one." It's not surprising that Gomez once ordered a vanity license plate that read "GOOF."

Carl Erskine, who threw two of the seven National League no-hitters in the 1950s, recalled, "Gomez was a funny guy. He didn't try to be a comedian, but he'd break you up. Gomez and Tommy Henrich went together to the 1965 World Series. Sandy Koufax was scheduled to be the opening day pitcher for the Dodgers, but if a game happened to fall on a Jewish holiday, Sandy was excused from coming to the ballpark. The opening game was on a Jewish holiday so [manager Walt] Alston had to move Don Drysdale up to pitch. As the game progressed, Minnesota got to Drysdale and Alston had to make a pitching change. As Alston was walking off the field with Drysdale, Gomez turned to Henrich and said, 'I know exactly what Alston is saying to Drysdale. I can tell you word for word.' Henrich said, 'How would you know that? What's he saying?' Gomez says, 'Why couldn't you have been Jewish instead of Koufax?'"

During a game in the 1936 World Series, Gomez gazed at the sky. The flabbergasted spectators wondered what was so interesting. It was an airplane fascinating Gomez back when air travel was much less common than now. His manager reprimanded him, saying his behavior could have led to the batter homering, but Gomez, quite logically, shot back that nobody could hit the ball if he didn't throw it.

He spoke about his role as a reliever. "A lot of things run through your head when you're going in to relieve in a troubled spot. One of them was, 'Should I spike myself?'" When Gomez was asked if the curveball was merely an optical illusion, he replied, "All I know is, when I lost my optical illusion, I had to quit."

After being offered a contract that cut his salary by $12,500, down from $20,000, he shot back, "Tell you what, you keep the salary and pay me the cut." He also joked about his inability to hit, saying the only time he ever broke a bat was when he drove over one pulling out of his garage. In his hands, a bat was about as solid as a dandelion's stem. When he hit a rare double once, he got picked off. His manager wanted to know what happened. Gomez answered, "How should I know? I've never been on second before."

During a gloomy game, Gomez batted against the sizzling offerings of Bob Feller. Gomez lit a match and held it in front of his head. The umpire told him to cut it out, that Feller could see home plate. Gomez replied, "I'm not worried about the plate. I want to make sure he can see me." Another time he watched three straight pitches from Rapid Robert blow by for strikes. Traipsing back to the dugout, he mumbled, "That last one sounded a little low."

Toward the end of his career, Gomez often was bailed out by reliever Johnny Murphy. Wells Twombly wrote that sometimes Yankee manager

Joe McCarthy would sidle up to Gomez and ask if he was okay, could he start. Gomez would walk over to Murphy and ask if he felt good and strong. When Murphy said yes, Gomez would return to McCarthy and report that, yes, *we* feel like pitching today.

After leaving baseball, he filled out a job application that required him to state why he had left his last job. His reason was simple—he stated he could no longer get batters out. Later, his doctor asked him to compare his chest pains to the dread as he prepared to throw a fastball. From 1 to 10, how bad was his pain? Gomez responded, "Who's hitting, Doc?"[5]

One last Sultan of Silliness from the cobwebbed earlier days of baseball is Frenchy Bordagaray, a man who once wore a monocle in the outfield and who doubled, but was out because he did a sort of happy tap dance on the bag and was tagged between taps. One time Casey Stengel was managing from the third base coaching box and he waved Bordagaray on to try to score. The throw had him beat so badly he didn't bother to slide. Stengel told him he would be fined $50 for failing to slide. Bordagaray countered, "You should be fined for such a lousy coaching job."[6] Later in that game he hit a home run and vowed childishly to himself, "Hmmpf, he's not going to fine me again for not sliding." He sarcastically made his point by circling the bases, sliding into each base. When he made the last leg of his journey from third to home, Stengel ran down the line with him. Bordagaray did a swan dive into home plate where Stengel fined him $100 for showing him up.

Bordagaray once hit Stengel in his head with an errant warmup throw. They won that day and before the following contest, he said that hitting him proved to be good luck. So his plan was to hit Stengel in the head again—this time intentionally. Simple cause and effect.

In the minors Bordagaray once forgot to take his position in the outfield to start a new inning, and it went unnoticed until an opposing player cracked a double to where Bordagaray should have been positioned (more later on a similar move by Manny Ramirez). Another harebrained move he made came when he was chasing a deep drive and his cap flew off his head. Abandoning the baseball momentarily, he retrieved his hat. Only after it was back in place did he again pursue the ball.

In 1947, Bordagaray was a Class A player-manager. His days in pro baseball died on July 15 when he punched an umpire and spit on him. For that, he was fined $50 and suspended for 60 days. When he learned of his punishment, he supposedly commented, "I deserved some kind of fine, but this is more than I expectorated."

So, from men named Frenchy, Dizzy, Casey, and Yogi through some of today's players, baseball has never been devoid of colorful characters.

2

KINGS OF THE HILL

The Most Colorful Pitchers Ever

In John Thorn and John Holway's sensational 1987 book, *The Pitcher*, the authors contend that pitchers account for twice as many flakes as position players. They quoted Branch Rickey, who said pitchers' arms were way ahead of their brains.

There's no doubt that pitchers concoct myriad wild and funny ways to while away the downtime, which often results in idle hands (or arms) becoming the devil's tool, creating much mischief.

Bert Blyleven speculated that pitchers, especially the inhabitants of the bullpen, are more colorful/crazy than players at any other position because they have more time to kill. Reliever Skip Lockwood put it this way: "A lot of relief pitchers develop a crazy facade that helps them deal with the pressure. Of course, maybe it's only the crazies that want to be relief pitchers." Nearly 30 relievers are featured in this book.

Also, fair or unfair, southpaws have a reputation for being screwy, and a good handful of them are chronicled here. It's noteworthy that more than 30 percent of the pitchers profiled are lefties, while only around 10 percent of the general population is left-handed.

Rather significantly, only nine of the slew of players in this book are Hall of Famers, suggesting that as a rule the greats don't have the time or inclination to see the flaky side of baseball. Author David Nathan states that the players who tend not to be funny and colorful "were the superstars—very few of them said anything super funny. Occasionally, somebody like Reggie Jackson or Pete Rose came up with a funny line, but they weren't usually your go-to guys for [funny] quotes."

If a list of the 10 most colorful characters of all time existed, it would probably include five pitchers, of which four would be relievers. Two or three of the others would be bench players.

At any rate, this chapter takes a look at men such as Roger McDowell, who reached the pinnacle of practical joking; the uninhibited Sparky Lyle; Larry Andersen, baseball's Henny Youngman; and many more wild and crazy guys.

BOBO NEWSOM (1929–1953)

Newsom, whose big-league career bridged four decades, was a modern wandering troubadour, plying his trade for 26 seasons, 20 in the majors, moving around so often he made 17 uniform changes. He was with the Senators five different times, prompting him to say he served more terms in D.C. than Franklin Roosevelt. Forget the slogan, "Join the Navy and see the world"—Newsom's luggage was threadbare after just several seasons. In all, he switched jerseys 28 times, as he also played for 10 minor league teams.

Still, he was valuable, winning 146 minor league games and 211 in the majors versus 222 big league losses. He is the only modern-era pitcher to win 200-plus games, yet finish with a losing record. Newsom even lost when he had a no-hitter going through nine innings. He won 20+ games in 1938, 1939 (a season in which he got traded), and 1940, but he was a three-time 20-game loser who led his league in losses four times. He also was the second pitcher to win 20 with an ERA exceeding 5.00.

In 1940, Newsom pitched in a game he would never forget, and not just because it was in the Fall Classic. His Tigers met the Reds, and 21-game winner Newsom won the opening game of the Series with his father in attendance.

The following day his father passed away, which led Newsom to vow he'd win his next outing for his dad. Working Game 5 on short rest, Newsom threw a seven-strikeout shutout, giving up just three singles and permitting only one man to reach second. Normally a rather obstreperous man, after his win he somberly returned to his clubhouse and immediately sought solace and solitude in the trainer's room, finally letting his emotions and tears flown freely.

There was no Disney movie ending for his Tigers, though, as the Reds won it all in seven. Disregarding that, Newsom had pitched the greatest game of his life and had paid a fitting tribute to his father.

* * *

Newsom was, said Bobby Bragan, "crazy and colorful. In 1943, he was pitching to me [as his catcher] in Brooklyn. We were playing Pittsburgh and the bases were loaded. He throws a spitball on a 3–2 count on Albie Fletcher and the ball went by me and went to the backstop because I didn't know he was going to throw a spitball. Leo Durocher was the manager—he was the best manager I ever played for, very aggressive—and he got Bobo real good; Mr. Rickey traded him about 48 hours later. When I saw Mr. Rickey, he said, 'I know you were very quiet during the whole thing and I appreciate that, but if you've ever seen anybody busy, you should have seen me in here trying to find somebody who would take Bobo, a guy that would stand up there and try to embarrass his manager in front of all the players.'"

Bragan continued, saying that Bobo would shag fly balls with the other pitchers during batting practice and "instead of rolling the ball back in, he hit one of the infielders on the head throwing the ball in from the outfield. The infielder was Bobby Bragan. I was out at shortstop taking some ground balls."

Newsom lost a game versus the Yankees when he experimented with Joe DiMaggio, throwing him a different type pitch each time he faced him. In their first encounter, DiMaggio homered and the next three at bats resulted in doubles, causing Newsom to quip, "His weakness is two-base hits."[1]

Newsom, who twice chose to wear uniform jersey #00, often spoke in the third person when referring to himself—as in, "Bobo's going to win today." Always flamboyant, after signing a big contract, he reported to his Tigers spring camp driving a sporty car sporting custom-made lights that spelled out "BOBO" and whose horn played the tune "Hold That Tiger" ("Tiger Rag").

DIZZY DEAN (1930–1947)

It's a statistic that's seldom mentioned, but in 1934 Dean won more than 80 percent of his decisions, going 30–7, with four victories (and seven saves) coming in relief roles. He remains the last National League hurler to reach the 30-win plateau. From 1933 to 1936, he even toiled 143½ innings in relief over 62 appearances.

Dean clowned around, but he was far more than a clown. He was highly competitive. Billy Herman said Dean would cheat at a card game just to win 50 cents, then take the player he had just cheated out on the town and spend $100 on him.

When he was just 22, Dean owned both a 20-win season and the record for the most strikeouts in a game, 17. He called it quits after throwing in one 1941 contest, but six years later worked in one last game, throwing shutout ball for four innings with the St. Louis Browns.

* * *

Like Casey Stengel, Dean was famous for distorting the English language. He was colorful in a Muhammad Ali manner (funny and boastful) long before the boxer emerged onto the sports stage.

As a young player Dean was a flash on the baseball scene, very much like when Vida Blue, Mark Fidrych, and Fernando Valenzuela first came to the majors. Dean would tell different writers different tales. For example, he told three writers in separate interviews different birthplaces. "I just wanted to give each one a story all his own. Them ain't lies. Them's scoops," he explained. Someone once said of Dean, "Diz just says whatever comes into his head . . . even if it's nothing."

During spring training of 1931, Dean bragged that he was going to win 30 games that year, but the Cardinals shipped him to the minors before camp broke. A teammate who was a believer in Dean said to a friend that they had just seen history being made: "This is the only time in the history of the game that a club lost 30 games in one day."[2]

When Dean strolled into a hotel lobby at 2:00 a.m. and spied his club's president, he said it appeared like they'd *both* catch hell for being out so late. "But I won't say nothin' if you don't," the unperturbed Dean added conspiratorially.

One classic Dean quote came after he had been hit in the head by an infielder's throw as he tried to complete a double play during the 1934 World Series. Dean didn't slide soon enough to avoid getting drilled in his forehead. After getting examined, he told reporters, "They X-rayed my head and found nothing."

In the 1937 All-Star Game, he was struck on the foot by an Earl Averill liner. A doctor informed him a toe was fractured. Dean shouted, "Fractured? The damn thing's broke."

Ethan Allen, the creator of a popular game called All-Star Baseball (sometimes called Spinner Baseball by kids), was a roommate of Dean's. Allen said that after one Cardinals practice session, he was ready to dry himself off after taking a bath when Dean stuck his head in the bathroom and told him not to bother draining the water because he was in such a hurry to bathe for a date that night, he'd just plunge right in.

Even in his 1953 Hall of Fame induction speech, Dean was honest and funny: "The Good Lord was good to me. He gave me a strong body, a good right arm, and a weak mind." Perhaps the only flake with a more fitting name was pro football's unconventional and wild star, Joe Don Looney.

Outfielder Wally Westlake praised Dean. "He was just a great guy, Old Dizzy, quite a pitcher in his day. There was a doubleheader he and his brother Daffy were pitching. Well, in the first game Dizzy threw a one-hitter [holding the Dodgers hitless for 7⅔ innings]. Then Daffy came behind him and threw a no-hitter, and Dizzy told his brother, 'Whyn't you tell Ol' Diz you were gonna pitch a no-hitter? If I'd a knowed that, I'd of pitched one, too.'"

That season, 1934, Dizzy had predicted he and his brother would combine for 45 wins. They didn't. They won almost 50, as Daffy won 19 and Dizzy won his 30. As Dean once crowed, "It ain't bragging if you can do it."

Before the 1934 Series began, Dean told his manager that he wanted to pitch in every game. Frankie Frisch responded by saying Dean couldn't possibly win four games against the Tigers. The ever-confident Dean replied, "I know, but I can win four out of five."[3]

In a World Series with no off days, Dizzy started three games over one week and the Dean brothers secured all four Cardinal victories to conclude a season in which they won 52 percent of their team's 95 victories.

Fans in St. Louis threw lemons at him one time, just as Detroit fans once tossed assorted fruits at Joe Medwick. Dean felt slighted because nobody threw any grapefruit, apples, or oranges at him. "I rate just as many kinds of fruit as any guy on this here club," he griped.[4]

In a 1931 minor league contest, Dean hit a solo homer. Later, his manager yanked him from the mound, so Dean stormed to the center field scoreboard and removed the "1," the one-run slate from the board. It was as if he said, "Pull me from the game and I'll take back my run and go home."

Brash as could be, before a 1937 contest Dean bet a friend named Johnny Perkins that he would strike out Vince DiMaggio the first time he batted. He did, and Perkins and Dean agreed to go double or nothing on the next DiMaggio-Dean confrontation. Dean won again, and repeated the bet for the third time he faced DiMaggio. Finally, Dean took on DiMaggio in the ninth inning, up by one run. DiMaggio fouled a ball behind the plate, but before catcher Mickey Owen could corral it, Dean emphatically shouted for him to drop it (or, according to one version, Dean jostled Owen's arm to prevent the catch). Dean then struck DiMaggio out, winning yet another lucrative wager.

On at least one occasion Dean's humor put an upstart player in his place. After observing an opposing batter who had taken his time digging in at the plate preparatory to facing the highly competitive Dean, he admonished, "You all done? You comfortable? Well, send for the groundskeeper and get a shovel because that's where they're gonna bury you." One concise message came when Dean, always confident of his ability, faced a rookie and, after peering down at him from the mound for a second or two, bellowed, "Son, what kind of pitch would you like to miss."

Norman Lumpkin, who played for the Atlanta Black Crackers in the Negro Leagues, said, "You know what you do with crazy guys like that? If you get a hit off a flaky pitcher, treat him nice because he'll remember you if you were showboating."

When Pee Wee Reese kidded Dean that he wished he had faced him so he could have pelted his high fastball, Dean shot back, "You might have hit it, pod-nuh, but you'd be on your ass."[5]

Dean even shamed Hall of Famer Hank Greenberg. Leading 11–0 with one out in the ninth of Game 7 of the 1934 World Series, Dean saw Greenberg approaching the plate. He shouted to the Tiger dugout, "Ain't you got no pinch hitter?"[6] Moments later, Dean fanned Greenberg, then finished his shutout to clinch the championship. Dean's rapid-fire fast-balls were as devastating as shots from a Gatling gun.

On yet another occasion, he grew impatient with an enemy batter who had stepped out of the box for a lengthy time to check on the signals from his third-base coach. Dean snapped, "Damn it, get up to bat. He done gave you the bunt sign three times."

He summed up his opinion of Giants first baseman Bill Terry by saying, "Could be that he's a nice guy when you get to know him, but why bother?" He put a scientist, who said a curveball was an optical illusion, in his place by saying, "Tell that scientist to go hide behind a tree and I'll optical illusion him to death."[7]

He remained colorful during his stint in the radio booth. Once when he tried to mention the name Ed Hanyzewski on the air, he confessed, "I liked to have broken my jaw trying to pronounce that one, but I said his name just by holding my nose and sneezing."

One game Dean worked with Reese, who asked Dean what a pitcher was throwing that day. Dean deadpanned, "Well, Pee Wee, I have been watching him for four innings, and I believe that's a baseball."[8]

Dean was not well educated; he dropped out of school in second grade and later remarked, "I didn't do so hot in first grade, either." Someone compared him to Jethro Bodine from television's *Beverly Hillbillies*, but Bill James said Dean was more clever than Bodine. Let's compromise: Dean was a clever Bodine. Dean's lack of formal education showed up in the way he colorfully butchered the language—for example, his line: "Don't fail to miss tomorrow's game." Upon hearing the word syntax used by a reporter, Dean reportedly said, "Sin tax? What will them fellas in Washington think up next?" He described a pitcher who was getting rocked as having nothing on the ball except the cover.

His thinking was backward when, upon arriving at a gas station, he said, "It puzzles me how they know what corners are good for filling stations. Just how did these fellows know there was gas and oil under here?"

While broadcasting a game during World War II, the game was called off due to rain. Wartime rules dictated he could not mention weather conditions on the radio, so he announced that he couldn't say why the game was over, but all a listener had to do was stick his head out the back window "and when it's wet you'll know." Then there was the time he told his listeners that a 1–0 game had been "closer than the score indicated."

After Carl Erskine threw his second no-hitter on May 12, 1956, Dean, broadcasting the contest for *The Game of the Week*, interviewed Erskine. Dean asked who had originally signed him. When "Oisk" answered Branch Rickey, Dean retorted in disgust, "Mr. Rickey? Branch Rickey is the cheapest man that ever lived. I worked for him in St. Louis and he was a cheapskate. I'll bet he starves you just like he did me."

Erskine replied, "Well, actually, he gave me a bonus to sign because the Boston Braves were trying to sign me at the same time [for $2,500]. Nobody got cash bonuses in those days, but Mr. Rickey paid me $3,500 to sign and $5,000."

Dean swiveled to face the camera and said, "Now, folks, this here young fella deserves to be in the Hall of Fame. Not because he pitched two no-hitters. Because he got two bonuses out of Branch Rickey." Incidentally, Erskine's first no-hitter was nearly a perfect game. With rain about to fall in the fifth inning, he hurried to get three outs so the game would count as an official no-hitter. The result was he gave up a walk. A rain delay followed, but when play resumed Erskine retired every remaining Cubs batter.

Erskine said Dean was truly as colorful as baseball lore has it, speculating that Dean's "director screamed every time Dean went to the microphone. Teachers used to write to him and say, 'You're using this bad grammar and my kids are picking up on it. Could you please not use the word ain't so much?' Dizzy read one of the letters on the air and said, 'Now I want to tell this teacher that a lot of teachers that ain't saying ain't, ain't eating.'"

SATCHEL PAIGE (1948–1965)

Paige's age was never positively pinned down, but he didn't think age was consequential, saying it was a case of mind over matter: "If you don't mind, it don't matter." Paige was baseball's undisputed Methuselah. When Bill Veeck signed him to a major league contract with the Indians in 1948, Paige became the oldest rookie ever, a distinction he still holds. After all, how many teams want a rookie in his 40s?

Paige went 28–31 lifetime in the majors. His win total is the lowest among Hall of Famers. However, counting wins in the Negro Leagues and during his barnstorming days, he won nearly four times as many games as the man with the most career wins, Cy Young (511). Paige pitched for 44 years and claimed he worked in more than 2,500 games, winning 2,000 times, laboring 5–7 days weekly. He said he once pitched in 165 consecutive games. Paige stated he had 250 shutouts and 45 no-hitters. He also stated he wasn't too concerned about pitching in the majors, because he could make more money barnstorming than he could in the Bigs.

It didn't take Paige long to convince critics that his signing was far more than a Veeck publicity stunt. Using tricks such as a hitch in his windup for his hesitation pitch, he went 6–1 in 1948 and held opposing batters to a measly .087 batting average, helping the Indians win the World Series.

* * *

One writer observed, "When Paige wound up to pitch, he looked like a cross between Ichabod Crane and Rip Van Winkle. . . . He was easy to imitate and funny to watch, unless you were the batter trying to hit against him." With his prowess, Paige naturally exuded self-confidence. In a Negro League game, after giving up a two-out triple, he intentionally walked the bases loaded to set up a crowd-pleasing confrontation with prolific slugger Josh Gibson, who represented the winning run. He then proceeded to inform Gibson of the speed and location of each ensuing pitch. Paige, a showman on a par with P. T. Barnum, came through. After facing a cannon volley of fastballs, Gibson timidly sat down.

Paige began some games by waving his outfielders in. They say he'd then strike out the first nine batters before putting his outfield back in place. By the way, Rube Waddell had pitched with his outfielders sitting near the infield with the bases jammed in 1904, nursing a slim one-run lead, but he "only" whiffed three straight batters. Of course in some of Paige's barnstorming days, he showed off by requiring defensive support only from a shortstop, a first baseman, and two outfielders.

Joe Cunningham owned a lifetime .403 on-base percentage, which still ranks in the top 50 of all time. His on-base percentage hit a personal apex of .453 in 1959 when he led his league. Cunningham faced Paige, recalling, "That was with the Rochester Red Wings. I think he started that game for Miami in the International League. I hit a triple off of him. I only faced him a couple of times. He threw a *good* fastball and he had that big windup, but he didn't always use that. I think he was trying to fool the hitters with his different windups."

Former big leaguer Wally Westlake concurred. "I was with the Oakland Oaks in 1942 and Paige came to Oakland for an exhibition game. He was good. He had a loosey-goosey windup—he was hard to follow." Paige employed an exaggerated windup, often spinning his pitching arm around and around, windmill-like, in a large circle before actually making a pitch.

Robert Williams, who played in the Negro Leagues, attested to how hard Paige was to hit. "He faced Roy Campanella in a Negro League All-Star game. Campy got a single and was so happy to get a hit off Satch he ran down the line jumping and doing crow hops."

When Carl Erskine hosted a radio show, he interviewed Paige. "I told him he had a great reputation for control and asked about his pitches. He had a unique way of answering you. He said, 'Well, I had a little piece of fastball, had a little piece of curve, and then I'd throw my do-daddies [off speed stuff].'"

Paige pitched with the precision of a Radio City Music Hall kickline, and he asserted that his control was so good he brushed back hitters by throwing under their chins and ripping the top button off their shirts with whistling fastballs. Paige claimed that he had a basket in his home, which he filled with players' buttons. And when one player complained Paige had torn the second button off his shirt, Paige apologized, "My control was a little off. I was aiming at your top button."[9]

His control was impeccable. In exhibition contests his catcher would sometimes handle his pitches while sitting in a rocking chair. One of his receivers cautioned, though, that he had to be rocking toward the pitch to catch it—otherwise the force of the pitch would knock him to the backstop.

Paige created names for his pitches such as the trouble ball, wobbly ball, alley oop ball, the midnight rider, bat dodger, the pea ball, and the "be" ball, named because it hummed as it approached the batter and because, said Paige, "it always be where I want it to be." He had his "Long Tom," the best fastball, and "Little Tom" for a somewhat slower fastball. A pea at the knee was a low fastball, while smoke at the yolk was his terminology for a fastball up by a hitter's noggin.

Paige was blessed with a rubber arm. They say he pitched 27 years, more than any other pitcher ever (tied with Nolan Ryan). Sam Jethroe, a veteran of the Negro Leagues and the majors, reflected, "He was a thoroughbred fella. He liked to kid around, shoot pool, but the amazing thing is he pitched three innings or so every day." Paige set big league records for the most wins (12) and the most strikeouts (91) thrown by a 45-year-old hurler (both later broken by Phil Niekro).

On September 25, 1965, when he was believed to be 59, he started and worked three shutout innings for the Kansas City Athletics in a regular-season contest against the Red Sox on Satchel Paige Night, a promotion dreamed up by Athletics owner Charlie Finley. When Finely asked Paige if he could handle throwing three innings, Paige said it all depended upon how many times in a day Finley meant.

Paige faced ten batters, striking out one, and giving up only one hit, a double by Carl Yastrzemski, whose father had once faced Paige in a semipro game. Never before or since has anyone pitched in the big leagues at an older age than Satch. At the time of the game, he had nearly 40 years' experience on countless professional mounds, but his last pitch in the majors had been a dozen years earlier. Among the 9,289 in attendance that day was future pitching star Rick Sutcliffe.

Erskine said, "Nobody ever knew how old he was. The writers would ask him over and over again what his birthday was. He answered in a very offbeat way and they figured out he didn't even know his birthday. He simply said, 'Fellas, you want to know how old I am. How old would you be if you didn't know how old you wuz?'" Erskine also recalled one of Paige's rules for living, probably the most quoted one: "Don't look back. Something might be gaining on you."

The ageless Paige had a great sense of humor. Hack Wilson once said that Paige's fastball started out "like a baseball and when it gets to the plate it looks like a marble." Paige quipped, "You must be talking about my slowball. My fastball looks like a fish egg." Once he said he threw to a catcher who was so old, there was no need for him to hunker down into a crouch.

A few other Paige classics:

- Regarding his control, he bragged, "It got so I could nip frosting off a cake with my fastball." Norman Lumpkin, who played against Paige in the Negro Leagues, said, "Early in his career, he'd spot his fastball as his only pitch, but he'd hit his spots. He threw the curve late in his career. When he was in a good mood he'd put on a show. He'd put down a handkerchief [as a makeshift home plate] and the catcher put out a target, and he'd hit it."
- Always trying to conserve energy, he said, "I believe in training by rising gently up and down from the bench." While not a philosophy modern coaches would espouse, it's difficult to argue with Paige. He may never have taken a test such as the ACT or the SAT, but even in retirement his achievements qualified him as an emeritus professor of pitching.
- He claimed that he had never thrown an illegal pitch, then said slyly, "The trouble is, once in a while I tosses one that ain't been seen by this generation."

Buck O'Neil was Paige's teammate when the legendary pitcher invited a girl named Nancy to spend the night with him. One version of the story has it that when she pulled up to the hotel in a taxi, a bellman took her belongings to Paige's room while O'Neil sat in the lobby. That same day, Paige's fiancée, Lahoma, had decided to pay Paige a surprise visit. O'Neil greeted her, stalled for time, then excused himself to instruct a bellboy to warn Paige.

Now, O'Neil's room was next to Paige's, and a room on the other side of O'Neil was vacant, so O'Neil told the bellboy to put Nancy in the unoccupied room. Later that night, Paige knocked on Nancy's door, whispering her name. There was no response so Paige knocked again, saying the girl's name louder. Again no reply, so Paige raised his voice, "Nancy!"

It was then that Lahoma flew out of the room she was sharing with Paige. Knowing he had to cover for Paige, O'Neil leaped out of his bed, went into the corridor and said that, yes, it's me, Nancy. Paige caught on and asked O'Neil something like, "I just wanted to check what time the game starts tomorrow, Nancy." Of course, their impromptu collusion meant from that day forward Paige had to call O'Neil "Nancy," and O'Neil had to remember to respond to that.

One quote can serve as a sad commentary on Paige's career, which should have been spent entirely in the majors. Author Lew Freedman wrote that when Paige was elected to the Hall of Fame, initially there was talk of honoring him, but in an auxiliary wing. That prompted Paige to muse, "The only change is that baseball has turned Paige from a second-class citizen to a second-class immortal."

BILLY LOES (1950–1961)

Trivia item: from 1950 to 1961, there were four occasions when a major leaguer hit four homers in a game. Loes, the man teammates called "Cuckoo," was on hand in uniform, all four times.

Loes was born and raised a half-hour from Ebbets Field; his neighborhood also produced Whitey Ford. Loes threw five no-hitters in high school, and one came in a city championship game.

From 1952 to 1955, Loes was on fire, winning 50 games and registering a .750 winning percentage. He won 30 more games and lost 38 after that, but he chalked up complete games in more than half of his decisions.

* * *

Dick Groat, the 1960 National League MVP, says he faced Loes as a rookie. "I came back from the College World Series in 1952, joined the Pirates in New York, watched the first game, pinch-hit the second game, then started against the Giants. I faced Loes and I was in awe. He just had magnificent stuff—he was overpowering with the fastball, had a great curveball. I don't know this to be a fact, but I've heard he was as wacky as a bedbug."

One salient fact about Loes's defense: he played in 316 big league contests and committed 13 errors, one per every 11 games he worked—no threat to a guy like Bobby Shantz, who won 8 Gold Gloves and who committed 16 errors over his 16 seasons, or 18-time Gold Glove winner Greg Maddux.

There's a famous story that makes fun of Loes's fielding ability, but the entire story wasn't revealed. Brooklyn teammate Carl Erskine elaborated: "For a World Series day game at Ebbets Field, I think Vic Raschi hit a ball back through the box at a critical time in the game, kind of a high hopper. Loes ducked his head and the ball went right by him. Well, at Ebbets Field I can testify this is true, at a certain time in the late afternoon the sun would come between the upper deck and the lower deck and would be right in the face of the pitcher. For about two or three minutes there was a blinding sun shining. After the game they asked Loes what happened on the ball hit back to him. He said he lost it in the sun. Well, how could you lose a ground ball in the sun?" On the surface, a player can't do that, so Loes's reputation grew. Groat said that crazy stuff like that happened to Loes a lot.

However, as Erskine pointed out, "The truth was the high hopper happened right at that critical time when the sun [blinded him], so it was true—he lost a ground ball in the sun. When he died, that was one of the tags that everybody who had covered him remembered. He had a lot of bizarre answers to [media] questions, but it was the truth."

On another occasion, dealing with the media got him involved in a bit of controversy. Loes was asked to take a stab at the outcome of the 1952 World Series involving his Dodgers and their nemesis, the Yankees. Instead of saying the predictable, that his team would have to fight hard but would prevail, his prophecy was that the Yankees, not his own Dodgers, would win in six games. After the Series concluded, he was asked again about his curious betrayal/prediction. His indignant justification was, "I never told that guy the Yanks would win it in six. I said they'd win it in seven." That was the correct outcome.

Erskine said that when fellow Dodgers first heard Loes had picked the Yankees to win, they were dumbfounded, saying, "'What team are you on, anyway?!' He was a different kind of cat. He never tried to be funny, but his makeup was such that he'd come up with bizarre answers to the press."

Another Loes tale concerned the time his general manager, Branch Rickey, asked him not to disclose the amount of money he had just signed his new contract for. Loes's response: "Don't worry. I'm just as ashamed of the figures as you are."

In a World Series contest as he was preparing to start his delivery, the baseball dropped out of his glove so he was called for a balk. When asked how the ball escaped him, he explained, "Too much spit."

Erskine said Loes had a lot of superstitions. "He would not wear the same shirt, he sat in the same place in the dugout, and when we held our meetings to go over hitters in the open area of the clubhouse, Loes wanted to sit at his locker on the days he was pitching—another superstition." Usually, the day's starting pitcher "was right there in the middle of the meeting saying, 'Here's how I'll pitch to Dark and here's how I'll pitch to Mays.' With Loes, all you'd hear was a voice from way in the back of the locker room. You'd never see Billy, just hear him." Loes would never take to the mound until the opponents' first- and third-base coaches were situated in their coaching boxes.

Loes bristled at modern players who, for example, wore earrings, saying, "If I was still pitching, I'd throw one in their earring."

Loes was famous for saying he had no desire to win 20 games in a season because his front office and manager would expect him to match that every year. Mike Gibbons, executive director of the Babe Ruth Birthplace and Museum, noted that "when Billy pitched for the Orioles, he had outstanding stuff but was content to win eight or nine games a year."

Over 11 seasons, Loes won 80 contests. He shared his theory of not overachieving with another starting pitcher, teammate Connie Johnson: "If you win 10, they'll want 12. If you win 12, they'll want 15. Fifteen, they want 20." He went so far as to say if the goal got too high and expectations weren't met, the team would cut the pitcher. Gibbons said, "He told Johnson, who had just won 14 games in 1957, that he was winning too many games. He warned Johnson that he would soon be dumped. He was right. The following year he won six games and the Orioles cut him."

As for Loes, his determination not to win big began in 1952 when he expressed no desire to have a clause added to his contract that would award him a bonus if he won 20 games. Coming off a 13-win season, and with no such clause, he won 14, 13, then 10 games and never again had more than a dozen wins.

Former catcher Hal Smith shared another Loes story: "One time Loes told me, 'When Ted [Williams] comes to bat, you tell him that I think he's the greatest hitter that ever lived, and I will throw two right down the middle. Tell him to take those, then I'll throw him another one and tell him to pull it, and pull it in the stand away from me. Don't hit it back at me in other words. Tell him to make me look good before he hits one.' I said OK and then said to Ted, 'Goofy wants you to take the first two pitches cause he's going to lay them right in the middle for you. Make him look good and then he'll throw you another one, and he said you can pull it out of the park but don't hit it back at him.'

"Williams started laughing. He said, 'I'm going to knock him off the mound.' So Loes threw the first pitch right down the middle, nothing on it. Ted took it, strike one. Strike two. Loes said, 'OK, Ted. This one's for you,' and threw it right down the middle. Ted hit a line drive past Loes's head. And Loes took off running after Ted going down to first. He was saying, 'You're not my hero anymore. You knew what the deal was and you tried to kill me.' Ted called him the biggest goof he ever saw."

MOE DRABOWSKY (1956–1972)

Drabowsky was the winning pitcher in Baltimore's first-ever World Series game. With the Orioles up 4–1 over the Dodgers in the bottom of the third, starter Dave McNally walked the bases loaded with one out. In came Drabowsky, already warmed up and about to become as hot as a blistering funeral pyre. Mike Gibbons said, "Moe got out of the inning and wound up going 6⅔ innings, giving up 1 hit and striking out 11, including 6 in a row, a World Series mark." The 11 Ks remains an Autumn Showcase record for a reliever.

* * *

Drabowsky said he had been a normal, average kid, but his concept of normal included breaking some windows with stones and having police sometimes show up at his door, although not for anything major. He displayed his pitching talent early on, around the age of six, throwing mud pies at sheets neighbors hung on clotheslines and stones at streetlamps.

Merv Rettenmund was a teammate of Drabowsky in Baltimore and spoke of an unwritten baseball rule: "As long as it doesn't get personal, you can do stuff like he did. He was always doing crazy things."

When 19-year big league veteran Dick Schofield was asked about colorful players, he pondered a moment, going through his mental Rolodex. Suddenly he blurted, "Oh, oh. The best. Moe Drabowsky. He was an all-timer. He had to stay up at night to think about stuff he'd do. I remember he was with Baltimore when Earl Weaver was growing tomatoes in the bullpen. He took a syringe and shot vodka in the tomatoes. He would buy goldfish and put them in the visiting team's water cooler. When they went to get a drink, there would be the goldfish swimming around the water." He also put sneezing powder in air-conditioning vents that fed into visitors' clubhouses.

People occasionally confused him with Al Hrabosky, asking him if he was the Mad Hungarian. He stock answer was, "No, I'm the Polish Prince of Pranks." He was wrong—he was the king of them all.

Labeled "the biggest flake in baseball" by Jim Bouton, Drabowsky was more than that—he was a virtuoso. He took advantage of the telephones located in bullpens. He was known to use those phones to order pizza delivery, to get weather reports from foreign cities, to make long distance calls to friends, close family members, as well as to distant relatives spread all over the country. Hardly a one-dimensional character, he majored in economics and was a stockbroker in the off-season, so he kept abreast of the market by calling for quotes from the bullpen. He was teased that he had a copy of the *Sporting News* under one arm and the *Wall Street Journal* under the other.

He also called people he didn't even know, and then there were times he called places such as Hong Kong to request 25 orders of egg foo yung or fried rice—to go, of course. When he got hungry for hot dogs, he'd swap an autographed ball for his snack.

Former Oriole Elrod Hendricks told the tale of Drabowsky being responsible for one of baseball's most clever pranks ever. "We were in Kansas City at the old ballpark in 1966, and he had just been traded from them over to us. He called from our bullpen to their bullpen because he knew the phone number, and he imitated [Kansas City manager] Alvin Dark's voice and had Lew Krausse get up."

Mike Gibbons said Drabowky was convincing as he barked to coach Bobby Hofman to "get Krausse hot in a hurry." This baffled everyone because there was no apparent reason for the move. Another version of this tale has it that Dark spotted Krausse the first time he was warming up and phoned the bullpen, barking words to the effect of "why the hell is Krausse throwing? Tell him to sit down." Shortly after, the pseudo-Dark called again, demanding to know why Krausse wasn't throwing.

Hendricks recalled, "Finally those guys looked out from the dugout, looked out there to their bullpen and saw all the activity. They then looked over to the O's bullpen and figured it out."

It should be noted that this is not quite the version Drabowsky tells. He has stated that a few minutes after he tricked Hofman, he called back and said, "That's enough. Sit him down," and quickly hung up before Hofman could hear any laughter. Drabowky's niece, Carole Smith, said the Athletics didn't catch on until the next day when he tried his trick again. In between those calls, Drabowsky made another call to Kansas City's bullpen, pretending to be A's owner Charlie Finley. He grilled Hofman, demanding an explanation for the fake call that got Krausse throwing unnecessarily.

When Drabowsky was living near Chicago and his Cardinals were in town to play the Cubs, he called his wife Liz—naturally from the bullpen—to tell her a couple teammates wanted to come by for dinner. Liz picked up the story: "I took a couple filets out of the freezer and got some salad and potatoes. About 10 minutes later he called again to say a couple more players were coming, then a couple more. Finally, he calls again and says, 'The whole bus is coming up.' And they did. That was Moe. He was spur of the moment and you had to live by that."

Drabowsky was Adam Peterson's minor league pitching coach. One night the two went out drinking and closed the bar. They borrowed a hose from a gas station on their way back to the hotel. Peterson said, "I went to my room. Moe had other plans." The next morning Peterson discovered he had been tied to the bed with the hose. After he struggled and wriggled for about an hour, the maid entered the room and let out a piercing scream. A moment later she began laughing. "Then, rather than help me, she got her friends." That began a parade of maids, pretty maids all in a row, marching by as if to see a circus sideshow. "They came in and laughed, and after what seemed like the entire staff had come through, they untied me."

In the off-season Drabowsky sometimes called other teammates and, imitating Finley's voice, negotiated contracts. He would, for example, offer a low salary to a player, knowing that he would respond by requesting how much he wanted. In that way, Drabowsky was at times able to gauge what some holdouts were earning, knowledge that might help his negotiations. Another time, using his Finley voice, he called Baltimore's Brooks Robinson to inform him he had just traded for him.

Boog Powell said Drabowsky would apply extremely hot lotions like Capsolin to player's uniforms, "even in their jock straps. It was like getting an instant hotfoot," although not exactly on the foot. "He put dead rats in your shoes, too." One day he clandestinely put some hydrogen sulfate on Powell's shoulder, causing him to go around all day reeking like rotten eggs. Powell said people avoided him, believing he had just passed gas. Drabowsky also hid dead fish and Limburger cheese in players' cars.

Drabowsky's brother-in-law, Frank Freidhoff, tells of an incident when Drabowsky was coaching in Sarasota for the Orioles. "They used to keep a big jar of boiled eggs in the kitchen area and the players would grab a couple and eat them before they went out to practice to get some protein. Moe would put a bunch of raw eggs in with the hard-boiled ones so every once in a while a player would crack it open and raw egg would spew all over him."

Drabowsky's daughter Beth Morris said when he and his teammates lined up for their physicals, "My dad went in and they drew blood. He came out with about eight Band-Aids on each arm and freaked the players out. He said, 'Don't go to the nurse that I went to. Look what she did to me.' They were afraid to get their blood drawn after that."

Prior to another team physical on a sweltering spring day, the players were told to report to a building with no air conditioning. The men had been given plastic cups to use to provide a urine sample. They complied, then waited in line to be called into an office one by one. The line was long and the heat oppressive. Drabowsky grumbled openly, complaining about the long wait. He also griped repeatedly about how thirsty he was. Finally, he said, "I'm dying of thirst and I can't stand it anymore." With that, he unscrewed the lid on the cup and took a deep gulp of its contents. The players' reactions were predictable—some averted their eyes, some groaned in sheer disgust, some muttered, "That's sick, man," or words to that effect. In reality, he had only guzzled apple juice.

Drabowsky once called for a baseball commando strike to take place at the military time of 2130 hours. He and some other relievers gathered rocks and shaped dirt balls, took blackened cork to their faces, and carried out their strike on their opponents' bullpen, pelting the roof of the pen like an aerial onslaught.

Another story has it that Drabowsky once sat on a high hotel balcony overlooking a pool. Some teammates called up to him saying he should join them, that they had refreshing water and cold drinks, and all they were missing was a television for entertainment. Minutes later a television set hurled downward and plopped into the pool.

Gibbons recalled, "Drabowsky had a crazy streak that propelled him to cause clubhouse havoc by placing pretend, and sometimes real snakes in teammates' lockers and bat bags." The first victim was Frank Robinson. Drabowsky placed a long rubber snake inside an attaché case that Robinson carried. On seeing Robinson inadvertently seize the snake then fling it away in terror, Drabowsky figured if he began to use a real snake, the fun and mayhem would increase. So he came into the clubhouse wearing a boa constrictor around his neck. Paul Blair saw it and assumed it was another rubber snake—that is, until he saw its tongue lash out. That's when he bolted, seeking and finding refuge in the dugout. And that's where he dressed after a batboy fetched his uniform. One evening, when Brooks Robinson noticed a Florida kingsnake rapidly flicking its tongue at him from his berth in a basket of rolls near his chair at a banquet, he turned pale.

Elrod Hendricks remembered another snake incident. "He knew that Orioles teammates Luis Aparicio and Blair were afraid of snakes, so he'd bring them in and put them in their uniform shirts. Back then we didn't have warm-up shirts and all that, we had one shirt we practiced in and one we played in, and it was wool so the snake felt the comfort, the warmth of the wool and he just stayed there.

"Those guys would reach in and put their arm in the sleeve, and there comes this snake. They were always harmless snakes, but nonetheless those guys [nearly] hurt themselves trying to get out of the way of the snakes." Once Drabowsky placed a live snake in Aparacio pants pocket. Not long after putting the pants on, Aparicio's felt something crawling around and nearly had a seizure. Sometimes the snake was placed in a teammate's pocket.

Drabowsky put a boa constrictor on a clothes hanger in Charlie Lau's locker knowing the snake would wrap itself around the hanger. He then replaced Lau's uniform shirt on the hanger, buttoned the shirt up, then sat back to watch his mischief unfold. Another time when Lau was sitting in a bullpen, Drabowsky found a long pipe. From about 20 feet away he placed the pipe on Lau's shoulder several times, causing an irked Lau to bat it away. Drabowsky persisted until Lau gave up and allowed the pipe to rest on his shoulder. That's when Drabowsky unleashed a snake, allowing it to slither down the pipe. When its head emerged next to Lau's ear, he swatted the pipe away and fled in terror.

On the road Drabowsky sometimes kept his snakes on his bed, beneath the sheets, which meant he frightened many maids over the years. However, at least once Drabowsky incited fear by an act of omission. Merv

Rettenmund related that story: "We were in Florida for Green Week, for fantasy camp. Drabowsky was down there as an instructor and he went walking around Clearwater, and he found a pet shop and he got a big, old snake. On the way out to the ballpark every morning he'd stop in a restaurant for breakfast. The first morning he said, 'I got my snake here,' and he showed the waitress a bag holding his snake. Did that every day." Once again, the prank craftsman Drabowsky had set the stage.

"The last day some guys got their breakfast and the snake's bag is on the floor, but it's not in it this time. So he calls the waitress over and says, 'Hey, my snake is loose, but we'll find it.' The waitress told the owner and he empties the restaurant. As soon as they got it empty, his phone rings and Drabowsky's wife says, 'Moe, you forgot the snake.' Well, he didn't forget it. He just took the empty bag over for a prank. That's the way he would operate."

Before the start of Game 1 of the 1969 World Series between the Mets and the Orioles, Drabowsky, then with the Royals, hired a plane to fly over Baltimore's ballpark. Trailing the plane was a banner reading, "Beware of Moe." The following day the warning became a reality when he had a package delivered to his old teammates. Inside was, of course, an ominous-looking snake.

The Braves once had a teepee located near their bullpen. A Native American going by the name of Chief Noc-A-Homa would pop out of the structure and do a dance to celebrate Atlanta home runs. Drabowsky once lobbed a smoke bomb into the teepee, causing the mascot to evacuate his spot, rubbing his eyes and holding his nose shut. That's when Drabowsky threw a cherry bomb by his feet. Joe Torre, a teammate of Drabowsky in 1971, said, "He used to hang cherry bombs by your door at night. Moe was crazy."

On time he threw an M-80 with a slow burning cigarette as its fuse. He wanted it to detonate behind the outfield fence, but it landed on the field. About 12 minutes later it exploded, causing Lou Brock to jump and Drabowsky to point to an innocent fan in the stands, shouting, "There he is!"

Nobody was safe around this prankster. After the Orioles won the 1970 World Series, he gave baseball commissioner Bowie Kuhn a hotfoot by situating a book of matches near his shoe then laying down a path of lighter fluid from the matches to a distant, safe spot. There, he ignited the fluid and watched the flame travel to and ignite the matches. Liz said that one got her husband in trouble: "The ball club wasn't real happy with that. They told him he had to hold down his pranks."

He also liked to administer hotfeet during the playing of the national anthem to vulnerable players whose eyes were on the flag and not the skulking Drabowsky. A clubhouse doorman at a ballpark was another victim. Drabowsky caught him sleeping and poured lighter fluid in a circle around the doorman's chair and lit it. The poor guy woke up terrified, encircled in fire.

He even targeted people outside baseball's inner circle. Steve Murfin attended the Orioles fantasy camp when Drabowsky was on the staff. Murfin was in a bathroom stall when Drabowsky struck, tossing a smoke bomb in. "It stunk up the place and filled it with smoke," stated Murfin. "I had to run out with my pants around my ankles. My mother came to see me play and saw me with my pants down, alternating between laughing and coughing." After he told her what had happened, she hunted Drabowsky down and reprimanded him. He apologized, saying he had mistaken her son for his intended target, Brooks Robinson. Murfin said, "She hugged Moe and walked away, shaking her head knowing she had been had by Moe, too."

Drabowsky waited for teammates to get in the shower or into a bathroom stall, then tossed in smoke bombs. He gave one writer a hotfoot so often when he was engaged in conversation with other players that the poor guy took to glancing at his feet frequently while interviewing players. To counteract that, Drabowsky lit the reporter's notes as he held them.

He called hotels' front desks to leave wake-up calls for the team trainer, instructing the operator to call at 1:00, 3:00, 5:00, 7:00, and 9:00 the next morning to remind the trainer to take prescription eye drops because if he didn't take the medication, he would lose his eyesight. Drabowsky also told the operator that if he didn't respond to the calls, she was to send someone up to the room and pound on the door. Thinking of every contingency, Drabowsky even said that if he answered the phone and ordered her to cease making calls, it would be because he would be half asleep, so she was to disregard any such requests. Drabowsky slept well, but the trainer sure didn't.

Beth Morris tossed in another story. "One time Dad and Charlie [Lau] were at a hotel in Los Angeles and Charlie had gone to bed early, so my dad was out with a couple players. There was a big statue of Buddha in the lobby and *somebody* brought it up and put it in front of Charlie's door so when he opened it the next morning there's this statue staring at him."

Liz Drabowsky let it be known that the old $20 bill on a fish line prank dates back to when her husband and Bob Uecker "used to do that at the airport, and sometimes people would reach for it and fall over."

Dick Schofield said, "He just did *everything*. It wasn't anything bad. He was supposed to get a pizza after a game and bring it to where I lived for my kids and us. We opened the box and Moe ate the pizza on his way home. There were only a few pieces left in the box. He's at the top of my list, the funniest man I ever met. His favorite trick at hotels was to find a room service cart in the hallway and push it, get it going and then let it go and just *crash*. He was crazy, man, I'll tell you." Additionally, his usual demeanor and appearance gave no hint as to what lurked inside his mind. "He was quiet, but when it got dark, he was dangerous."

Another hotel-related story from Liz: "Bobby Thomson and Moe roomed together once. They'd have their luggage downstairs and Moe would always go out to lunch, and Bob—they called him the Hoot Man— would go up to the room and order a sandwich then take a nap. Moe would give him four or five dollars for the porter when he took the luggage up to the room. And Moe always joked on the bus how Hoot Man took the luggage up and kept the tip because, being of Scottish descent, he was so cheap. He never was. He was a wonderful guy."

All-Star second baseman Brian Roberts dug through his memories and said, "I never played with somebody as wild as Moe Drabowsky. He was one of my coaches in the minor leagues and to listen to his stories— you can't even comprehend some of the stuff that they did when he was playing. I don't think stuff like that happens any more nowadays. That kind of relates to it [being] a whole different generation [versus] what goes on now, what you can get away with."

Roberts said that the stories he heard "went way beyond [today's pranks]. When I was in Delmarva he was our pitching coach in A ball. One of our guys had put a huge trash can full of water, like a big industrial size can, on Moe's hotel door room and knocked on it. He opened it and it flooded his whole room. So he was mad for the entire season. The last day of the season he decided to come in with a fire extinguisher and sprayed it all over the whole clubhouse. The fire alarm went off, they had to evacuate the fans. Our game started, like, 30 minutes late—and that was when he was 65 years old, so you can imagine what he did when he was 20."

Jay Johnstone said that when he first met Drabowsky, he went to shake hands with him. Drabowsky was holding a cocktail glass, but, in order to shake hands he simply let the glass drop and shatter. Johnstone said he immediately knew that this was his kind of guy.

Drabowsky once observed a contrast between starting and relieving, saying a starter might work two hours before leaving the game, knowing he had pitched poorly. When he worked out of the pen, he said he sometimes threw only two minutes before he knew he was crap.

Carole Smith said he even joked around with family members. "Oh, always." She also told about the time her uncle took a charcoal grill to his bullpen to prepare hot dogs and hamburgers for his buddies while their game was going on. Beth Morris said, "He got us to do practical jokes, too. He wouldn't give us hot feet, but he put fake bugs in food, like if he didn't want us to eat an apple pie, he might put a few fake flies in it."

Drabowsky's wife said, "Even around the house he always had the snakes—that was his middle name. He just had a great sense of humor." After his playing days ended, he still traveled extensively. "As soon as we got into the hotel, Moe would open the big drawer on the nightstand between the beds and look in the Yellow Pages. And I knew exactly what he was looking for—he was looking for pet shops where he would ask if he could borrow a snake. And every time he was able to do that. They were very accommodating. They knew his reputation, I guess." Everyone did.

At an Orioles fantasy camp, Brooks Robinson and Drabowsky were sitting together signing autographs for fans. Morris said, "Brooks signs his signature with 'HOF,' standing for Hall of Fame, and the year he was inducted there. My dad would sign his with 'PHOF.' When Brooks asked him what that meant, Dad told him, 'Polish Hall of Fame.' He was so proud of that and of showing Brooks, 'This is how I sign my name.'"

Upon his retirement, Drabowsky was even the answer to the trivia question about which player born in Poland owns the most career homers. Drabowsky led the way with three.

BO BELINSKY (1962–1970)

Belinsky preceded Joe Namath on the sports scene by several years, and while they shared the same playboy lifestyle and the same source of income—throwing a ball—Belinsky didn't possess Namath's talent. He also hurt himself by abusing alcohol and drugs. Once, out of control, he shot his wife in the hip, then pointed the gun at his head.

Belinsky is yet another flaky lefty, which almost qualifies as being a redundant phrase. He never played high school sports, but he was destined to have a meteoric career and impact on the game. Even before his first big league appearance, Belinsky was a holdout. Offered the minimum salary of $6,000, he demanded $8,500.

* * *

Always looking for action, he was once the biggest ladies' man in baseball. Rocky Bridges called such players nightcrawlers. Even as a young man Belinsky was a hustler, so it was fitting that he was born in New York, the City That Never Sleeps, and died in Las Vegas, aka Sin City. He began his major league career as a Los Angeles Angel, an ironic nickname for him, and it was soon apparent that California was made for him and vice versa.

It was also evident that he wasn't made for baseball, despite having skill and owning a no-hitter as his fourth big league win. That game came less than a month after his call up to the majors, and was only the second no-hitter thrown by a rookie. After the game Belinsky said, "My only regret is that I can't sit in the stands and watch me."[10]

He went 7–1 over his first eight decisions, but ended up at 10–11. It took him seven more seasons to eke out 18 additional wins. His lifetime pitching log was a less-than-lustrous 28–51, and that's after starting his career at 5–0. His ultimate baseball flop conjures up a line Oscar Levant said when he learned Joe DiMaggio's marriage to Marilyn Monroe had failed: "It proves that no man can be a success in two national pastimes."

Belinsky confessed that he got more publicity for accomplishing less than any major leaguer ever. He had only one season above .500 (a modest 9–8 mark in 1964). He also stated that if he had done everything people said he did, he'd have wound up in a jar at Harvard's medical school. A team trainer mused, "Do you think baseball will shorten Bo Belinsky's career?"[11]

When he pitched for the Angels, this playboy of the Western world tooled around Hollywood in a candy-apple Cadillac with the top down and with a starlet such as Mamie Van Doren on his arm. He even took her to spring training once, calling her his physical trainer. He boasted that for one year the town was *his,* and that was something money couldn't purchase. With his bold ego, he really was Namath before most sports fans knew of a Namath.

Steve Blass, a teammate of Belinsky, recalled, "He was married to Jo Collins, the Playboy [1965 Playmate of the Year]. When he was with the Pirates, she came around to our apartment where a lot of us stayed asking for money for a charity, very legitimate, very worthwhile. I opened the door and she said what she was doing. I said, 'I'll give you everything I own—the house, the car.' She was very pretty, a nice gal. He was a very nice guy, very personable. It was Bo and Jo."

Belinsky's roomie, Dean Chance, said he went 51–1 in high school and threw 18 no-hitters. He set a record for the most losses (18) in a year which preceded a Cy Young Award–winning season. Chance borrowed the Ping Bodie line about Babe Ruth, pointing out that rooming with Belinsky was actually like rooming with his suitcase. And Gene Mauch, who managed the bon vivant, stated, "I wish I had 10 pitchers with Bo Belinsky's stuff and none with his head."

One story from 1963 has it that Belinsky was getting tattooed 8–0 after two innings. He angrily marched into the dugout, done for the day. Asked why he was so incensed, he snorted, "How do you expect a guy to win if you don't get him any runs?" Of course, that basic story is also attributed to Bobo Newsom, so who knows?

Belinsky once shared a phone number for a hot date with a fellow pitcher. However, when the teammate dialed the number, it turned out it belonged to the team manager Bill Rigney. Worse, Belinsky gave another teammate the phone number of what he said was a real beauty—that person turned out to be a drag queen.

In 1964, Belinsky was fined and suspended by the Angels after he knocked out 64-year-old sportswriter Braven Dyer. Four days later, Belinsky was assigned to the Angels' Triple-A farm team, Hawaii of the Pacific Coast League. In December the Angels dumped Belinsky in a trade with the Phillies for Rudy May and Costen Shockley.

After playing with the Phillies, he came up with the great line, "Philadelphia fans would boo a funeral." He wasn't far off, as fans in the City of Brotherly Love booed Santa Claus and pelted him with snowballs during a 1968 Eagles game. Speaking of snow, once Belinsky was late reporting to spring training camp and gave the excuse that a snowstorm caused his delay—a snowstorm in Texas.

In a 1965 interview, he again displayed poor judgment by saying that if he had been with the Phillies the year before when they blew a seemingly insurmountable lead down the stretch, he would've taken action to take the pressure off the folding Phillies. His solution? "I would have gone out and got some big blonde and punched her out . . ." His becoming a scapegoat, he contended, would have taken the heat off the team.[12] This is the same man who, just a few years earlier, had argued with a date, pulled over to the curb, and unceremoniously dumped her out of his car at 5:00 a.m. She wound up with cuts and a black eye and said he had assaulted her, and so he was taken into custody by Beverly Hills police.

Belinsky said he knew he couldn't beat the piper, but he felt sorry for "all those poor bastards who never heard the music."[13]

BILL FAUL (1962–1970)

Faul played his college ball at the University of Cincinnati, where he shattered the school's record for strikeouts in a game (19). He went on to top that with his NCAA record 24 whiffs. Coincidentally, he happened to be pitching when his Cubs turned three triple plays in 1965.

* * *

Broadcaster Ernie Harwell remembered Faul as being very flaky. "He wanted to take fully inflated balloons back to the kids at home, but he couldn't get them in his suitcase." One spring training Faul chose to use a bicycle to get around rather than a car. After that season ended, Faul didn't show for a team party, causing a teammate to say that he supposed the chain on Faul's bike must have broken.

Baseball lifer Jimy Williams said Faul, a man who never showered even after working in a game, "used to hypnotize himself, self-hypnosis before a game." When asked if what Faul did was similar to what John

Smoltz did, Williams beamed, "Oh, no, I've been with both of them. Smoltz couldn't hold a candle to Bill Faul." Faul was, in fact, a licensed hypnotist while Smoltz was into mental preparedness. In 1991, a struggling 24-year-old Smoltz was saddled with a 2–11 record and a 5.16 ERA when he sought the advice of a sport psychologist, a move which helped him turn himself and his career around.

"Faul used to lay down on a lounge chair before he was going to start a game," said Williams, "and he used to cover his head with a towel and hypnotize himself. I can remember hearing him yelling, talking, screaming before he went in to pitch, just to get himself psyched up." Asked if he did any of this in the trainers' room, Williams grinned, "They wouldn't allow him in there."

Coot Veal played with Faul in Detroit and said he "was in a different world. He wasn't dangerous, just different. Players stayed away from him." He convinced roommate Ken Rudolph that he would hypnotize him into believing he was a dog and then compel him to jump out their 19th-floor window. Rudolph soon got a new roomie.

Williams went on, "He was a dandy, something a little different. I would have to call him eccentric. He certainly didn't think he was a flake, but, then again, maybe my definition and his are a little bit different."

Faul occasionally crossed the line between eccentricity and utter nuttiness. He also swallowed live toads, believing that doing so put more hop on his fastballs. Former All-Star Larry Dierker said, "They said he would eat things in the bullpen like frogs. He was a real sick guy. As a rookie he pitched a couple of good games and said it was because he hypnotized himself and had the hitters at his mercy. He wore number 13, and he'd turn around and stand on the rubber with his back toward the hitter. He was jinxing them, see. But a couple of times the umpire had to go out and make him turn around and start pitching. He was pretty weird."

A minor league teammate told Faul he'd give him the phone number of a girl he had dated if Faul would eat a live toad. He did it, crunching away and swallowing, but the teammate said that wasn't enough. So eventually they went to shops which sold pets and bought a white mouse, which Faul (suddenly acquiring discriminating taste?) said he would not eat. He also purchased a parakeet which promptly pecked him. The clerk asked if Faul needed any feed for the bird, and he answered no, that the parakeet would be dead long before he'd get hungry. At the ballpark Faul agreed to bite the head off the bird and when it pecked him again, he made good on his promise.

One day after being yanked from a winter league game, Faul stormed into the clubhouse, seething. A teammate suggested he simply put on another player's uniform, return to the field, and resume pitching. He supposedly almost got away with doing just that.

If a player today disclosed that he was doing yoga exercises, he would evoke no strong reaction. When Faul did this back in the 1960s, he was considered to be a flake. In a way, though, Faul's preparations, especially his self-hypnosis, put him way ahead of his time when it came to what more recent players call visualization.

Regardless, Faul's methods did not help him become a star, as his lifetime record was 12–16 and his ERA nudged the 5.00 mark (at 4.72). Moreover, he was susceptible to serving up the longball, giving up about one and a half home runs for every nine innings he worked.

TUG MCGRAW (1965–1984)

McGraw never went by his real first name, Frank, so when his kindergarten teacher called roll, he didn't respond to that name. Later, when she realized she had missed one child, she found out why when McGraw told her that his name was Tug. He also told her that it was his father who was Frank and, furthermore, that Frank had already been to kindergarten.

Much later, McGraw created a cartoon character named Scroogie after his best pitch, the screwball, which somehow seems a perfect pitch for this screwy lefty. He also created two celebratory gestures: in key moments when he came off the mound he slapped his glove on his thigh and, after getting out of jams, he patted his hand over his wildly palpitating heart.

There was a time when McGraw, father of country singing star Tim, was known to sleep in the bullpen during games. His defense was simple: he stated that, hey, by the seventh inning he was awake. He certainly was ready to go when he was on the hill. Four times he ranked in the top 25 for MVP voting and in 1980, when his 4.6 Wins Above Replacement (WAR) was the seventh best among pitchers, he came in fourth in Cy Young balloting. On seven occasions he was among the top 10 relievers for saves, though one year he tied a record by yielding four grand slams.

* * *

Veteran New York sportswriter Mike Vaccaro said McGraw was "probably one of the original flakes. He was a guy who didn't take himself very seriously, but the 1973 Mets probably wouldn't have been as colorful as they were if he hadn't coined the phrase, 'You gotta believe.' That phrase was hatched because the Mets were in last place in the late summer and Don Grant, the chairman of the board, came in the clubhouse to try and cheer up the boys. He kind of gave this pep talk—and you have to envision this old-time anchor who was trying to rally this group of 25- and 26-year-old kids that they can do better. So McGraw had had enough, and with Grant standing there, he started to yell, kinda maniacally, 'You gotta believe, fellas. You gotta believe.' He was really making fun of this button-down symbol of the establishment. What ended up happening out of that meeting was that 'You gotta believe' became one of the great rallying cries of all time. It almost carried the Mets to the World Championship."

McGraw was quick. When a reporter asked him if he preferred grass or Astroturf, McGraw smiled mischievously and said, "I don't know, I never smoked Astroturf." Equipped with a devil-may-care attitude, McGraw loved throwing water balloons out of hotel windows, and he once wanted to situate a camper outside Shea Stadium for his place of residence during the season.

One time after McGraw earned a chunk of money as a bonus, he mulled over how he would spend his loot. "Ninety percent I'll spend on good times, women, and Irish whiskey." He paused, then came the punch line: "The other 10 percent I'll probably waste."

Jerome Holtzman wrote of the time Pete LaCock hit a homer to send a Cubs-Phillies game into extra innings and McGraw vowed to pay LaCock back. His payback turned out to be nothing like a knockdown pitch. When he faced LaCock in the 11th inning, he stuck his tongue out at him.

In short, McGraw was fun to be around. Marty Appel, author and former Yankees public relations director, called McGraw "a great oversized personality. My encounters with him were always delightful and his personality just shone through." Former big league coach Dan Warthen noted, "He was always doing something off the wall. If there was mischief, Tug was behind it."

FRITZ PETERSON (1966–1976)

A 20-game winner, Peterson owns the lowest career ERA ever for games pitched in old Yankee Stadium at 2.52, just ahead of Whitey Ford's 2.55. Peterson led his league five consecutive seasons for the fewest walks per nine innings pitched, something nobody had done since Cy Young (1893–1901).

Peterson is infamous for his involvement in a wife-swapping scandal with Yankee teammate Mike Kekich, but he put that behind him as best he could. There is certainly more to the man than that shocking event from his younger days.

* * *

Former teammate Tom Grieve critiqued, "He did strike me as the kind of guy who was very witty, very clever, very bright. Some guys are just crude with their practical jokes, but Fritz impressed me as the guy who would be a little more sophisticated and clever." Yankees historian Marty Appel verified that: "He was an elaborate practical joker."

Take the time in 1975 when his Indians were in their spring training camp. Duane Kuiper, a teammate, picks up the tale: "The clubhouse man would leave the weekly bill for clubhouse dues, say for $30, on each player's chair. Fritz wrote a '1' in front of the '30' on the rookies' bills. They'd see it [a bill apparently for $130] and almost die. They'd believe anything." Of course as recently as 2016 players got almost that much a day ($105) in per diem money, a sum since slashed, but in 1975 a bill for $130 truly was enough to induce a stroke for a rookie.

Speaking of big money and of playing tricks on rookies, former star first baseman Chris Chambliss said, "I think the game's a little bit different now. The money that they make now is so much different. So some of those traditions have started to fade away." He divulged that there were times when a rookie's ordeal was to serve the veterans when a group of players went out to eat. Sometimes a rookie would be invited to eat at a fine restaurant with veterans. Proud to be included, the first-year player would readily accept. Then, at the end of the evening, the vets would have the waitress hand the exorbitant bill to him. Later, of course, they would *usually* let him in on the joke and pay the tab. However, says Chambliss, even having a bunch of teammates eating out together is dying out. So, as he put it, "Some of those pranks don't really exist anymore."

Joe Charboneau also felt that by the time he reached the major leagues in 1980, many veterans, instead of being pranksters, became unofficial coaches for young players. "Rod Carew took me under his wing, talked hitting with me. He was a good mentor, for lack of a better word." Charboneau joked that on one occasion Carew was offering advice even as "he was struggling a little bit—I think he was only hitting about .350 that year, but he was a fabulous person and player. He was always willing to help anybody and everybody on their hitting. He was a real class act. . . . Reggie Jackson would work with me and talk to me, too—there were a lot of veteran players willing to help you during the game and pre-game. Ralph Garr helped me a lot when he was with the Angels, and Willie Horton, Bucky Dent, and George Brett helped a lot, too."

Returning to Peterson and an era of numerous pranks, he once played a complex trick on Thurman Munson after Munson had filled out an order form for an expensive western-style holster. Peterson intercepted the order and altered it so Munson would get a holster all right, but it would be for left-handers, and way too small to fit Munson's waist.

When Munson received the holster, he tried to return it, asking club-house manager Pete Sheehy to mail it back to the company. Peterson again intervened, substituting a letter of thanks and asking for directions to help him learn how to draw a pistol out of a left-handed holster. A representative from the company wrote back apologizing that they had no literature on how to use such a holster.

At that point, a very irate Munson told Sheehy to return the holster for a refund. Again, Peterson went to work. He took possession of the holster, kept it over the winter, then when Munson reported for spring training, there on his chair at his locker was the ubiquitous holster.

On another occasion, Peterson signed Mel Stottlemyre up to purchase encyclopedias from various companies. When Stottlemyre returned home from a road trip, tons of boxes of expensive tomes awaited—and they just kept on coming for days.

Sparky Lyle called Peterson the best practical joker around. One example was the time Lyle was one of his victims. The Yankees were in a Minnesota hotel almost 30 minutes away from the ballpark. A car pulled up near the team bus outside the hotel, and the driver went inside to deliver a package. Seeing this, Peterson went over to some teammates and, gesturing toward the car, offered them a ride. Four Yankees accepted, hopped in the car, and waited for Peterson to join them. Moments later the owner of the car popped out of the hotel and noticed strangers in his vehicle. He may have thought they were car thieves, but then again, how many criminals pack into a car with no getaway driver at the wheel?

Knowing that teammate Gene Michael was horrified by just about anything that moved, Peterson and Mel Stottlemyre placed a large bullfrog in Michael's jockstrap. When he got dressed and felt something moving, he belted out words to the effect of, "Something just kicked my privates."

During games Peterson would sneak back to the clubhouse and disturb a teammate's belongings in or around his locker. He then would tell that teammate, let's say Munson, that he had just seen another Yankee, for instance Roy White, messing with his locker. Munson would rush to his locker while Peterson told White that he had spied Munson messing with *his* locker. Therefore, when White made his way to the clubhouse, sure enough, there was Munson slinking about. Very Machiavellian.

As was the trick Peterson pulled on the Twins clubbie who had prepared a couple dozen deviled eggs. Peterson discovered the clubbie's cache and gobbled eight, about seven more than what was his fair share. He then returned to the dugout and tempted Jerry Kenney by telling him about his tasty clubhouse discovery. Before Kenney could act, Peterson warned the clubbie that Kenney had eaten a bunch of the eggs and would probably return for more. When Kenney finally got around to eating an egg, he got caught and was forever doomed to be in the clubhouse attendant's doghouse.

Peterson duped Kenney again when he sent him a forged letter asking if he'd do a commercial for Gulden's Mustard, just as Elston Howard had done. He offered Kenney $5,000 for the spot, great money for a player earning $9,000 as a Yankee. Howard, who was in on the joke, told the ecstatic Kenney he should ask Gulden's for more. The next day Roy White told Peterson to tell Kenney the truth because his mark had just ordered a new Mustang convertible.

Many years later, again using official letterhead—this time of the Hall of Fame—Peterson sent Moose Skowron a request for him to donate his pacemaker. He made it clear the donation would come after Skowron had passed away, of course. The patient Peterson didn't bump into Skowron for quite some time, but at an Old Timers' Game in 2006 when he knew

Skowron was within earshot, he casually told Stottlemyre that he had received a letter from the Hall of Fame asking him to donate his shoulder joint replacement after he died. That prompted Skowron to join the conversation, screaming that it took some nerve for the Hall to make such requests and that he had already chewed out the group's president, Dale Petroskey. Even after Petroskey insisted he had no knowledge of any such request, Skowron continued his tirade.

Roy White, who knew that the Yankees had taken an exhibition trip to Japan a few years earlier, was also victimized by Peterson. Using the Yankee letterhead, the ultimate prankster posted a notice about a new tour of Japan, indicating that there were 25 openings for those who wished to sign up. The bait was so tempting—a two-week trip for players and wives, travel expenses covered, plus $1,000 spending cash—White naturally bit.

Now, the wildest thing Peterson ever did, as touched on earlier, was take part in the shocking 1972 act of swapping wives with a teammate, Mike Kekich. Using a broad definition of what constitutes a baseball trade, *this* trade was the most bizarre ever. The two pitchers had become close friends and their families interacted a lot (too much, it would prove). The two men not only traded wives, they exchanged the entire families—kids, dogs, and all. When Yankee general manager Lee Mac-Phail learned of the swap, he said, "There goes family day."[14]

In 1973, the staid Yankees organization, embarrassed by the scandal, sent Kekich to Cleveland. The next year they swapped Peterson there as well, but they would not become teammates because that move came almost exactly one month after the Indians had released Kekich. In the end, only two players who never made it to a World Series as Yankees ever wore the pinstripes longer than Peterson—Horace Clarke and Don Mattingly.

SPARKY LYLE (1967–1982)

Lyle, who racked up 238 lifetime saves, is one of only a handful of relievers to win the Cy Young Award, and he was the first to cop that honor in 1977. He didn't play baseball in high school, but he did play Legion ball and he once fanned 31 batters in a 17-inning sandlot game. Lyle pitched 899 games, none as a starter, a job he said he had no desire to perform. His nickname was Sparky, but his job was to extinguish even the slightest of fires. "The thing about Sparky was that he was opinionated. He wrote a book called *The Bronx Zoo*, so you know what the Yankee clubhouse was all about," said sportswriter Mike Vaccaro.

Lyle was as effective as he was funny. In 1977, he helped his Yankees win 100 games, en route to winning the World Series, by appearing in a league leading 72 games and by notching 26 saves (number two in the American League) to go with his 2.17 ERA. He even won 13 games out of the bullpen and wound up sixth in the voting for the MVP.

* * *

The aftermath of his finest season featured a classic line about Lyle's eventual fate. Vaccaro recalled, "He had won the Cy Young Award in 1977 when he had this fantastic year, the culmination of a great five or six-year run in New York. Then he was driving cross-country in a rainstorm when the news came over the radio that the Yankees had obtained Goose Gossage, so basically Sparky's [closer] job was gone. He was going to be Gossage's setup man, a mop-up man. Later [after Lyle got traded], Nettles said, 'He went from Cy Young to sayonara.'"

Lyle was a great jokester, but that was only one facet of the man. "Sparky was just a delight to be with," said Marty Appel. "Every conversation, every encounter with Sparky, you'd come away smiling because of his winning personality and his great attitude on life. He was one of my heroes just for the way he led his life and carried himself. If things weren't going well for him, that's okay—tomorrow would be better. That was a great way to approach life. I still have nothing but great fondness for Sparky."

Nevertheless, if awards were given out for crazy behavior, Lyle probably would have copped quite a few of them. Dick Schofield said, "I played with Sparky Lyle in Boston, and if he could do something that would be different, he was right there and he did it."

Yankee teammate Bucky Dent reminisced, "Sparky was a beauty. He used to sit on birthday cakes that came [to the clubhouse] when it was a guy's birthday. They put them on a table so we could eat them, but we never got a chance to." Nor would they want to, as Appel explained, "Lyle would strip off all his clothes and ceremoniously squat on the cake to the delight of teammates." One could say Lyle sat on birthday cakes while wearing his birthday suit.

When Yankee teammate Jim Mason was fast asleep one day at the team's hotel, Lyle took the opportunity to move him to the pool, remove his clothes, and tie him to a chair. He then called the police to say a potential suicide attempt might be imminent. Teammates gathered around for the impending spectacle, but Mason freed himself to end the caper.

Lyle once broke into a hotel room packed with fellow Yankees and blasted them with spray from a fire extinguisher. Unbeknownst to fellow Yankee Mike Kekich, when he was administering a hotfoot to Phil Rizzuto, Lyle was simultaneously giving him one.

Another time Lyle noticed a teammate, Rick Sawyer, had a post-game routine of coming off the field, grabbing a towel, folding it in a precise manner, then placing it on a rack. After his shower, he always took his towel, mechanically unfolded it, then dried off, starting with his face. So Lyle slathered black shoe polish all over the part of the towel hidden by folds. When Sawyer emerged from his shower and began to towel off, the polish smeared all over, requiring a serious scrubbing to remove. Typically, players and even their expensive clothes weren't safe when they showered and Lyle was lurking about.

Elston Howard was asleep on a plane ride so the opportunistic Lyle squirted a pile of shaving cream on top of his head. Only when Howard noticed he was getting a lot of peculiar looks from other travelers in the airport concourse did he discover Lyle's handiwork.

Lyle once had a doctor place his pitching arm and a leg in a cast—nothing was wrong, but Lyle wanted to see how his manager, Bill Virdon, would react upon seeing his pretend plight. One time when a young female jumped aboard a Yankees team bus and asked for autographs, she permitted players to sign her bare buttocks. When it was Lyle's turn, he took his time, signing Albert Walter Sparky Lyle Junior. Another time Lyle described Munson, who was often labeled as a moody person. Lyle's portrayal was different: "Thurman's not moody. When you're moody, you're nice sometimes. He's just mean."

Lyle relied on his wicked slider, but in one game he repeatedly shook off Munson's sign for that pitch. They met on the mound and Lyle asked, "Hey, you think I can get him out with my super fantastic change?" Confused, Munson basically said, "Changeup? You don't have one!"

Lyle's logic was, "That's the last thing they'd think of getting from me. They know I don't throw one."[15]

Yogi Berra often bummed Lyle's toothpaste. So, using a syringe, Lyle injected White Heat, a scalding ointment, into the toothpaste, then sat back waiting for the fun to begin. Berra was an inveterate mooch who also borrowed Whitey Ford's roll-on deodorant. The only problem was the container didn't hold deodorant—it was full of a mix of sticky, gooey ingredients Ford used to doctor baseballs. Berra had to cut his armpit hair to solve his problem.

A fan complained to the Yankees brass that Lyle had promised him a ball during batting practice, then didn't make good on his promise. Lyle was told to sign a ball and mail it to the disgruntled fan. He complied, signing, "Kiss my ass. Sparky Lyle."

In away games against the Indians, he often played in front of sparse crowds, which led him to borrow an old line: "If anybody called up and asked what time the game started, [they'd] ask, 'What time can you make it?'"

JERRY REUSS (1969–1990)

Reuss, a 220-game winner, came in second in the 1980 Cy Young Award voting. That season his .750 winning percentage was second in the National League. Three times his WAR for pitchers had him in his league's top 10.

Reuss is yet another of many, many zany southpaws. Carl Erskine said, "He's another guy who saw the funny side of life. He had that kind of personality."

* * *

When Steve Yeager and Reuss were teammates with the Dodgers, they enjoyed some crazy times. Former Dodger coach Dick McLaughlin recalled when the two men "were in a helicopter being taken to West Palm Beach for a dinner—they were going to be speakers that night. On the way to the airport they stopped and bought some balloons and filled them up with water. They were about one-half mile from the spring training complex and had the pilot fly over the Dodgers field, and they dumped about 20 balloons." He said the ensuing scene was reminiscent of the movie *Tora, Tora, Tora* as startled players scattered from the balloon barrage.

Reuss and Jay Johnstone loved to team up to terrorize and torment fellow Dodgers, especially manager Tommy Lasorda, with their practical jokes. Many a hotfoot was applied by these men.

Fred Claire was the Dodgers general manager from 1969 to 1998. He said Reuss posted one of his most colorful moments on Facebook. Reuss persuaded some groundskeepers to give him one of their uniforms. Donning the outfit, he got in a cart and began to drag the infield. "Jerry told the story that after Tommy [Lasorda] recognized what was happening, he quickly called him to the sidelines, but that didn't stop Jerry because he went out a second time. He found another partner to do this again a year or two later. And that would be, of course, Jay Johnstone." McLaughlin said that after driving the cart, "Jay and Jerry started mooning the crowd and Lasorda, who didn't recognize his players at first."

Reuss, Ken Brett, and Don Stanhouse also performed an act like that. Shortly before the visiting Reds were to take batting practice, they were clustered in their dugout. All of a sudden, a cart rolled by and, as it neared the dugout, the three pitchers shot moons at the Reds in a most unusual drive-by shooting.

Fred Claire continued, "I've heard Jerry tell this story—when we flew into New York, and I guess we were there the day before we were to play, he went to Yankee Stadium. This sounds unreal, but he took his Dodger [equipment] bag and went into [Yankees manager] Lou Piniella's office to say, 'I'm here and ready to help your team.' Piniella said, 'What the hell are you talking about?' Jerry said, 'Well, you know. I've been traded to your team.' Piniella went crazy and said, 'Nobody tells me anything about what's happening here.'" Classic Reuss.

McLaughlin shared the story about when Reuss was at Vero Beach on a rehab assignment. His Dodgers had broken camp, so Reuss was the only veteran in camp. "He decided he was going to run the practice with the minor leaguer kids, stretching, everything. We were all standing around when he said, 'We're going for a little run,' and his group didn't come back for an hour. I never found out where he took them—maybe under a tree to catch some shade."

Referring to blustery Candlestick Park, Reuss said, "This wouldn't be such a bad place to play if it wasn't for that wind. I guess that's like saying hell wouldn't be such a bad place if it wasn't so hot."

BILL LEE (1969–1982)

Lee, a true out-of-this-world Spaceman, and another lefty (naturally), pitched for the University of Southern California as a teammate of Tom Seaver. He reached a personal high of 17 wins three times. In two seasons his total of complete games and his ERA ranked in the top 10. A veteran of 14 big league seasons and many more years of pitching in various leagues after he left the majors, his lifetime record in the big leagues was 119–90.

* * *

Lee said that all of the drinking and carrying on at USC made it tough for him to become oriented there, but it was great training for what was to come in the majors. After winning the College World Series, a teammate drank gasoline directly out of the pump. He was fine for a while, then passed out. Someone commented that the guy was wasted. Lee said, "No. He just ran out of gas."[16]

During the middle of an intense pennant race, Lee was asked how much pressure he was feeling. He replied, "Thirty-two pounds per square inch at sea level." Lee stated that he sprinkled marijuana on his pancakes, and when asked how he liked Montreal, he answered that it was fine "once I get past customs."[17] His take on mandatory drug testing was, "I've tested 'em all. But I don't think it should be mandatory."[18] He said that he was glad he was a starter for one reason: "It's a lot easier when you're starting, because when you're starting you can pick your days to drink."

Definitely off kilter in his thinking, he requested jersey number 337 because when turned upside down, that numeral "spells" LEE. He settled for number 37 which, coincidentally, was the number also worn by fellow flakes Casey Stengel and Jimmy Piersall.

It's been said that when he first set eyes on Fenway Park's Green Monster, which loomed a bit more than 37 feet over the left field playing area, Lee asked if the imposing wall was kept there during the games. Going into Game 7 of the 1975 World Series, he was asked how he'd describe the Series up to that point, and he answered succinctly: "Tied."

Fittingly, Lee, known as the Spaceman, titled a book he wrote *The Wrong Stuff*, and the cover of his book *Have Glove Will Travel* featured him dressed like an astronaut, but one with a beanie adorned by a propeller on top.

He also said he was running for president for what he called the Rhinoceros Party. He said he'd limit campaign donations to a quarter, because his was merely a two-bit bid for the White House.

By the way, Lee may have been off-center, but Joe Charboneau was impressed by his intelligence. "He could speak French because he played in Montreal. He was into philosophies and stuff like that."

Marty Appel said, "I got a kick out of him. I remember esoteric things with him, like I read once that he walked into the trainer's room and Carl Yastrzemski was on the table lying on his side. Yaz's number eight, sideways, looked like the symbol for infinity which Lee thought was perfect because Carl Yastrzemski was going to go on forever. That's the way his mind worked."

"He didn't like the Yankees," said New York sportswriter Mike Vaccaro. "He didn't like Graig Nettles and he despised Billy Martin in every way possible. He called the Yankees 'Martin's Brown Shirts.' He liked to say that as a pitcher he didn't really know when a ball was hit [well] by seeing it come off the bat, but he could *hear* it off the bat. Lee was driving home listening to Game 7 of the 2003 ALCS, about five minutes away from his home, when he heard the crack of the bat through the radio of Aaron Boone's homer a split second before the announcer said, 'It's high, deep. It's going, it's gone.' He could tell from the sound of the crack of the bat that it was gone.

"As a longtime Yankee hater, even more than being a longtime Red Sox alumnus, he was bummed about that. He walked into his house where he had been tortured that entire summer by a Norwegian rat which had broken into his fridge and had left droppings everywhere. He hated the rat so much, he gave him the name Billy Martin. One of his intricate traps had gone off, and there were the remains of Billy Martin, the rat. He told me, 'I was still feeling pretty pissed, but killing Billy Martin made me feel a little better.'"

Lee felt speedy Cool Papa Bell was impressive for his ability to turn out the light in his bedroom, then dash into his bed before the light went out, but Lee topped that, sometimes passing out before he even got back to his hotel room.

AL HRABOSKY (1970–1982)

Hrabosky's intimidating Fu Manchu made an impression on batters who faced him. Hrabosky just *knew* it helped him get men out. When one manager informed him he would have to shave it off, the man known as the Mad Hungarian snorted, "How can I intimidate batters if I look like a [profanity] golf pro." He insisted there would be no Delilah to sap his power.

There was another side of Hrabosky when off the field. During a 2018 interview, former big leaguer Joe Cunningham said, "I was managing Modesto, California, and the Mad Hungarian was the short relief pitcher for me." Many years later, Cunningham was asked by some law enforcement officials to get some former Cardinals together to create an antidrug elementary school assembly program. "Hrabosky did this for about 10 or 15 years, and he is still in the Cardinals front office."

* * *

Cunningham said when Hrabosky, who was an intense linebacker in high school, pitched, "He had a little antic, a thing where he tried to throw the hitter off and [pump himself] up a little bit. That was part of his act—and it worked. Of course, he had a pretty good fastball, too."

Hrabosky's version of a self-hypnosis act frequently featured storming several strides off the mound toward second base to meditate. He snapped out of it by violently and crisply firing the ball a few inches into his glove as he strode back to the rubber, steam seemingly spurting out of his nose like a deranged dragon. Once he tried to slam the ball into his glove but he missed, which only infuriated him more as he had to retrieve the ball from the grass.

Lee Smith, one-time holder of the record for career saves, said he believed Hrabosky "was psyching himself out." Firing himself up was, said Hrabosky, a way to prepare for the next pitch with confidence and determination. Goose Gossage said, "I definitely think it was an act." Regardless—it worked.

Once, though, his tactic resulted in a famous stalemate. Ken Griffey Sr. recounted a time George Foster was batting. "Every time George stepped into the batter's box, Hrabosky would go behind the mound and turn his back on him and rub up the ball. Then he'd slam the ball into his glove and go back up on the mound, and George would step out. They did that for about 10 minutes. The umpire told George 'Get in the box, and [to Hrabosky] you pitch.' I said, 'Look at these two out there arguing and they haven't said a word to each other.'"

Hrabosky got into a similar sort of standoff with umpire Bob Engel. The ump tossed a new baseball out to the mound, but Hrabosky didn't like the feel of it so he lobbed it back to Engel, requesting another ball. Engel got upset at Hrabosky's pickiness, so glaring at the pitcher who was about to reject another ball, he fired a ball toward Hrabosky, who made no effort to catch the errant throw. Disgusted, Hrabosky rolled the ball he had been inspecting toward home plate. Engel countered by taking yet another baseball out of his ball bag and rolling it near the mound. The Mad Hungarian, by now the furious Hungarian, was not about to bend over to get either of the two balls, which were on the grass. A much calmer teammate gave him a ball, and play resumed.

However, the next pitch, which was ball three, resulted in Dodger batter Reggie Smith taking first base. In the turmoil of the situation, several people had lost track of the count, but not Hrabosky. When he told Engel that the pitch was only ball three, the ump basically replied, "How do you expect me to know that—you had balls all over the place."

One year, Hrabosky had a birthday cake delivered to Jerry Reuss. Knowing Reuss planned on sticking his face into the cake, Hrabosky garnished the cake with manure from horses he owned.

BERT BLYLEVEN (1970–1992)

Blyleven was born in Zeist, Netherlands, but moved to a home two miles from Disneyland when he was five years old. He made it to the majors when he was just 19, making him the youngest player in the majors. The year he retired, he was the sixth-oldest player. His path to the majors was smoothly paved because he had developed one of the greatest curveballs in the history of baseball—a pitch so toxic to batters, it was deserving of the nickname Deadman's Curve.

Carl Erskine, who also had a great pitch that dropped straight down, said Blyleven had one of the best curves he ever saw and "I've watched a lot of pitchers. He threw his kind of high three-quarters [release], not as extreme as my straight overhand pitches." Now in his 90s, Erskine says he very rarely watches all nine innings of a game, but "when I see a pitcher like Blyleven, I stay with the game to watch him pitch."

In 1986, Blyleven dished up a homer to light-hitting Jay Bell in the latter's big league debut. It's one of those interesting coincidences that Bell was one of the players Blyleven was later traded for. Bell's belt lifted Blyleven's total of home runs surrendered to a new season record of 47, and he gave up three more that year. Blyleven is still the single-season record holder for homers surrendered, but he could joke about that: "It's pretty bad when your family asks for passes to the game and wants to sit in the left-field bleachers."

Only eight men, all big-name pitchers, have ever been taken deep more often than Blyleven's 430 times. That simply meant he was around the plate with his pitches and that he lasted a long time at baseball's highest level. Nothing, however, stopped him from becoming a Hall of Famer (Class of 2011).

Through 2018, Blyleven stands fifth on the all-time strikeout list, third for career 1–0 victories (15), and ninth for shutouts (60). One season he only won 12 games, but had a record 20 no-decisions. Seven times he was in the top five in ERA, and he won 287 games in all.

* * *

Tom Grieve, once a teammate of Blyleven, remembered, "Bert was one of the funnier players. He was constantly doing practical jokes. The thing that always made it work for him was he's such a good guy. He has no ego. He's one of the guys, a great teammate. So when he's pulling practical jokes and making fun of people, no one ever took it the wrong way. I don't think you'll find anyone who didn't genuinely like Bert Blyleven. He was definitely a prankster, and he was one of the two or three best pitchers in the league at the same time so he was able to pull things off in a way that, as far as I could tell, never offended anybody.

"One of the things he's known for is his fascination with farting. He wears a T-shirt that says, 'I Love Farts,' so that pretty much says it all. When we were playing together, he would make this little contraption— he would get a coat hanger, cut off the ends and hook up big rubber bands with a washer. He'd wind the washer up so that when he let it go, the rubber bands would cause it to spin fast. He'd sit on it with a book so when he lifted up a little bit, it sounded exactly like he was passing gas.

"I remember one instance when I was sitting next to him at a restaurant. The hostess came over to ask us what we wanted to drink, and he lifted up and [made the noise] and then looked at me and went, 'Oh, dang, what are you doing?' At that point in time, I wasn't in a position to say, 'That wasn't me, that was you,' you just kind of suck up the joke."

Once Grieve was in a Chicago movie theater with about 20 other people. "It was pitch black and I heard someone on the other side of the room passing gas throughout the movie. A couple of us said to each other, 'I guarantee you that's Blyleven.' And the movie ended and the lights came on and there's Bert walking out of the theater."

He pulled a trick on Cleveland teammate Von Hayes in 2001 when Hayes got a broken bat single for his first big league hit, albeit a cheap one. Blyleven retrieved the baseball but substituted it for another one, which he presented to Hayes. The ball had this message: "First hit off [expletive] right-hander Jim Slaton, on a broken-bat quail to center field."[19] Of course he later gave the proper ball, untarnished, to Hayes.

Grieve said, "He also liked to play practical jokes at the airport. He would hook up a dollar bill to a fish line and toss it where people were walking. When someone bent down to get the dollar, he'd yank the fish line so they couldn't get it. . . . But one of the more cruel ones he did was he would get a silver dollar and heat it up with a match then drop it on the floor. When someone tried to pick it up, they'd obviously drop it because it was so hot." He also taped clubhouse boys to tables and turned them upside down, or to a ladder which faced a wall, dooming the kid to a poor view and a lengthy stay in his prison.

Grieve helped turn the tables on Blyleven when both were announcing games. "In Texas our home [broadcasting] booth is next to the visitors' booth. Bert was announcing for the Twins and we knew Rene, the girl who was serving as his stage manager. We brought in a remote-control fart contraption—you could put it in your pocket and press a button and it would make all sorts of fart noises.

"We gave it to her to put in her pocket, but we had the control in our booth. We would press it and at first he kind of just looked at her out of the corner of his eye like he wasn't sure that really happened. And we did it again during the game and he started laughing. Then he said something to her and she said, 'Oh, I'm so sorry, Mr. Blyleven. I must have eaten something bad today.' This went on the whole game. When the game was over, he had made a new friend and was actually proud of the fact that for the whole game she did this. When we finally told him what the joke was, he looked like he had just lost his best friend—he was crestfallen, genuinely disappointed when he found out it was all a joke. He thought he found someone of the opposite sex who loved [farting] as much as he did."

His nationality coupled with his propensity for lighting people's shoelaces on fire spawned his nickname, the Frying Dutchman. Blyleven even joked about where he sometimes aimed his pitches. "I've never played with a pitcher who tried to hit a batter in the head," he began. "Most pitchers are like me. If I'm going to hit somebody, I'm going to aim for the bigger parts."

Grieve was never surprised at such quips. "He was clever on the bench. He was witty. He was funny. Once when he knew the camera was on in the dugout, he gave the one-finger salute to the camera. Someone asked, 'What were you doing,' and he said, 'I was just saying that the Rangers were number one.' He was the first one that I ever heard say that although it's been repeated many times since then."

Nobody was immune to his pranks. Still, at times he was chastised for his actions like when he and some other pitchers got caught putting on their makeshift mini-golf course in the bullpen. They were detected when their action was captured on the Jumbotron.

LARRY ANDERSEN (1975–1994)

Andersen was a relief pitcher who bounced around, making pit stops with six big league clubs. Playing for that many teams and for 17 seasons in the majors makes Andersen the very definition of a journeyman player. He made two trips to the Fall Classic, and he was the only Philly to appear in both the 1983 and the 1993 World Series.

A clever comedian off the field, on the field he was as serious as a biopsy. He worked in 699 contests and registered 49 saves and an ERA of 3.15. When the durable righty retired, only one player in the majors was older.

One of his claims to fame is his involvement in a lopsided 1990 trade, going from the Astros to the Red Sox in exchange for Jeff Bagwell. Andersen would pitch in only 15 games and record a single save for Boston. Bagwell proceeded to win innumerable games for the Astros with his 449 home runs and 1,529 runs driven in.

Yet when the trade was first consummated and Andersen, coming off two good seasons, was told whom he had been traded for, he asked incredulously if this nobody minor leaguer named Bagwell was all they got in return for him. That's a comment that in retrospect is as funny as it is ludicrous. Now Andersen can truthfully brag that he was traded for a Hall of Famer.

In 2012, when the MLB Network compiled their top 25 baseball personalities of all time, Andersen checked in at number 12 on that list.

* * *

Another Hall of Famer, Alan Trammell, said Andersen was "a team prankster and very much a comedian." Andersen reminds many observers of stand-up comic Steven Wright, known for his dry sense of humor. In addition to being a huge devotee of soap operas, Andersen was a big fan of humor and produced some great comedic material. Some of that is evident in Andersen's one-liners, such as:

- "Roses are red, violets are blue. I'm a schizophrenic, and so am I."
- "How can you tell when you're running out of invisible ink?"
- "Why does *sour* cream have an expiration date?"
- "How come 'fat chance' and 'slim chance' mean the same thing?"
- "Why does your foot smell and your nose run?"
- "What do they package Styrofoam in?"
- "What do they call a coffee break at the Lipton Tea Company?"
- "Why do we park on a driveway and drive on a parkway?"
- "Why do we sing 'Take Me Out to the Ballgame' when we're already there?"
- "Was Robin Hood's mother known as Mother Hood?"

- When told to be careful with a power hitter, Andersen remarked, "If he's a good fastball hitter, should I throw him a bad fastball?"
- "You can only be young once, but you can be immature forever."

That final comment could be taken as his personal motto. After all, this is a guy who boasted about his ability to burp loud and long. He even claimed he could hold a burp for about 15 seconds, and he could talk and sing *while* burping. Obviously, he doesn't march to the beat of a different drummer—he gallops.

He said that being isolated in the bullpen meant he couldn't take part in dugout celebrations after, for example, homers. He compared himself in that regard to the television castaway, Gilligan.

Andersen is also comparable to Steve Martin from his early stand-up comedy. Former big league coach Joel Skinner said that Andersen "is a guy that would enjoy putting on the funny glasses and the mustache, things like that." He did much more than that.

Anyone who knew Andersen has many memories of the man. Five-time batting champion Wade Boggs said, "I played with him in Boston. He had great one-liners." However, Denny Walling, a big league coach and former player, said that quite a bit of Andersen's humor goes beyond the witticisms, that some of his antics remind him of "Roger McDowell and his off-the-wall stuff." (More on McDowell later.) Walling once was an Astros teammate of Andersen, and he recalled, "He used to do a lot of different tricks. He'd do the thread on the $20 bill in the airport thing. Set it down and yank on the string when someone went to pick it up."

Boggs continued with his take on Andersen: "His sunflower seeds on the face was probably the neatest thing that he did. He opened them up and sort of pinched them to his face." It wasn't unusual to see Andersen plaster around 80 to a personal high of 87 seeds on his face at a time until he looked like a beekeeper sporting a swarm of bees on his face. When asked what was the point of it all, Boggs chuckled, "I don't know, just crazy." Walling, though, said he felt Andersen sometimes did it simply "for the camera to get a look at." Many players have been known to do something wild to get some television face time.

Andersen once distributed 40,000 masks of his face to the home crowd. He later joked that this led to him being accused of holding up convenience stores around the city for about a year. All-Star Phil Garner commented, "Larry was always doing pranks in Houston. One of his favorites was in airports when he'd wear cone heads. He also had a big rubber fly that he would carry around all the time. He would put it in his food on the airplane then he'd call the stewardess over and complain about the fly in his meal. The stewardess would be scrambling, trying to get him good food, but he'd just carry on and on about it."

Once, he and two Seattle teammates got into their manager's hotel room and removed all the light bulbs, piled the furniture into the bathroom, and filled the toilet bowl with cherry Jell-O.

In 1997, the Phillies hired Andersen as a coach. One day, Phillies pitcher Matt Beach surrendered a mammoth home run to Butch Huskey of the Mets. The ball smacked down into the 600 level of Veterans Stadium. The last time a man had hit a ball into that uppermost region had been 26 years earlier when Willie Stargell, a bona fide big bopper for the Pittsburgh Pirates, deposited a ball there.

Andersen came up with a unique description of the longball: "You know . . . the commander of that Mir space station? I think that ball landed in his seat." Andersen also said that he went to Beech after the Huskey blast. "I told him, 'Don't feel bad. This is a small stadium. That wouldn't even have gone out of Houston.' He said, 'Yeah, the city.'"

Earlier that season, Beech had also served up a pitch that Atlanta's Andruw Jones drilled, just missing the 600 level in center. This time Andersen noted, "I've always told Beechie that if you're going to give them up, you might as well make them memorable." He skipped a beat, then concluded, "Obviously he's a quick learner."

Walling added that he felt baseball "needs guys like Larry. It adds a little bit of color and it certainly adds some fun and releases [tension] in the clubhouse." The term "flake" used to call to mind baseball characters who were charming, colorful, and/or humorous in a crazy yet fun way. The word was used with affection. Years ago, a player like Andersen would have been labeled an irrefutable flake, but somehow over the years that word has taken on a negative connotation and is no longer in wide usage. Near the turn of the twenty-first century, former big league manager Terry Collins expounded, "Years and years ago, there were probably a lot of guys who were considered flaky or colorful, but now there's so much focus and so much attention on the players that a lot of them have toned it down for a lot of reasons. They don't want to be the center of attention all the time, so I think players today are a little bit different in that sense." He believes a lot of the clowning doesn't take place on the field as it once did, but rather in the clubhouse, "in private, not where the fans or media get to see it."

Maybe so, but Walling chimed in on what he sees as the distinction between labels such as "flake" versus "colorful character," saying, "Times change, so the terminology changes. Colorful character sounds a little better than flake now, but there are a lot of them around." Distinctions aside, Andersen, a veritable King of Comedy, contributed much to the lore of baseball.

RICK SUTCLIFFE (1976–1994)

Sutcliffe enjoyed an 18-year career, winning 171 games and a Cy Young Award in 1984. That year was a remarkable one in that he had a 4–5 record with the Indians, then was shipped to the Cubs and spun things around with the mighty force of a vortex. With Chicago, he went 16–1 for an astronomical winning percentage of .941. Down the stretch he reeled off 14 victories in a row and helped the Cubs win their division. Astonishingly, his ERA plummeted from 5.15 with Cleveland to 2.69 in Chicago. He went from just 5.5 strikeouts per nine innings to 9.3 with Chicago, and his walks per nine innings were cut in half.

* * *

Former pitcher Jamie Moyer said, "Over the course of my career I've had some interesting teammates who liked to have fun. [Ryne] Sandberg, as quiet as he was, he was a prankster, and Jay Buhner liked to have fun with the guys. Nothing malicious, it was all in fun and it all stayed in house. It's just part of the camaraderie of the team."

Moyer said some veterans would "pick on guys in a fun way. I wouldn't call it hazing but, especially with the younger guys, kind of allow them to feel a part of the team. Sutcliffe was always a fun guy to do pranks like the rookie thing, dressing guys up." Moyer was referring to a tradition of making rookies wear outrageous clothes such as superhero outfits or ballerina's tutus, then marching them through public places like airports. "I remember after my first major league start in Chicago, I won and, of course, you're doing interviews after the game. I go in the shower, go to my locker, and look for my clothes and they weren't around. I look around the clubhouse and nobody was around. I probably searched for about a half an hour to find my clothes. It was all in fun."

Denny Neagle, a one-time 20-game winner, said his favorite player "who had me cracking up was Rick Sutcliffe. The guy can do some stand-up and he's so quick with one-liners he had me cracking up. He's big on practical jokes, too. Hotfoot, you name it, he'd do it."

In 1991, a Cubs rookie catcher named Erik Pappas banged out his first big league hit. The ball was lobbed into the Chicago dugout for safekeeping, later to be given to Pappas as a memento. Now, if Babe Ruth was the Sultan of Swat, then Sutcliffe was a Colossus of Craziness. He got possession of the baseball and inscribed Pappas's name and the date of his first hit on the ball. When Pappas returned to the dugout, Sutcliffe presented him with a ball. Pappas remembered, "He used an old ball instead of the real ball from my first hit. He purposely spelled my name wrong."[20] Seeing that act of vandalism on what he thought was his treasured trophy, Pappas was shocked. Naturally, after an appropriate amount of time had passed, Sutcliffe told Pappas the truth and gave him the real ball. On other occasions, a rookie returns to the dugout to claim his souvenir only to be handed a soiled, muddy, and/or grass-stained baseball.

Craig Counsell, a member of the 2001 World Champion Arizona Diamondbacks, related another prank. "Mark Grace was a rookie and Sutcliffe was with him on the Cubs. Sutcliffe had some red Gatorade and he had poked a hole in [the drink's container] and covered up the hole with his finger. He walked over to Grace with two outs in the inning and said, 'Kid, can you hold this Gatorade while I tie my shoe?'

"He hands it to Grace and ties his shoe; the stuff is pouring all over Grace; and the batter makes the third out so Grace doesn't have time to go and change his pants—he's got red Gatorade all over his pants and he's going out to play first for the Chicago Cubs." He laughed, saying it was a case of a veteran telling a rookie, "Welcome to the big leagues."

Even batboys fell prey to Sutcliffe's devious ways. Mike Hargrove, who played with Sutcliffe on the Indians, said the devilish pitcher would ask batboys to fetch him the key to the batter's box. Other players were in on the joke, so when they were approached by the batboy, they'd tell him to try looking in some other location, and off the youngster would traipse again, trying to please Sutcliffe and never realizing he was being given the old runaround. Hargrove smiled, "Sometimes he'd send a guy for a bag of knuckleballs or curveballs." The scavenger-like hunt, tediously going from clubhouse to clubhouse trying to locate the treasure Sutcliffe had requested, was a gag which worked at times and, said Hargrove, to Sutcliffe's way of thinking, "It never hurt to try."

MARK FIDRYCH (1976–1980)

Fidrych was a comet that streaked across the skies of major league baseball, then left the scene forever. Extending that metaphor, when Fidrych died at the age of 54, a line from Shakespeare was apropos: "When beggars die there are no comets seen; The heavens themselves blaze forth the death of princes."

His first start wasn't until one month of 1976 was shot, yet the 21-year-old righty went 19–9 and won the Rookie of the Year Award after topping his league in ERA (2.34) and complete games (24 in 29 starts). He even averaged 8.6 innings per start. Although he appeared in just two seasons during which he pitched 10 or more games, he was a two-time All-Star. Somehow he owned a losing record as a high school pitcher.

* * *

Fidrych got his nickname, "the Bird," for his gawky resemblance to television's Big Bird. At 6 feet, 3 inches and 175 pounds, Fidrych was one of the most demonstrative players on the diamond. He used to dart over to teammates and shake their hands after they made a defensive gem. In the middle of a game he'd drop down to his hands and knees to manicure the mound, patting and rearranging the dirt to his liking. He nervously paced around the hill like a cat on a caffeine-laced catnip bender, circling endlessly. Call him jittery, hyperactive, or manic, he was always entertaining.

However, his main claim to spacey fame may have been the fact that he talked to the baseball before pitching, believing that made it go better. He'd clutch the ball then extend his hand toward home plate in a straight line. It was his version of giving pre-flight instructions, programming the ball where to go, but if a baseball then went for a hit, he shunned it, asking the ump for a new one. He believed some baseballs somehow or other had a hit in them—those he avoided. When asked if a ball ever talked back to him, he said only the ones flying out of the park. They bellowed back to him that he should never have thrown such a pitch. Incidentally, Lefty Gomez said he spoke to baseballs long before the fidgety Fidrych did. Asked what he said, Gomez grinned, "I said, 'Go foul, you [expletive], go foul!'"[21]

John Lowenstein plotted to ask the umpire to check a ball just before Fidrych pitched to him. He planned to get the ball from the ump, place it to his ear, and hear what instructions Fidrych had given it.

Cy Young Award winner Vernon Law said the one flake "that really stands out in my mind was Fidrych. I know I've never considered talking to a baseball. Maybe some of the hitters talked to the bats, too." He was correct. In his first at bat against Fidrych, Graig Nettles stepped out of the box as the Bird began his windup. He began talking to his bat, saying something like, "OK, now don't listen to that ball."

Fidrych also talked to himself. As teammate Alan Trammell noted, "That's just the way he was. He would talk to himself as a motivational tool." Fidrych was, in fact, the first colorful character who popped into his head when asked about special characters. Trammell indulged in polite understatement when he said, "He was a little different with his antics on the mound. That's just the way he was. It was kind of a cute story because it caught baseball's [attention] for a couple of years."

Baseball icon Don Zimmer said, "Fidrych was a crowd pleaser and a good pitcher. I mean, a lot of people thought he was a clown—he was no clown. When he got hurt, it was a great loss to baseball because he put people in the ballpark." In his rookie season, the gangly drawing card with boundless energy helped boost the Tigers attendance to 1,467,020, a jump of 408,184 for a team that finished fifth in a six-team division. The team drew about 13,000 spectators per home game in 1975, but Fidrych's magnetic pull attracted 51,032 fans, then 51,041, and 45,905 to Tiger Stadium over a three-start span and 605,677 in his home game starts. Hysteria was omnipresent, and some fans took to dressing up like Big Bird for games. Taken with the ways of the ingenuous Fidrych, his fans became known as Bird Watchers. Joe Charboneau, the 1980 American League Rookie of the Year, said Fidrych "made baseball fun and exciting—good for baseball."

Terry Collins had many Fidrych memories, too. "You know, I'm from Michigan so I remember seeing Fidrych a lot on TV talking to the ball, fixing the mound, and running on and off the field. He was voted Tiger of the Year and he attended the black-tie banquet. He came in wearing blue jeans and a T-shirt. That kind of said something. His attire wasn't very proper, but this is the same guy whom they applauded the free-spirit aspect of. That was *him*. He was carefree, and for his brief time he was an outstanding pitcher."

Trammell recalled, "He went down on his knees to fill up the hole [created on mounds at times] with dirt with his hands, but the guy was all business. Somebody would make a good play in the infield and Fidrych would go all the way around the infield to shake everybody's hands even *in between innings*. But that was him."

The Bird even applauded his players when they made a good play behind him. Collins stated, "They loved playing behind him. He was a *great* teammate. I've talked to a lot of the Tigers who played with him and they said, 'You'd make a play behind him, he'd be the first guy to shake your hand, the first guy to pat you on the back. If he made a mistake, he'd be the first guy to admit it.' Those kinds of guys are respected by your teammates. He was a breath of fresh air, absolutely." Fidrych vigorously pumped more hands than an aspiring presidential candidate. At times (even during a game) he shook the hands of fans, groundskeepers, and the security police working the contest.

Fidrych said he got many reactions to his behavior. "Once in Cleveland, they threw bird seeds on the mound before I went out to the mound, and in Minnesota they released 13 pigeons the day I was going for my 13th win. In some cities they wrote a message on the ball I got at the start of an inning."

"No matter what we say, and it is an athletic game, this is still an entertainment business," Collins explained. "And when you have those kinds of guys, people like him and enjoy watching him. They come to watch him play—they come to see those kinds of players. So if there's one or two guys out there that are like the Carlos Perezes, the fans enjoy that, they enjoy watching [such] antics."

Pitcher Steve Foucault was a Tiger teammate of Fidrych who remarked, "Mark Fidrych was a colorful character. He was one of a kind. I mean he comes along probably once in 50 years. He was very animated and he absolutely loved to pitch. He was just hilarious; he was a funny guy. He was kind of a clown, he liked to play jokes and he was wonderful. In the few years that he was successful, he was as good a pitcher as anybody in the game. He was super competitive and he had great stuff and he came right at you and he did it all night.

"After he pitched, and he pitched almost a complete game every night, and after the game he would go in the clubhouse, rip his jersey off, drink a beer, then come running out. He wet his head down to get his frizzy hair [soaked], *then* he came out. He'd have his head all wet with sweat or water and just kinda shake it around then he'd do a lap around the stadium. He waved to the fans and kinda jogged around the field. People were yelling, 'We want the Bird,' and nobody ever left until after he did this, then they'd start filing out."

Tigers announcer Ernie Harwell said that he recalled Roger Maris getting a curtain call request when he broke Babe Ruth's season home run record, but he also stated, "The first time I remember it to any extent was Mark Fidrych in the '70s, and the curtain call has been fairly regular at Tiger Stadium after Fidrych."

Fidrych's personal catcher, Bruce Kimm, later played for the White Sox. When he faced his former teammate, Fidrych tipped his cap to Kimm, beamed, then grooved a pitch for him to pulverize. Kimm ruined the Bird's good intentions, promptly popping it up.

Fidrych lived simply, staying in a small apartment that had no phone. He commented, "Sometimes I get lazy and let the dishes stack up. But they don't get stacked up too high. I've only got four dishes."

Not long after Fidrych passed away, trapped underneath his dump truck that he had been working on, his widow Ann and his daughter Jessica were asked to throw out the first pitch at a Tigers game. They walked out to the mound where the Bird had given fans so many thrills and, before making the ceremonial lobs, manicured the mound as an homage.

PASCUAL PEREZ (1980–1991)

Baseball writer Dan Schlossberg said, "Pascual 'Perimeter' Perez got lost going to a game in Atlanta because of the network of highways around the city. The Braves started Phil Niekro instead of Perez and he pitched a great game. That started the '82 Braves to the West Division championship."

The exact details of Perez's version of the Flying Dutchman were these: On the day he got his driver's license, he got lost on I-285, a 60-mile interstate highway that encircled Atlanta. He went around the city several times before he ran low on gas. Finally he was steered in the right direction by a gas station attendant. A 20-minute ride turned into one lasting almost three-and-a-half hours. He arrived at the ballpark 10 minutes after the game had begun.

In the days that followed, he was teased for his poor sense of direction, but he went along with the joke, wearing a warmup jacket with "I-285" inscribed on the back as if that were his jersey number. Further, his wild adventure seemed to loosen up the Braves, who had lost a 10½ game lead after dropping 19 of their previous 21 decisions. After the Perez escapade, they went on a winning tear that vaulted them into first place, where they finished the year.

* * *

One of the first to wear jewelry while on the mound, Perez festooned his neck with countless gold chains. He wore enough of them to fasten together a chain-gang crew of prisoners. Pascual is actually just one-third of a three-flake family that includes brothers Carlos and Melido, also big league pitchers. It was Melido who accepted a bet with Pascual about the number of games Pascual would win in 1988. The wager was not for money, but rather a cow, one of four Pascual owned—and all of them had the same name, Perez. Sounds like he borrowed a page from George Foreman, whose five sons are all named George.

One man's goofy is another man's colorful, and superb closer Jesse Orosco was somewhat forgiving of uninhibited pitchers such as Perez. After striking men out, Perez sometimes blew on the tip of his right index finger as if it was the mouth of a smoking gun. Other times, after recording a strikeout to end an inning, he sprinted from the mound to the dugout as if bolting from a track star's starting block, arriving there well ahead of the other eight fielders. Orosco stated, "He's very animated, but not many players say anything because he started that way. Rickey Henderson's the same way." Still, Orosco also made it a point to say, "It's not good for a pitcher to scream at a batter after he's struck him out. I come from the old school. Hit the ball, run, throw, catch it—that's the way the game should be played."

In 1997 Terry Collins said, "Perez is real colorful, *real colorful*," especially his "actions after he strikes you out or when he catches a ground ball up the middle. He's got a little flair to him." He was referring to Perez's herky-jerky motions and his arm-pumping action after getting batters out, upstaging the opposition. He even threw an occasional hesitation pitch a la Satchel Paige, and an eephus pitch. Only a few men, Rip Sewell being the most famous, have ever thrown an eephus pitch, also called a blooper pitch. Sewell's was thrown in an arc with a parabola, like the St. Louis Gateway to the West. It soared about 25 feet into the air before floating down, tempting batters to flail away at it, not unlike the way batters swung wildly and missed Bugs Bunny's changeup. Only one man, Ted Williams, ever homered off Sewell's tantalizing pitch.

A video on YouTube featured the time Perez, working out of the stretch, did a deep bend from the waist, so low he actually peered over to first base from between his legs. He then fired the baseball underhand, like a football center snapping the ball, through his legs for a pickoff throw. The background music used for the video could well have been Perez's theme song—it was "Don't Worry, Be Happy."

Even his comments reflected his casual, rather laissez-faire attitude. After winning his fourth straight game one year, Perez said, "The last time I smiled so much was for a jury." However, when his actions led to controversy, he wasn't so easygoing. In a game against the Cubs, he was struck on his hand by a line drive off the bat of Jerome Walton. Angered, he threw a ball into the Chicago dugout, and a Cub player, in turn, threw two out at him (one accidentally struck an umpire). Furious, Cubs manager Don Zimmer called Perez a clown.

In the end, Pascual was more a bit more colorful than effective as he finished his career with a 67–68 record, despite a two-year stretch in which he went 29–16.

ROGER MCDOWELL (1985–1996)

McDowell's playing career began with the New York Mets. While he and his wicked sinker probably gained most of his notoriety there, his travels also took him to four other clubs. Possessor of a baffling sinkerball, he once led the league in an obscure statistic, games finished (60).

He wasn't a spectacular reliever, but in 1986 when he went 14–9 with a 3.02 ERA, he saved 22 games for one of his four seasons with 20+ saves, and he made the top 20 in MVP voting. His 159 lifetime saves ranked 76th of all time at the end of 2018.

* * *

B. J. Surhoff, a one-time All-Star, said, "McDowell is a free spirit." That was a huge understatement. McDowell redefined the term prankster.

Billy Ripken, a colorful guy himself, said there are scads of stories about McDowell and his hijinks, "but you can't put them in a book." Pressed to expose a few incidents, Ripken came up with a few nuggets, but he first prefaced his thoughts with, "Roger's good with practical jokes. Some people think that I have a reputation for being a practical joker, but I don't do anything practical. I'm just loud, and what you see is what you get every day. With Roger, well, I've heard stories of him putting mice and parakeets in somebody's room by breaking into their room. He'd take out all the light bulbs in the room so when the player came in, everything would be scurrying around in the dark, and he'd have no idea what was in there with him. And obviously when the door would crack open and there was some light [streaming in], that's what would make all the critters scurry around and scare the player." This was a reprise of a trick the Red Sox did long ago when they placed a possum in the bathroom of a clubhouse boy, removed the bathroom's light bulbs, and when the poor kid tried to escape from the room, a player named Dusty Cooke held the doorknob from the hallway, preventing his escape.

Another McDowell tale related by Ripken involved the time the ace jokester "put a fish in somebody's suitcase, and then he super-glued the lock holes shut." Obviously it was a dead fish which gave off quite a stench, leading to a predicament that wasn't easy to solve. It also helped make McDowell legendary.

Ripken added that McDowell was quite cagey in that his victims weren't, say, the typical target—rookies. Rather, it would be "anybody who crossed him first, but, for the most part, he left the, shall we say, 'colorful' people alone because he knew they had resources and the type of mind to get him back."

Will Clark, a former teammate of McDowell, agreed with Ripken's assessment. "He definitely is a practical joker and a prankster. One day in San Francisco when he was pitching with the Dodgers, they accused him of scuffing up the baseball. Roger Craig, the Giants manager at the time, did. As a matter of fact, they accused him in the newspaper of scuffing the ball.

"So the next day Roger [McDowell] came out of his clubhouse, and when you come out in Candlestick Park, you have to walk down the right-field line, and that's where the Giants' dugout was. You have to walk in front of that dugout to get to the visitors' dugout. Roger went by wearing a utility belt with a hammer and a chisel and screwdrivers. And he had sandpaper stuck in his shoes. I thought that was pretty good."

Dwight Gooden, a Cy Young Award winner and a Met teammate of McDowell, said, "He was the funniest guy I knew, by far. You could never turn your back on him—he was always coming up with something. Every day he had something going on, whether it was giving somebody the hotfoot or doing his upside-down man. He was definitely a guy who you didn't want to get on his bad side."

McDowell had more comedy props than comedian Carrot Top. Two-time All-Star Gregg Jefferies said McDowell had a repertoire of tricks and an array of wild wigs. "He had different masks, too. The best thing he did was put his uniform on upside down so he looked like he was standing on his hands."

Veteran pitcher Orel Hershiser, who called McDowell an "A-number-1" flake, elaborated, "It was great when McDowell puts his jersey on backwards, puts the pants on his upper body and the jersey on his lower body [legs going through the sleeves] and walks round 'on his hands.' I think that's pretty cool." He packed a mask with a towel to give it shape, and he tied his "head" to his waist, allowing it to hang upside down. The outfit made it appear as though he was constantly walking on his hands while his real hands were over his head inside his shoes. He'd even walk on just one leg, which made it appear as if he were standing on one hand. To top it off, he would do knee bends with one leg to make it seem like he was doing one-handed push-ups.

"But," continued Hershiser, "I've seen him do some really crazy stuff that I wouldn't even want kids to read about." He was no doubt alluding to such events as one of McDowell's most outrageous moments—when he was spotted urinating in the outfield prior to the start of a game.

It was not unlike American League outfielder Rick Bosetti's goal of relieving himself on the home field of every team that played on natural grass. That, he said, is why he favored interleague play. A teammate said Bosetti even did this during pitching changes, facing the outfield wall and using his glove as a shield. He also said when he got caught and punished for doing some childhood vandalism, he learned two lessons: to do things right and, more vital to him, to make sure not to get caught.

One day McDowell drew the attention of a group of fans to a door located in the bullpen. He then thrust open the door with a magician-like flourish, and "presto"—on display was Jesse Orosco, perched on a toilet reading a magazine.

Bleacher fans in Wrigley Field took a liking to McDowell. On afternoons that sizzled, he'd get the grounds crew hose and spray the crowd. McDowell was also capable of pulling off routine tricks as well. Former big league infielder Jeff Frye said, "He was always coming up with something funny. He's a great practical joker, lighting guys' shoes on fire, giving them the hotfoot. He's great." He also loved to explode fireworks in the bat rack.

When it came to smoke bombs, McDowell added a personal touch. He had some that came in plastic vials. On flights he'd take a Band-Aid, gently tape a vial to the bottom of a toilet lid, then depart. When the next person sat on the lid, the vial would break, releasing a gag-inducing stench. Obviously, this was long before acts of terrorism changed things for air travel.

Longtime coach Sam Perlozzo concurred. "I was with the Mets when he was there. He was the team prankster and the best hotfoot artist I've ever seen. He could put a hotfoot on the back of your shoe better than anyone. He took some time at it. I've actually seen him crawl underneath a bench during a game to get to somebody's foot. He'd crawl about twenty feet on his belly just to get a guy." McDowell was willing to become a commando—anything to get his man. "I've had a hotfoot from him while coaching third, and I've had one from him at home plate when I was giving a lineup card to the umpires. I remember myself and Bill Robinson, who was the Mets first-base coach—the first thing we'd do every inning before we'd go out to coach was to look back at our heels. He had hotfoots made and lined up, ready, all the time.

"He'd get a pack of matches, roll it into a circle, tape it, stick a cigarette up in there and light it so it was almost to the tip of the matches. And he'd get a little piece of tape and stick it right on the back of your heel upside down. Then the cigarette would burn up toward the matches and go off so that when you're out in the field coaching it goes off then. It scares you, and if he gets it on there right and you don't know it, and it's burning pretty good, it can get you. I've seen him ruin a few people's shoes," concluded Perlozzo with a chuckle.

McDowell's antics, including his pyromaniacal tendencies from giving hotfoots to exploding firecrackers in the dugout, weren't confined to off-the-field and pre-game time frames. Like a hyperactive child with too much time on his hands, it didn't take McDowell very long to think up ways to get into mischief. Longtime major league shortstop, coach, and manager Larry Bowa said, "They didn't use him until the eighth or ninth inning, so he'd sit on the bench and before you knew it, your foot's on fire. He'd always be lighting shoes *during* the game."

Perlozzo remembered another one of McDowell's tricks: "He uses that shoe goop, gluing people's flip-flops to the bench. You couldn't get them off—it was almost like nailing them down. But they would get him back. They'd pile up all his shoes in the middle of the clubhouse and squirt lighter fluid on them and set them ablaze."

In 1991, right after Tommy Greene authored a no-hitter in Montreal, McDowell called him on the phone, pretending to be Canada's prime minister Brian Mulroney. Greene fell for it as McDowell added yet another prank to his resume.

McDowell even joined a mariachi band, which appeared on the diamond before a game, and in 1992 he appeared in the hilarious "The Boyfriend" episode of the television show *Seinfeld*. Along with his former Mets teammate Keith Hernandez, McDowell helped out in scenes parodying the Zapruder film, with McDowell cast as a second spitter lurking behind a shrub and expectorating a so-called Magic Loogie that hit two of the show's characters, Kramer and Newman. McDowell reportedly gets a royalty check for $13.52 every time that episode airs.

Bowa summarized, "He was *very* flaky, always playing around, but I just think that was his way of relaxing. A lot of guys like to listen to music; he'd do things like put on crazy outfits. I think every team needs somebody like that, but if you have two or three of them, you're in trouble." He's correct—too much clubhouse anarchy can lead to managerial firings, for example, but nothing stopped the incorrigibly sly McDowell.

MITCH WILLIAMS (1986–1997)

Left-hander Williams was a flamethrower, pure and simple—a throwback to the rear-back-and-fire-the-ball pitcher of long ago. Twice he earned some Cy Young Award consideration, and his 192 saves along with his lifetime 8.6 strikeouts per nine innings pitched testify to his talent. Of course, he also gave up 7.1 bases on balls per nine innings. In five of his eleven seasons, he was in the top 10 for mound appearances. As a rookie he worked in 80 of his Rangers' 162 contests to lead the league.

* * *

Al Nipper, who was a teammate of Williams on the Cubs, once observed, "If you put his brain in a blue jay, it would fly backwards." Nevertheless, Williams was quick-witted, too. Larry Andersen said Williams put a heckler in his place saying, "Hey, I don't get on you when you're picking up my garbage at six in the morning."

Williams had more ups and downs than the Dow Jones Industrial Average during a volatile market. He had his dominant moments when he was unleashing virtually unhittable heat, especially from 1989 through 1993 with the Cubs and Phillies. On the other hand, he suffered through many spells of extreme wildness, earning him the nickname "Wild Thing." He even wore the number 99, like Rick Vaughn in the movie *Major League*.

Asked what change he'd love to see in baseball, he lobbied for a requirement calling for seven balls before a batter earned a walk, but only two strikes needed for a strikeout.[22] John Kruk joked that if he faced Williams, he'd stand right on home plate because that way he'd never get hit by a pitch. In five seasons Williams was among the top 10 pitchers for plunking batters.

Williams threw violently, wildly falling off the mound. Should a coach have tampered with his technique? Reliever Mike Stanton commented, "You can't change the way somebody throws. Everyone's mechanics are their own. You can tinker with them, but usually full overhauls on mechanics don't work." Williams, who experienced the heartbreak of dishing up a World Series–winning home run to Joe Carter in 1993, never changed. His lack of control gave him a lot in common with the very hitters he faced—neither of them knew where the ball was going.

After losing that deciding game to Toronto in the World Series, the Phillies released him. He then embarked on a long trek of comeback attempts, trying to latch onto a job with numerous teams, but the end was near. He spent 1994 with Houston and 1995 with California, then sat out a year at his property, aptly called the 3-and-2 Ranch. In mid-May of 1997, the Royals traded him after he pitched just 6⅔ innings, had an ERA of 10.80, and averaged 9.5 walks per nine innings after averaging 17.7 with the Angels.

Prior to the start of the season he spent as an Angel, teammate Chuck Finley played golf with Williams and remarked, "He's everything I thought he'd be. His swing is violent. He drove the cart hard. He drank Coke hard. He throws hard. He's out of control, but fun to be around."

Alan Trammell saw Williams as "a guy who fell off the mound as much as anybody that I've ever seen in baseball. I remember watching on TV when Andre Dawson hit him in the back of the head with a line drive, which is not a very good position for a pitcher to fall off the mound." Trammell found it noteworthy that Williams's delivery was so extreme that the back of his head was vulnerable to the flight of the ball, allowing him to get smoked. "His mechanics, as we all know, were a little bit off. He was a little wild, a little erratic, but that's kinda what made him, because he was wild but effective."

Larry Parrish said, "I played with him and he was some kind of wild when he first started. He couldn't throw it in the batting cage consistently. But he turned out to be a premier reliever. He was always going to be in trouble every time he pitched. I mean there was no such thing as a one, two, three inning. He was going to walk a couple, hit a guy, then strike a couple of guys out."

Former teammate Mickey Morandini remembered the time when Larry Andersen was beginning to go bald. There was a product, rather like spray paint, which when applied to bald spots was meant to resemble hair. "So Mitch did that to Larry and it almost looked like Larry [suddenly] had a full head of hair. It looked colored on his skull. Mitch was just a nut."

Parrish shared a story about a game Earl Weaver managed against Williams's team. Weaver loved to platoon, so ideally he'd have right-handed hitters face the lefty Williams. "But he had already made a switch and had his left-handers in the lineup. They brought Mitch in and he plunked a couple of Orioles. Weaver comes to the plate wanting him ejected for hitting his players. The umpire says, 'Earl, he's not *trying* to hit any of them. He's *trying* to throw the ball over the plate. He's just *that* wild.' And Earl goes, 'I know that, but he's more dangerous than smoking cigarettes!'"

JOHN WETTELAND (1989–2000)

In 1999, longtime baseball man Jim Lefebvre was asked who he believed was the hardest throwing reliever around. He went with Wetteland, saying, "He's just a great pitcher. He goes out there and, 'Here it is, man.' He comes after you hard with his fastball, curveball, slider. If you're going to face him, you're going to have to hit his best stuff." Wetteland was hitting around 96 miles per hour, a speed few could match back then.

He was the MVP of the 1996 World Series when he saved four games for the Yankees, a record that can't be broken. His four seasons with 40+ saves tied him with Dennis Eckersley at one point.

Fred Claire recalled, "I did trade him, but I had great respect for John." The two men once talked about Wetteland's interest in music and how he related that to pitching and how for starters, as opposed to relievers, "everything wasn't at such a rapid beat. He was trying to make the point in terms of the tone of what he was doing. His record speaks for itself. He was a tremendous pitcher."

Wetteland certainly did enjoy a great deal of success. After breaking in with the Dodgers and saving only one game over three seasons and with a way-too-high ERA, he saved 80 games over his next two seasons with Montreal. He wound up with 330 saves and a lifetime ERA of 2.93. He also led his league in saves with 43 in 1996. When he attained the 300-save level, he did so in a span of fewer games (533) than any player except Eckersley (499). He was chosen as the top reliever of the 1990s. In addition, it was he who groomed Mariano Rivera to become his replacement.

* * *

One of Wetteland's former Yankee teammates, Paul O'Neill, used what sounded like a euphemism for flakiness in speaking of Wetteland: "He's kinda out there." Meanwhile, Wade Boggs described Wetteland as being "a taco short of a combination." Both of their insights were, of course, correct.

Former infielder Sean Berry said Wetteland had some unusual superstitions. "I played with John for three years. He never took off his hat—the same one he had for spring training, he kept the whole year, and he used to get the same bullpen ball from a coach who would throw it to John."

Boggs had more: "He'd put on rollerblades and skate around the concourse and around the clubhouse. That's about as colorful as it gets." O'Neill chipped in that he didn't get to appreciate Wetteland's creativity too much because most of his wild behavior was often restricted to "stuff he did in the bullpen."

The bullpen is a well-known haven for craziness. As a versatile player who mainly handled catching chores, Jim Leyritz was a frequent bullpen inhabitant. He spent time with Wetteland when both played for the Yankees. Leyritz said that Wetteland was "part of the bullpen committee. He'd play little games down there like if you didn't clap when your team got ahead, he'd throw water on you. Or guys would spit chew at each other's shoes every now and then. If you missed the shoe and hit the guy in the leg, the guy threw a cup of hot coffee on you. You'd have guys catching a reliever who was ready to come in a game and his white uniform would have turned brown. They did some crazy and funny things down there."

From 1997 through his final big league season of 2000, Wetteland was working his wild ways with the Texas Rangers. In a 1999 interview, teammate Rick Helling said, "He's got all these rules in the bullpen." Wetteland wielded dictator-like power and presided over a kangaroo court, charging players for virtually any real or imagined infraction. Helling said one broad charge many were hit with was "being an embarrassment to the bullpen." That might entail fraternizing with opponents during batting practice back when that was still a scorned activity or, said Helling, "if a guy's got a no-hitter going and somebody in the bullpen might slip up and mention that."

Wetteland created an environment in which players would laughingly narc on one another. As Helling noted, "A guy in the bullpen can bring up a teammate [on charges] like, 'I was embarrassed—he was talking to the enemy.'" That was all it took as mock mayhem ensued.

Helling spoke of the punishment Wetteland doled out. "He's got guys running the gauntlet or getting 'the chair.' The last thing you want to do is get 'the chair.' If you get brought up on [kangaroo court] charges and you plead innocent but are found guilty, 'the chair' is about the worst punishment you can get." Even the phrase "the chair" connotes dread, much like the punishment administered in the movie *Cool Hand Luke* in which misbehaving prisoners were doomed to spend "a night in the box."

The Rangers version of a Texas figurative death penalty was, in fact, an ordeal. "You get strapped into a chair and are blindfolded," Helling continued. "Every guy in the bullpen can mix up his own concoction to dump on you, on your head, your whole body." The stuff poured on players included things like nasty-smelling heat rubs and tobacco juice. "We do this in the first inning and you gotta stick with it, the smell and everything for a half inning. After that, you can go in and change your jersey and all that, but it's a good way to keep the guys loose. You definitely mind your p's and q's out there when he's in charge of the pen."

Interestingly, Wetteland did have a serious, very professional side. One of his managers, Johnny Oates insisted, "He's not a flake. He's all business." In a 1999 interview, Wetteland refused to go into details about his colorful ways. He was coldly analytical, almost somber, saying, "I just don't talk about this kind of stuff. The clubhouse is our world." Thus, the persona he displayed to teammates was quite the opposite of what he said in the brief interview.

He did touch on his creative pranks, saying, "If you're spontaneous, you just can't think about something off the top of your head because it just happens. Stuff happens nightly." It did when Wetteland was around, that was a certainty. However, after his playing days were over, he did show his serious side once more when he became a coach—fittingly, a bullpen coach.

Unfortunately, the Wetteland story turned ugly. In 2019, he was indicted on three counts of sexual assault of a child.

TURK WENDELL (1993–2004)

Six of Wendell's first 13 big league assignments came as a starter. He then relocated to where he belonged, in the outer regions of the bullpen—

he would never again get a start. Overall, he won 36, lost 33, earned 33 saves, and posted a 3.93 ERA. He did take the ball quite a bit, working in 77 games in 2000 (fourth in the National League) and in 80 games in 1999, second only to Montreal's Steve Kline.

* * *

There's little question about Wendell belonging among the game's most colorful characters ever since his flake credentials are unimpeachable and his behavior on the field genuinely zany. Wendell belongs in the Strange Habits Hall of Fame with his baffling assortment of superstitions.

Jim Lefebvre cataloged them: "When he runs to the mound, just before he gets to the foul line, he jumps up and down and does a little corkscrew. Just before he pitches the ball, he has to turn around and make the sign of the cross. He charges back on the mound, turns around and points to the center fielder. He's gotta point back or Wendell doesn't throw. Then he points to the first baseman. After the inning's over, he does another corkscrew and runs back to the bench. He eats [black] licorice and brushes his teeth in between every inning." Naturally, he spit out the licorice before each brushing—after all, he wasn't *that* crazy. Some took to calling his perplexing ways "Turk's quirks."

Wendell also drew three crosses in the dirt on the back side of the mound, and before his first pitch he would lick the hand that etched the crosses. He wore two watches, with one set to the time it was in his Massachusetts home. Sean Berry said, "I owned a shirt of his that listed the 30 things he did before he would pitch. If the ball came out to him, he had to wait until it stopped rolling to pick it up. I don't know if they were superstitions—they were things he did."

New York Post writer Mike Vaccaro said, "He used to wear a necklace of [animal claws and] teeth. I joked with him that one of these days he's going to throw a curveball and it's going to take his eye out. He said, 'Oh. I hope so.' And I wasn't sure if he was kidding or serious."

Author Mike Blake listed other idiosyncrasies: Wendell felt he just had to make throws to first base—even when it was empty. He had the habit of going behind the mound, then circling it in a counterclockwise direction. Next he squatted on the rubber, but if he gazed in and saw his catcher was in his squat, he made the catcher stand up. Then his catcher was permitted to hunker down, and at that point Wendell would finally stand, now ready to pitch. Finally, he refused to catch the baseball before he got to the mound because he wanted somebody to roll the ball to him. Even after a foul ball was hit, he wanted the ump to roll a new baseball out to the mound.

A skunk lived in the Padres ballpark and occasionally popped up in the bullpen, causing normal people to scatter. Not Wendell. He chased it saying, "Here, skunky, skunky."[23] Not at all surprisingly, he also got sprayed by it when he got too close.

Actually, though, after Wendell left the Cubs and after he had aged a bit, his manic behavior tapered off. Still, for most of his pro career (after first demanding uniform number 13) he wore jersey number 99, an odd number for a baseball player, but he was obsessed with that number. He wanted as many 99s in his contract as feasible for good luck. It is obviously the highest number ever worn, three higher than that worn by pitcher Bill Voiselle, who hailed from a town named Ninety-Six.

Hall of Famer Chipper Jones said, "I would categorize Turk as colorful and not a flake. He's just different with the little quirks and habits he has. That makes him different." Rather reminiscent of Mark Fidrych and his actions.

The final take on Wendell came from Terry Collins, who said, "I remember he used to jump over the foul lines and he wore no socks even during the game." That fact was hidden from fans, Collins explained, by his wearing "his pants tucked inside his shoes."

Collins added that players can get away with eccentricities such as "the licorice thing when things are going well," but said most players resent such behavior. Players like Wendell often get the message to settle down eventually, and many do mend their ways. As Collins said of the flamboyant Wendell, "I know he toned it down quite a bit." Even at that, a toned-down Wendell was quite a sight.

FERNANDO RODNEY (2002–)

From the start of his career through 2019, Rodney had pitched for 11 different teams over 17 seasons. A three-time All-Star, his most glowing season was 2012 when he compiled 48 saves and had a nearly invisible ERA of 0.60. He matched that save total in 2014 when he led the

American League in that category. His 325 career saves through 2018 placed him 18th on the all-time list.

Marty Appel believes Rodney's accomplishments weren't publicized enough. He chuckled, "It's like I say for Trevor Hoffman—he had 601 saves and none of them were on national TV."

* * *

Other than his many career saves, Rodney be may best known for a celebratory signature move he did after concluding another successful appearance. From 2012 on, he pulled an imaginary arrow out of an imaginary quiver on his back, then fired the arrow from his imaginary bow while looking skyward. Of course, many weren't enamored by such a display. There was such an occasion when Mike Trout had a moment of payback. After his Angels rallied against Rodney in the ninth inning, Trout shot his own pretend arrow directly at Rodney. Steve Blass said, "Rodney's a very talented player who I wish had a little more respect for the game."

Jeff Francoeur played with Rodney while with the Marlins. "I used to laugh because I played against him, and had looked at him from the other side, like, 'What in the world is this guy doing? He's got his hat sideways. He's nuts.' But I can remember like it was yesterday when I got traded over there [to Miami], he came up to me and started talking. I asked him about the hat sideways and shooting the bow and arrows, and I liked it that he just said, 'That's who I am. And if you don't like it, then screw it.' I thought, you know what, this is a guy who is confident of himself. I tell you what, he was some kind of fun to watch. He was such a good teammate, such a funny guy, you just appreciated the way he went about things. And he was reliable—he pitched every game. If you wanted him to pitch, he was going to pitch."

Gus Garcia-Roberts, an investigative reporter who wrote the book *Blood Sport* about Alex Rodriguez and steroids, doesn't mind such displays. "I feel like baseball could use more personality like you see in basketball, where you really sort of see a player celebrate—they're not holding back. You get to know them, personality-wise. People celebrating, being ostentatious, and having their personal brand out there is good for baseball. Sports is all about personalities—that's really what captures the casual fan, in relating to these players as actual people. To me, as a fan and somebody who would love to see baseball reach even more people, anything that accentuates that, I'm all for it." Rodney fits that bill.

Rodney sported a baseball cap with a flat bill, placing it at a jaunty angle, off-center in relation to his face. And that angle is much more pronounced than many other lefties—men known to never have the hat on the head squarely, like CC Sabathia. As Jeff Francoeur said, "it was completely sideways. As an old-school baseball guy, at first you're kinda like, 'I don't like it,' but that's why I tell people I've learned you never judge a book by its cover." Case in point: Rodney said he tilted the hat to honor his father who died in 2002, just six days before Rodney threw his first major league pitch. His father was a fisherman who wore his hat leaning to the left to protect his face from the scorching Dominican Republic sun.

Rodney is a one-man menagerie, skilled at imitating animal sounds from roosters and other birds to dogs, with a Kermit the Frog impersonation tossed in. Writer Jake Mintz called Rodney "perhaps the most theatrical human being in the Major Leagues" and the possessor of "one of the league's most delightful personalities."[24] When Rodney pitched in the 2013 and 2017 World Baseball Classics, representing the Dominican Republic, he carried a large plantain with him, displaying it during pre-game team introductions. He called it Platano Power and his teammates bought into it.

Once, during an April snowfall in Minnesota, Rodney was on the mound and figured he could hydrate by eating some snowflakes just as easily as he could by drinking water. So, in the middle of the game, he leaned his head back and caught some snow in his mouth, amusing fans and teammates.

Rodney also evoked peals of laughter during a 2016 contest between his Marlins and the Braves. Coming off the field after pitching the eighth inning, he was so taken by the song "Cotton-Eyed Joe" playing over the PA system that he broke into an impromptu dance. The American country/folk song inspired Rodney to do his rendition of a sort of jig, with arms akimbo and legs kicking to and fro (worth a look on YouTube).

TREVOR BAUER (2012–)

In 2018, Bauer seemed to be really coming into his own. Before an injury shelved him, he had a shot at the Cy Young Award. An All-Star that year, he went 12–6 with a 2.21 ERA after going 17–9 but with a rather inflated ERA of 4.19 in 2017.

* * *

Mike Vaccaro was asked if Bauer had played in the old days, would he have qualified as being a flake. He chuckled, "I think in the new days he qualifies as a flake, too. He's never afraid to say offbeat stuff. In the old days I think he would have been less controversial because a lot of players were like that—certainly pitchers have always been known to be a little bit different. I think because now everything is public and every-thing is out there five minutes after you say it, sometimes it's just weird. Weird ducks, people who were a little quirky, used to be celebrated more than they are now. Now they're kind of looked at a bit differently."

Regardless, Vaccaro says Bauer is "great for the game because he's not only a terrific pitcher, but he's different. Different than the standard issue, 'Yes ma'am. No ma'am. Give 110 percent,' quote that you get. Players are kind of trained today to be more vanilla than they ever were before, which is unfortunate because that's how you get characters. What you're trying to find is great stories about great characters. Guys were encouraged more to be themselves in the old days.

"So, yes, he definitely is an old-school flake. That term definitely applies even today if we still used it. I'm not saying Bauer is Dizzy Dean, but it would be hard to think that Dean would be allowed to be Dizzy Dean in the modern era. He would have had an agent, a publicist, and a media relations director who would have gotten to him before he ever would have said something quirky or different to a guy with a notebook."

Bauer definitely comes across as eccentric, craving attention, yet un-concerned about being liked. He doesn't seem to care what others think of him and he's convinced he is just about always right. He told writer Ben Reiter that on first dates, he informs women he wants no emotional entan-glements and that they should know that he will be sleeping with other women.

Bauer is very much into rigorous workouts. In his early days in the majors his methods were particularly unorthodox. For example, beginning when he was 14, when he warmed up to start an inning on the hill, he concluded his tosses by moving one or two steps *behind* the mound before hurling the ball at full speed to the plate. That drew comparisons to the fictional character Happy Gilmore. Some of his catchers chose to dart out of the way of his final pitches—sizzling in at up to 100 miles per hour—rather than risk injury. That's fine with Bauer.

Once, using a three-ounce baseball in a workout session, he fired a pitch at 116.9 miles per hour. He took a running start and released the ball very near to the plate, but how many pitchers would try such a thing? Likewise, he has been known to throw six or seven days a week.

He butted heads with Diamondback coaches and, early on, with Cleveland's coaching staff over his beliefs about how best to prepare. *Toledo Blade* sportswriter Ashley Bastock said Bauer "is super eccentric. That was the thing with the Diamondbacks—that's why they traded him. They didn't want to listen to him, and he didn't want to listen to them. There was no give and take." In Cleveland, Bauer gradually gained more input concerning his training methods.

Bauer is a big proponent of the long toss, one who has usually defied injury as well as conventional thinking. He's stated that he can heave a baseball 420 feet and sometimes attain a speed of 100 mph doing so. Some teams insist a pitcher should not throw farther than 120 feet, and do so on a line, not on high arcs like the ones Bauer uses, nor for as long a time as Bauer does—at times 10–20 minutes longer than what many coaches desire.

Bauer displayed his ability to fire the ball a great distance on July 28, 2019, just three days before the trading deadline. After giving up seven earned runs on nine hits to the Royals in 4⅓ innings, his day on the hill was done, but not before he hurled a baseball in disgust into the netting behind home plate. Then, as his manager, Terry Francona, headed out to lift him, Bauer furiously fired the ball from a spot near the mound. It flew some 350 feet over the center field wall. After the game, he said his competitive drive just got to him. He promised it wouldn't happen again. He was correct that it would not occur again, at least not *while he was with Cleveland*—two days later the Indians, no longer able to tolerate his ways, traded him.

In 2018 Bill Livingston said, "I think his success this year quieted the views that he was flaky. He had his own opinions on how to do things and was at odds with [manager Terry] Francona at times, but he apparently has an elastic arm and can fill almost any role on the team. I think he pitched out from under the shadow he kind of brought with him." The ultimate point here is that his methods have panned out. "He had the courage of his convictions to stay with them. I found him to be kind of abrupt and brusque sometimes because he felt like he knew so much more than other people. But he probably did about pitching mechanics."

Bastock, who covers the Indians, said that during clubhouse celebrations Bauer "always wears a GoPro camera. You see him walking around with a camera strapped on his head and it's so bizarre because nobody else does that." He then edits and posts his footage.

Bauer also worked on another project with teammate Carlos Carrasco. "They made mini-baseballs [that were designed] to look like teammates. It was intense and very surgical because their big rule was they could use only stuff that they had on hand." The two men would do things like slicing a ball open then yanking some yarn up to the top of the ball to resemble a player's hairstyle.

Just before his Indians were to take on Toronto in the 2016 American League Championship Series, Bauer, the holder of a degree in mechanical engineering from UCLA sustained an injury while tinkering with a drone. His mangled pinky finger prevented him from making a scheduled start in Game 2.

In 2018, he caused another fuss when he got into a twitter turmoil with some of the Astros pitchers, hinting that they doctored baseballs to get better spin on pitches. Several annoyed Astros responded, most notably Alex Bregman. In late April 2019 the feud continued. Bauer tweeted a video in which he spoke to a bobblehead doll of Bregman. It went like this—close-up of Bauer: "What's up, little buddy? Did I dominate you last night?" Cut to Bregman doll: Bobbing its head up and down, "Yes."

3

KINGS OF THE DIAMOND

The Most Colorful Position Players of All Time

While pitchers may have produced more colorful characters than position players, they hold no monopoly on humor and craziness. From men such as the always entertaining Casey Stengel, who dates back to 1912, to the buoyant Francisco Lindor, who broke into the majors in 2015, the players featured in this chapter have triggered more grins, giggles, and guffaws than a barrelful of stand-up comics.

CASEY STENGEL (1912–1925; MANAGED 1934–1965)

Stengel got his nickname from a player who called him "Kansas City," after his hometown. That soon morphed to "K.C." and then "Casey." Stengel spent 14 years in the majors as a player and 37 more as a minor and major league manager.

Among his many accomplishments was his marvelous string of winning the pennant 10 times over his 12-year tenure with the Yankees, from 1949 to 1960. At one point he had won the pennant in nine of ten years and the World Series in seven of those seasons, a sterling achievement. Starting with 1949, his first year as their skipper, his dynastic team won five straight World Series, a feat never matched. No man managed or won as many Series games as Stengel. Strangely, in 1954 his Yankees won 103 games, a personal high for a Stengel team, yet they finished eight games out of first place, way behind the Indians who won a league record 111 contests.

Sportswriter Mike Vaccaro said, "The thing about Stengel is that he was pretty much known—before he became a raging success with the Yankees—as a horrible failure. But he's the only guy who ever wore the uniform of every New York team—the Giants, the Dodgers, the Yankees, the Mets."

Having studied dentistry, but reportedly giving up on that profession in part because he was left-handed and dentists' equipment is designed for righties, Stengel became an enormous part of baseball lore, seemingly to infinity and beyond.

* * *

Stengel was a pioneer on the frontier of flakiness, a forerunner to Jimmy Piersall and others. "He was a mischief maker all the way back to his childhood," said his biographer, Marty Appel. "As a kid in Kansas City, he enjoyed throwing snowballs at men walking down the street with pipes, trying to dislodge the pipe from their mouth. You read an anecdote like that and you say, 'This guy is going to be a colorful character in life.'"

Legendary even now, a baseball eternity after his departure from the game, Stengel began his career with the Brooklyn Dodgers way back in 1912. After the 1917 season, the popular Stengel, then an outfielder, was traded to the Pirates.

When he returned to Ebbets Field as a Pirate in a game played on June 6, 1918, the Brooklyn fans were getting all over Stengel even before the game got underway. Before Stengel came to the plate for his first at bat, he had come across his former teammate, Leon Cadore, standing in the bullpen, gently holding a sparrow.

A cartoon-like lightbulb suddenly glowed in Stengel's head, so he took the bird and put it under his cap where he could feel it thrashing around. Minutes later, he came to the plate and reacted to the crowd's catcalls by taking an exaggerated bow. Then he tipped his cap to reveal the bird sitting atop his head. The bird fluttered away, at first in a dazed, zigzag flight path, not unlike the comic strip character Woodstock sometimes does. Fans were momentarily stunned, then burst out laughing.

Incidentally, years later a notorious football flake, Tim Rossovich, embellished on Casey's routine. He sat down to a meal with his fraternity house buddies, tapped on a water glass to get everyone's attention, and then opened his mouth, allowing an almost comatose bird a chance to take flight. But instead of soaring to freedom, the small bird unceremoniously flopped onto Tim's "home" plate. In college, future big league flake Bill Lee sometimes hung out with Rossovich—a case of birds of a feather?

Back to Stengel, a man one scout called "a dandy ballplayer, but it's all from the neck down."[1] An old story has it that Stengel stationed himself in the outfield during an exhibition game by hiding under a manhole cover over a hole under the field. Peering from his unusual defensive spot under the manhole cover, he saw a flyball coming his way and leapt from the hole, catching the baseball.

He was a no-show in the dugout for an exhibition game because he was seated in the bleachers, dressed like a farmer. He began to heckle his own teammates, bragging loudly that he could hit better than them. This is almost assuredly an apocryphal story, because the kicker is his enraged teammates told him if he was so good, he should come out of the stands and take a swing. He did, belting a home run. Then, borrowing a glove, he played the field. It sounds like something he would have done if he could have gotten away with it. It also sounds like a story concocted by the writers of the day.

There are tales about the times Stengel wanted to persuade the umpires to call off a game because he felt it was getting too dark to continue play. To make his point, Stengel left his dugout while carrying a flashlight, or he'd have his relievers warming up while illuminated by the beam of a flashlight. And he protested another time under dark, rainy skies by entering the field with a lantern and an umbrella.

Around 1915, Wilbert Robinson boasted that he could catch a baseball dropped from an airplane. Stengel, then an active player, replaced the ball with a grapefruit. It plummeted around 400 feet to where Robinson managed to get under it. The grapefruit hit him in his chest and splattered sticky juice all over. Robinson was momentarily convinced the impact had opened a gash in his chest and that he was bleeding profusely.

Stengel didn't come off as a genius, but he was cunning. He employed a trick to catch his players who broke curfew. He would give an elevator operator a fresh baseball and instruct him to get autographs on the ball from any players who came back to the hotel after curfew. The ploy worked very well.

When he managed a poor Dodgers team in Brooklyn in the 1930s, he said his players were not very proficient, but they were capable of craziness. "Whenever I decided to release a guy, I always had his room searched first for a gun. You couldn't take any chances with some of them birds."[2]

Bob Cerv of the Yankees tells this classic story: "I was sitting on the bench all by myself, when Stengel came out and sat down not too far from me. . . . All of a sudden I heard Casey talking. He was saying, 'Well, I see where we're getting old Enos [Slaughter] back again, and I think his bat is going to help us. He was all crippled up when we had him last time, but he's gonna help us now.' Then he said, 'The only trouble is one of you guys will have to be going to Kansas City for him.' I looked around, but there was no one else on the bench but me!" Sure enough, one day later Cerv was with Kansas City. Another version of this has Stengel simply saying, "Nobody knows this, but one of us has just been traded to Kansas City."

As a player, Stengel was no superstar, but he wasn't a slouch, either. A lifetime .284 hitter, one year he led the National League with a .404 on-base percentage. He boasted that he was so feared, he even drew intentional walks during batting practice.

Stengel is also the answer to a trivia question: In 1923, who hit the first home run in World Series competition in Yankee Stadium, a walk-off, inside-the-park homer against the Yankees? The 32-year-old Stengel, minus one shoe and breathing heavily, beat the throw, signaling himself "safe" as he slid. Mike Vaccaro stated, "Casey was pretty old even when he was young. He was an aging player serving his apprenticeship under John McGraw. That inside-the-parker was a perfect capper to his playing career."

Even though Stengel, then with the New York Giants, averaged only about four home runs per season as a player of the dead-ball era, he hit two in the 1923 Series. As he made his tour around the bases on the second homer, which gave the Giants a 1–0 victory, Yankee fans cascaded him with boos. He responded by thumbing his nose at the Yankees bench and by blowing kisses to the spectators. Yankee owner Jacob Ruppert petitioned Commissioner Kenesaw Mountain Landis to suspend Stengel. Landis fined him instead, saying, "Casey Stengel just can't help being Casey Stengel," a quote which was altered decades later to fit the unpredictable Manny Ramirez. At times Stengel grabbed a newspaper and, from his outfield position, began to read it to the fans.

When asked about Stengel, Wally Westlake replied, "You got half an hour?" He then went on about the time he got out of the service and rejoined his Oakland Oaks in 1946. "Casey had become the manager. I came out of the batting cage early in the season and he called for me from the dugout. He said, 'Sit down here, Westlake. Young fellow, you got pretty good talent. Now I'm going to teach you how to play this game.' He did—when I hit the big leagues I realized how lucky I was to play for Casey because he taught me all the little things that you don't read in the paper. He saved my butt." Westlake was one who fully realized how good Stengel could communicate and teach.

Stengel could employ humor to get across a message, too. When one of his pitchers who had been shellacked threw a temper tantrum in the dugout, violently kicking the water bucket, Stengel told him to settle down. "If you break your leg, I can't trade you."

When the name Stengel came up with Carl Erskine, he spoke fondly. "Oh, yeah, Casey. I went to many, many Old Timers' Games and when Casey got the mike, they couldn't get him off. He had this Stengelese—somebody dubbed it that—when he talked about a player, he'd never use his name. He'd use something that, if you're in the know, he'd use some description of him instead of telling his name.

"For instance, he'd say, 'Now, this here fellow who just came in the room,' and he's talking about me. 'He's got that overhand curveball. He owns all them banks in Indiana.' I *was* president of a bank after I got through with my playing career. Or if he was talking about Whitey Ford or Mickey Mantle, he'd never use his name—he'd just say something that related to him. Most people couldn't understand him. If you didn't know [who he meant], you'd never make sense of what he said."

Marty Appel noted, "Casey was speaking in Stengelese long before he got to the Yankees and everybody became aware of him. He did it when he was managing the Boston Bees and nobody was particularly noticing. It was contrived very often, it was double talk, it was a way of stalling for time until he thought of what he wanted to say, or just talking so there was no meaning to what he said. But he did make a craft out of it—he was wonderful with that."

Stengel, he said, also used his patter to skirt a question "or to just have fun with the writers. When he was retired, I saw him many times making speeches at functions. If you'd seen him over and over again, Casey would get up to talk and people would head for the men's room or just roll their eyes like, 'Oh, here we go again,' but for those who had never heard it before, what a treat to hear Casey Stengel actually deliver Stengelese, his famous dialect. He was brilliant at it and he could go on without a comma or a period in sight. If he had been told he had to finish by 10:00 p.m., at 9:59 and 55 seconds, he'd say, 'And I thank you very much.'"

Casey clearly had a way with words, and at times what seemed like a confusing comment made perfect sense upon reflection. He once described Satchel Paige's success by saying, "He throws the ball as far from the bat, and as close to the plate as possible."

Appel said Stengel was sharp enough to know his audience. "He knew if he was talking to a morning writer or an afternoon writer. He knew their needs were different. He was very media savvy in that sense, and if somebody new was joining the team and had never covered the team before, Casey could either entertain if there were other writers around, just baffling the [new] guy with what he was saying, or if the guy was one on one, Casey would deliver non-Stengelese, perfect answers."

By the way, in more recent years Jim Gantner, nicknamed Gumby after the cartoon character, mangled the language so much that his verbal missteps became known as Gumbyisms. He'd say things like he forgot to do something because he had "ambrosia," or that he took a trip to a "Canadian proverb."[3] He said the capital of Argentina was Buenos Dias, and that you can't employ the daylight pick-off play during night games.

Dizzy Dean, another eloquent (in his *own way*) speaker, was once at a banquet with Richard Nixon and Stengel. Nixon was already well aware of Dean's speech habits; he had heard Dean inform his radio audience such things as a runner "slud inta third base." Stengel was the first speaker that evening. After hearing Stengel, Nixon was amazed at his oration and asked if Dean, too, could talk like Casey. "Naw," Dean drawled, "I ain't that good."

Stengel was good in many ways. As mentioned, he won a record 10 American League pennants over his dozen years as the Yankees skipper. The only other manager to win the flag over those seasons was Al Lopez with the Indians and the White Sox. In Stengel's 10 pennant-winning seasons he went on to win the World Series a sensational seven times, including five world championships in a row from his first season with the Yanks, 1949, through 1953. However, due to his years with several poor teams, his lifetime managerial winning percentage is only .508.

Despite his success with the Yankees, Stengel was fired after he lost the 1960 World Series to the Pittsburgh Pirates. The Yankees brass said that he was "let go" due to his age and not because of his lack of ability or his defeat at the hands of the Bucs. Stengel sarcastically stated, "I'll never make the mistake of being 70 again." Jimmy Piersall once mocked Stengel's age saying, "Everybody knows Casey has forgotten more baseball than I'll ever know. That's the trouble—he's forgotten it."

That line is somewhat similar to what Stengel told a reporter who asked him what people his age thought of modern players. Stengel, then around 75, had a terse reply: "How the hell should I know? Most of the people my age are dead at the present time."

He also used sarcasm, sometimes a bit too harshly, with his players. One of his pitchers complained that he was having trouble gripping the ball. Stengel countered with, "You're standing on two tons of dirt. Why don't you rub some of it on the ball?"

He could be particularly rough on his pitiful Mets. He scolded Mets pitcher Tracy Stallard, "Aim the ball right at the middle of the plate, because you can't hit anything you aim at, and maybe you will catch a corner." He told his inept outfielders, "When one of them guys hits a single to you, throw the ball to third. That way we can hold them to a double."

He was capable of snapping at other people, like the time a reporter asked him if the Yankees had choked after losing the 1957 World Series. Stengel exploded, "Do you choke on your [expletive] microphone?" His comments, though biting, were often right on the money, as was true when he chided a Met pitcher named Ray Daviault who had complained that he had made a perfect pitch but an opponent had still hit it out of the park. Stengel barked, "It couldn't have been a perfect pitch. Perfect pitches don't travel that far." Daviault lasted only one season (1962) as a member of the newborn Mets franchise. He must have thrown a lot of not-so-perfect pitches as he went 1–5 with a balloon-like ERA of 6.22. Remarkably, that lofty ERA wasn't all that much higher than Stengel's collective team ERA of 5.04.

Some of Stengel's pitchers complained that they had to work extra hard when they got themselves into a jam. Stengel's words of wisdom were direct: "If we pitched as hard when we're not in trouble, we wouldn't get in trouble."

One of his most famous lines about his woeful Mets was, "Can't anybody here play this game?" The answer was no—his team set a modern-era record with their 120 losses. A baseball axiom has it that *every* team wins a third of their games and loses a third of them; his 1962 Mets lost exactly three-fourths of them.

A sportswriter approached Stengel after the Mets had butchered yet another game. He asked the Ol' Professor what Stengel thought of his team's execution. Stengel pondered the question briefly, then supposedly replied, "I think it's a good idea." Before playing in the Astrodome where the roof originally gave fielders fits, he was asked if he'd make his players work on flyballs. He replied, "We're still working on grounders."

Stengel once evaluated Rex Barney, a pitcher who threw as hard as anyone but who had just an iota of control. Stengel said, "He has the power to throw the ball through a wall, but you couldn't be quite sure which building."

When Stengel first became the Mets manager, he was desperate to find talent, so he tried dipping into the college pool, figuring there, if nothing else, he'd find smart players. Yet he soon rued, "We got a lot from Johns Hopkins, but them we thought was from college turned out to be from the clinic."[4] He also came up with the line, "The only thing worse than a Mets game is a Mets doubleheader." Even many years after the Mets were no longer an abysmal club, Stengel was still capable of being heavy on sarcasm. He conceded, "This team plays better baseball now. Some of them look fairly alert."

Humor was a big part of Stengel's personality. He received a letter from a soldier who was fighting in Korea. The man had been complaining about Stengel's strategies, second-guessing him. Stengel shut him up by responding, "If you're so smart, how come you're still in the Army?"

During spring training Stengel once told one of his coaches to "take those players over to that other diamond. I want to see if they can play on the road." And just prior to the first game of the 1916 World Series, opponents Duffy Lewis and Ernie Shore passed by Stengel. He greeted them by saying, "Hello, boys. What do you think your losing share is going to be?"

At least once, though, the joke was on him. When he caught his Yankee pitcher Mickey McDermott trying to sneak into the team hotel at

4:00 a.m., Stengel muttered, "Drunk again." McDermott replied, "Me too."

Stengel truly was a master at dealing with the press, even when asked inane questions. Responding to a reporter's question about whether Don Larsen's perfect game in the 1956 World Series was the best game he'd seen Larsen pitch, Stengel succinctly said, while maintaining a straight, craggy face, "So far."

In 1965, reporters asked Stengel about two prospects on his Mets, Ed Kranepool and the 19-year-old Greg Goossen. Stengel predicted, "In 10 years Ed Kranepool has a chance to be a star. In 10 years Greg Goossen has a chance to be 29." Stengel was a pretty good oracle. Kranepool, though not a superstar, spent 18 seasons in the majors and was a pretty valuable member of the 1969 Miracle Mets who shocked the world by winning the World Series over the highly favored Baltimore Orioles of Frank and Brooks Robinson, Jim Palmer, and a host of other big names. As for Goossen, he did, in fact, reach the age of 29 late in 1975, but he had been out of the majors since after the 1970 season, having hit .241 lifetime with 44 career RBI over just 460 at bats.

The list of Stengel stories could go on and on, and in some other books they do. So with that in mind, and to avoid rehashing too much classic material from colorful legends such as Stengel and Yogi Berra, here's one last one. This is one Stengel often recounted, even though some of the details seem to be rather dubious.

On Independence Day of 1934, Stengel had Walter Beck on the hill for his Dodgers. A 20-game loser in 1933, Beck was getting lit up. In two-thirds of an inning, he gave up three earned runs and three hits while walking three and tossing two wild pitches.

That was enough for Stengel. He made a trip to the mound to yank Beck, who was so irritated he heaved the baseball with such force it banged off the right-field wall. The impact off the tin wall caused a booming noise which, so the story goes, snapped outfielder Hack Wilson, who was leaning on the right-field fence, out of a reverie. He was either hung over or simply lost in thought, but either way, when he heard the reverberation from the baseball banging off the wall and then spied the ball nearby, he assumed it was in play. He gathered up the ball and fired it, needlessly, to second base. From that day on, Beck became known as "Boom Boom" Beck.

BABE HERMAN (1926–1945)

A lifetime .324 hitter, Herman was as dependable and as steady as a metronome. In 1930, he hit .393 but lost out on the batting crown when Bill Terry hit .401 to become the last National League player to top .400. The year before Herman hit .381, which was good enough for second place in the league to Lefty O'Doul's .398. His season apex for total bases, 416, is ranked at 14 on the all-time list. He hit for the cycle three times, still a record, and did that twice in one season, something only three men ever accomplished.

Yet Herman is best remembered now for his myriad muffs. One year he led National League outfielders with an ungodly 16 errors. He was the embodiment of the player described as having "a good stick, no glove." Some say his glove was as useless as popping placebos to cure terminal cancer. As a trivia note, Herman was hired as an adviser on the film *Pride of the Yankees*, about Lou Gehrig, and was used as the double for Gary Cooper (as Gehrig) on long shots.

* * *

Herman's most famous incident came when he was said to have tripled into a triple play. Actually, this tale is exaggerated, but he did double into a wild double play. Somehow, his bases loaded, two-base hit which could have—and probably should have—scored three runs, wound up plating just one run.

Here's how it all came to pass. Herman's Dodgers met the Boston Braves back on August 15, 1926. That day an event occurred that forever assured Herman, then just a rookie, a berth in the Flakes' Hall of Fame. With Brooklyn teammates on every base, Herman spanked a blistering line drive off George Mogridge that caromed off the right-field wall. Hank DeBerry waltzed home from third, but Dazzy Vance, who had been on second, rounded third but headed back to that bag, uncertain about whether he could score.

In the meantime, the Dodger who had been on first, Chick Fewster, had seen Vance initially head for home so he was certain he could race all the way to third base. However, as soon as he saw that Vance had retreated, he was in no man's land. The ball came in and Fewster was soon to be tagged out at third base. Herman, hellbent on advancing, also chugged into that bag as determinedly as the little engine that thought he could. Only Vance had the right to be on third. Unbelievably, unless Herman's reputation for being involved in wild blunders is factored in, three men wound up trying to occupy the same base, and it's said that a befuddled defender simply tagged all three. On the plus side, Herman's hit wound up as the game-winning blow.

Now, it's not true, as lore has it, that Herman hit a triple that led to his gaffe. Ring Lardner commented, "Babe Herman did not triple into a triple play, but he doubled into a double play, which is the next best thing." This strange play gave birth to a famous story. Basically, the straight line was, "The Dodgers have three on base." Punch line: "Yeah, which base?"

Much has been written about his poor fielding. He was said to be as graceful as a circus dancing bear. There are stories about many a fly ball conking him on the head. Herman denied it, but did so lightly, saying, "Never once did I get hit on the head by a fly ball." After a pause he added, "Once or twice on the shoulder, maybe, but never on the head." In seriousness, he said he actually lost a fly ball that everyone brings up, one he insisted struck his chest, not his head. His denial didn't change the legendary version, so he good-naturedly went along with the jokes about his fielding though they were often exaggerated or fabricated. Not even his league-leading 392 putouts in 1932 could prevent the media's flood of jokes.

They say a player bet Herman that he couldn't catch 20 fly balls in a row without having one strike him on the head. Herman accepted after establishing one rule: "Remember, just the head; the shoulders don't count." John Lardner wrote that Herman "did not always catch fly balls on the top of his head, but he could do it in a pinch."

Baseball executive Fresco Thompson observed that Herman didn't fret about his fielding. "Babe wore a glove for only one reason. It was a league custom. The glove would last him a minimum of six years because it rarely made contact with a ball." One sportswriter assessed Herman's defensive prowess like this: "He greatly improved in his ninth season. He still hadn't caught a ball, but he was getting a lot closer." Somebody even claimed Herman once explained the reason he hadn't caught a pop fly was that he had lost the ball in "the moon." He used that excuse because it was a night game, so he couldn't use the usual line about losing the ball in the sun.

Then there's the time Herman misplayed a ball, first coming in, then going back, then slipping on the grass. He got up, chased the ball to the fence, fumbled, and kicked the ball around. Finally he threw the ball over the backstop. When asked what had happened, he simply replied, "When?!" The path he took on balls hit in the air resembled that of the flight of a bumblebee. At one point, an unscrupulous character had been passing himself off as Herman in some sort of scam. Herman joked, "The next time he comes [here], take him out in the back yard and knock a few flies his way. If he catches any, you'll know it isn't me."

The next story may be another contrived one, but it's a gem. Speaking to reporters, Herman pled, "Please stop writing those awful stories about me being crazy." He said that just seconds before he pulled a lit cigar from his pocket. Herman said the truth was he once did stow a lit cigar in his pocket, but only momentarily to smuggle it out of a room with a No Smoking sign.

Someone once told him they knew a person who had lost everything during World War II. Herman asked, "What did he do, bet on the Germans?"[5] Yet another good, though probably phony quote from Herman came when he was supposedly asked what he thought of the Napoleonic Era. He reportedly responded, "It should have been scored as a hit."

PEPPER MARTIN (1928–1944)

Martin's greatest glory came in the 1931 World Series, a seven-game victory for his Cardinals over the Philadelphia Athletics. The four-time All-Star amassed 12 hits to set a Series record. He hit .500 on the nose with five extra base hits, five steals (still seventh on the all-time list), and an on-base plus slugging average of 1.330.

Three years later, he again helped St. Louis win the Series, this time chipping in with 11 hits and scoring a seven-game Series record eight runs. No player with more plate appearances than Martin has a higher lifetime average in Fall Classic play than his .418.

Over his 14-year career, he led the National League in stolen bases three times, and on three occasions this catalyst was in the top 10 for runs scored. A lifetime .298 hitter, his personal high for runs was 122. His best season for doubles was 41, and for batting average, .316. He also briefly did some placekicking in pro football.

Martin didn't graduate from *elementary* school until he was 15 years old, and never got a high school diploma, but he held a doctorate degree in baseball.

* * *

Former big league player and manager Bobby Bragan told a story about Martin, prefacing it by saying that baseball executive Branch Rickey was an expert at recognizing talent. "You know, he had meetings late at night in Vero Beach when I was managing the Fort Worth Cats and Pepper Martin was managing Miami Beach in the Florida State League. Mr. Rickey would change players around—he had 21 teams at that time—and he would take a pitcher off Fort Worth and put him in Triple A, or one off Miami Beach and put him in Double A." Rickey asked Martin about a pitcher who had thrown only half a season and hurt his arm, "What's the story about the calcification?" Martin replied, "I think it's good—I haven't seen him take a drink all spring."

When Martin reported to his first spring training camp, instead of using the travel money his club had provided to buy a train ticket, he chose to ride the rails, bumming part of his 1500-mile trip by riding the brake rods under a freight car. He even spent one night in jail as a vagrant, and by the time he reported to the Cardinals camp, sans any luggage, he resembled a disheveled beachcomber, wearing dirty clothes; grease, soot, and cinders; and a shaggy, five-day-old beard.

Martin was a key member of the Cards hillbilly musical group, the Mudcat Band. It included a man on the washboard and another blowing into a jug. Martin said they could play any song at all, whether they knew it or not. It was fitting that Pepper was on the same team with a Dizzy, a Daffy, and a Ducky (Medwick).

In a game Dizzy Dean was pitching, Bill Terry lashed three line drives through the box, making Dean resemble Charlie Brown in the comic strips where comebackers disrobe him. Martin went to the mound to give Dean this sage bit of advice: "I don't think you're playing him deep enough."[6]

Another time, Martin displayed his spacey ways during a team meeting. Manager Frankie Frisch ranted about his team's bungling play, going on and on. When he finally paused, Martin shot his hand up like a schoolboy, saying he'd like to ask a question. Still fuming, Frisch grudgingly acknowledged Martin who said, "I'd like to know whether you think I ought to paint my midget auto red with white wheels or white with red wheels."

Martin devised a scheme that was either harebrained or deviously clever. He wanted someone to bake something with the consistency of a pie crust in the shape of a baseball. He planned on waiting until a runner had steamed into his position at third base on, say, a triple. Martin was to have possession of both the real and the fake baseball. He would lob the faux ball to the pitcher (he envisioned Dizzy Dean), wait for the runner to start to take his lead off the bag, then tag him out. Meanwhile, Dean was to gobble down the evidence to complete his foolproof con. Prudently, Martin never actually attempted this scam.

He summed up his views on two-a-day practices: "I got a jackass back in Oklahoma and you can work him from sunup till sundown and he ain't never going to win the Kentucky Derby." Then there was the time he decided to remove insoles from his spikes, explaining, "They make me too high and I'm hitting over the ball."

Thanks to his speed on the base paths and overall bold style of play, Martin earned the nickname "the Wild Horse of the Osage." In one game, Joe Medwick was on second when Martin laced a single to right. The throw went to the plate to try to retire Medwick. Seeing that, Martin lit off for third base, and knowing only one umpire was working the game, he took the short route, going first to third by racing across the mound. While Martin did have blazing speed, the ump knew *nobody* ran that fast—he called him out.

Carl Erskine, who had a great lifetime win-loss percentage of .610 with a dazzling season best of .769, considered Martin to be "a hustler, just a fireball player. He excelled at running hard, sliding hard, playing hard. He was very clever. Something that has disappeared from baseball is players playing pepper. The fields were not very attractive on color television because of bare spots where guys played pepper every day. So they quit doing it, but Pepper Martin was very clever in pepper games. He'd throw the ball between his legs, over his shoulder. He was fun to watch, and fans miss some of that pre-game stuff."

Often such pre-game sessions of the Gashouse Gang included Martin and teammates forming a circle, tossing the ball around with quick sleight-of-hand motions and faked throws mixed in. It was like watching baseball's version of the Harlem Globetrotters. Other times the players would make fancy "throws" with a phantom baseball.

What Dean and Pepper Martin reportedly did in a hotel once was like a manic Marx Brothers scene. They invaded a group of society women who were holding a meeting at a swank Philadelphia hotel. One version of this story states they obtained firemen's uniforms and some smoke bombs, and as the women were about to leave the banquet room, smoke erupted everywhere. Dean and Martin entered and thundered orders as pseudo-firemen. One report has them ordering some to stand up and others to sit down, creating chaos before things settled down. Another version has it that the duo disguised themselves as painters and, armed with paint cans and ladders, took over a ballroom, rattling around, disturbing the guests' event.

Martin once held the job of athletic director at a penitentiary where, one writer joked, he probably taught his players how to steal.

BOBBY BRAGAN (1940–1948; MANAGED 1956–1966)

Bragan was not too much of an offensive threat, but he did drive home 69 runs in his sophomore season. Still, he was valuable enough to keep around on a team, the Brooklyn Dodgers, in an era when they were respectable and won a pennant.

Bragan was a teammate of Jackie Robinson when the UCLA star broke baseball's color barrier in 1947. In that season's World Series, Bragan made the best of his only plate appearance. In Game 6, he crushed a ball for a double and drove in the run that put his Dodgers ahead for good in a 8–6 win over the Yankees. Bragan immediately gave way to pinch runner Dan Bankhead, and New York eventually prevailed, winning Game 7.

Bragan holds the distinction of managing both Roberto Clemente, "the best right fielder I ever saw defensively," and Hank Aaron, the man he singled out as "the best ballplayer," and a man he still considers to be the all-time home run king—"I wouldn't give a nickel for Barry Bonds."

As the manager of the Braves, Bragan had an illustrious handful of future Hall of Famers on his roster in Aaron, Eddie Mathews, Warren Spahn, a young Phil Niekro, and a man who would enter the Hall of Fame as a manager, Joe Torre. Bragan's best team, the 1964 Braves, won 88 games.

How does a marginal player like Bragan, a lifetime .240 hitter with just 89 extra base hits spread out over 597 big league contests, become a manager of so many talented players? Bragan said he first realized he was destined to become a manager because, as he put it, "I guess I didn't have enough ability to be a real outstanding player."

What he had been endowed with, however, was a strong baseball background after learning a whole lot of "Dodger baseball" in Branch Rickey's system. Plus, Bragan was a former catcher, a position many feel gives a manager a good shot at success, an edge over others. Not only that, he also spent time at shortstop (he was there more than he was behind the plate, actually), as a third baseman and, infrequently, as a second baseman.

* * *

Bragan shared a story about colorful baseball executive Rickey. He began by saying, somewhat like a word association game, that Rickey brought three things to mind: "Jackie Robinson, number one. Number two, first complex in baseball with five diamonds—at Vero Beach, Florida, Dodgertown. And he put the first helmets on ballplayers when he did that at Pittsburgh. He had four degrees from Ohio Wesleyan."

Rickey used his intelligence to outfox other teams as well as his own players when it came time to negotiate contracts. In a 2009 interview, Bragan looked back on one particular time when he fell victim to Rickey in 1943, shortly after he was swapped to Rickey's Dodgers from the Phillies, where he had begun his playing days. "I was traded to Brooklyn and I was looking forward to meeting Mr. Rickey. I was making $4,500 a year and I said, 'I'm coming from one of the poorest clubs in baseball to one of the more affluent teams, and that should warrant some kind of a token raise.' He said, 'You got it all wrong, Bobby. You played every day over there in Philadelphia; you're going to be on the bench over here so long they'll start calling you Judge. Sign that contract.'

"So I signed it. And then I played every day. So in June I stopped by his office on Montague Street again and his secretary said, 'He can't see you today, come back tomorrow.' So I went back the next day. I went in and he said, 'Bobby, my secretary said you came by to see me yesterday and I've racking my brain ever since—what could that young man want to talk to me about, and I prayed to God it wasn't more money. Either you're the kind of a person that can live up to your contract or you're not—isn't that right?' I said, 'You're exactly right, Mr. Rickey. I just came by to say hello.'"

Bragan wound up playing for the same salary he had in Philly. It took him until 1948 before his salary as a player reached a personal peak of $9,000. Actually, that was the year Bragan played in just nine games before he switched jobs, becoming a manager. Bragan related that Rickey called him into his office early in 1948 and informed him, "You're not playing, would you like to go to Fort Worth, Texas, and be a player-manager in the Texas League? Burt Shotton is down there and he recommended we make a change in the manager."

Bragan replied, "Yes, sir, I'm ready to go," and stayed in the league for five years. "Then I went out to Hollywood and did the same thing for three years in the Pacific Coast League, and then Mr. Rickey hired me to manage the Pirates in '56 where I worked with general manager Joe Brown, son of [comedian] Joe E. Brown." His Hollywood Stars of 1953–1955 won 106, 101, and 91 games with him serving as a player-manager.

Most of Bragan's most colorful moments came when he was a manager. At times he manifested his offbeat ways in confrontations and/or disputes with umpires. Bragan said he was working a game in the Pacific Coast League and "an umpire blew a couple of calls. I went out to protest. I said, 'You know you're making a joke of the game. I'm going to show you how to make a joke out of it.' I sent nine [consecutive] pinch hitters up for the batter. I told them, 'Don't let him pitch, just let them announce you as a hitter and I'll call you out and send somebody else up.' Right before a pitch, I'd call [each pinch hitter] back."

Bragan managed identical twins Johnny and Eddie O'Brien with the Pirates. "In spring training," recalled Bragan, "if it got to, say, the seventh inning and I needed a hitter, I would have John go in and put Eddie's uniform on, have him go out and pinch hit, tell [the umpire], 'Eddie O'Brien batting for the pitcher.' I never had the guts to do it in a regular season game, only in spring training."

Johnny O'Brien remembered a time the Pirates split their squad to play two spring training games, and Eddie was not at the same park as Johnny. Johnny not only played the entire game, but Bragan pulled his twins trick, having Johnny also pinch hit, pretending to be Eddie. When the brothers met up later, Eddie asked Johnny how he had done. Johnny replied, "Pretty good, but you went 0-for-1."

Then there was the time Bragan's Pirates were playing Chicago in Pittsburgh. "Bob Shaw was pitching against us. I think he was throwing spitballs, so I told the first three hitters, which were John O'Brien, Dick Groat, and Clemente, 'After he throws one pitch, tell the umpire to look at the ball.' Frank Dascoli was the umpire and I'm coaching third base. So O'Brien asked to look at the ball and he inspected it. Then Groat takes a pitch, asks him to look at it, then Clemente. When Clemente asks to see the ball, Dascoli takes his mask off and starts walking toward me.

"Larry Goetz is the umpire at third base. I started walking toward Dascoli but Goetz says, 'Come back, Bobby, don't go up there, it looks like rain.' I said, 'I'm not concerned about the rain, I'm concerned about spitballs.'"

Goetz, not wanting to delay the game with rain imminent, came back with, "You're not concerned about the rain? Take a hike," and he thumbed Bragan. At that point, said Bragan, "I went to the dugout and I told Danny Murtaugh, my coach, 'Get me a hot dog and a cold drink, I'm going out to talk to these umpires and find out what they have against me—that's the only crew that's ejected me all summer.' So I took a Coca-Cola [or orange drink] with a straw out to the mound and I said to three or four umpires, 'You ought to take a sip of my Coke, it's good.' They weren't interested, of course." Bragan was fined and soon dismissed for his colorful shenanigans.

When he worked for the Rangers, he attended a game versus Toronto that featured a promotional appearance by television's Clayton Moore, the actor who portrayed the Lone Ranger. Bragan punned, "It's not very often we get to see the Lone Ranger and Toronto the same night."

Bragan took part in an unusual gimmick when he was inserted into a minor league game as a manager on August 11, 2005, with the sole purpose of becoming the oldest professional skipper ever. John Dittrich was the general manager of the Fort Worth Cats. Bragan said, "It was his idea that I manage that team for one night and become the oldest manager because I was a couple of weeks [actually, one week] older than Connie Mack."

That night Bragan, at the age of 87 years, 9 months, and 16 days, also became the oldest manager to get ejected from a professional baseball game. *That*, he related, was no stunt. "I did it because the shortstop was ejected in the third inning—the umpire threw him out before he ever left home plate, still in the batter's box. So I was sitting over there with Maury Wills, my coach, and when he did that I just automatically got up and walked out to him. I said, 'That's the only time I've ever seen a man get thrown out that quickly, from the batter's box—did he call you a dirty name?' He said, 'No, he didn't.' I said, 'Did he use profanity?' He said, 'No, he didn't.' I said, 'What'd he say?' He said, '[The batter] said I was doing a lousy job.' I said, 'Well, I'll go along with that.' He said, 'You go with him.' Isn't that something?" Then, true to the managerial code, Bragan concluded, "Anyway, we won the game, 11–10."

Speaking of colorful older managers, the record for the oldest manager to be booted from a big league game belongs to Jack McKeon, who was tossed from a 2011 game at the age of 80, six years older than the previous record holder, Casey Stengel.

Bragan didn't take too much stock in statistics. "Say you were standing with one foot in the oven and one foot in an ice bucket. According to the percentage people, you should be [just] about perfectly comfortable."

A final Bragan story comes from, he believes, April in the 1954 Pacific Coast League season. This one was impressive enough to get portrayed in a famous *Life* magazine photo. Bragan related the story: "Emmett Ashford was umpiring behind home plate. I had recommended him to the big leagues [up from the minors] because he was an excellent umpire, but in this particular game, we're playing the Los Angeles Angels, our big rival when I was managing the Hollywood Stars. Mel Queen was my pitcher and he threw a ball to Bob Usher, the center fielder for the Angels, and there was a question as to whether the ball hit him or hit his bat. Ashford ruled that it had hit his arm and he awarded him first base.

"So I ran out to the plate and said, 'Emmett, would you do me a favor—would you ask your partner down at first base did he hear a wood sound or a meat sound. He said, 'I don't need to ask anybody anything, you understand that?' I said, 'You telling me you're God, is that right?' He said, 'That's right,' and I said, 'Well, I'm going to lay down and worship at your feet.'" That action was the grounds for yet another Bragan ejection.

YOGI BERRA (1946–1965; MANAGED 1964–1985)

When he retired, Berra held the record for the most homers (306) hit by an American League catcher. It took 24 years before Carlton Fisk surpassed him. At one point, Berra also owned the single-season high for homers by a receiver with 30—a record broken first by Lance Parrish, and one which Fisk also later shattered when he cracked 37.

A lesser-known Berra statistic is his home runs to strikeouts ratio, one of the best ever. Over 19 seasons, he struck out just 414 times and connected for home runs 358 times. Only he and Joe DiMaggio launched 350+ home runs without fanning at least 500 times, and only DiMaggio had a better K-to-HR ratio than Berra. In addition, 22 players enjoyed (45 total) seasons in which they had more homers than strikeouts, and only DiMaggio and Berra achieved this five or more times.

Further, on Yankee teams loaded with sluggers such as DiMaggio and Mickey Mantle, Berra led his team in RBI from 1949 to 1955. A three-time MVP, he ranked in the top four in MVP voting every year from 1950 through 1956. Furthermore, he made 18 All-Star teams, played in 14 World Series, winning a championship in more than half of his seasons (10 times), and established Series records for games, hits, and doubles. He was just the second manager to win a pennant in both leagues. Berra, who once accepted 950 straight errorless chances, became a Hall of Famer in 1972.

* * *

Berra was a bad ball hitter and a free swinger; perhaps that's partly why he rarely fanned—he could hit just about anything. On one occasion, Herb Score struck out Berra on a fastball so high Berra had to jump to take his cut, and he missed. When he returned to the dugout, he asked Stengel, "Casey, how in the hell can a pitcher that wild stay in the big leagues?"

Wally Westlake, a veteran of 10 seasons, affectionately recalled Berra. "He was one of a kind. He was quite a guy. I'll never forget when I was with Cleveland and we were in New York. We had our clubhouse meeting and we came down to how we were going to pitch and defense Berra. Bill Wight, the left-hander, was pitching and our manager says, 'Bill, whatever you do today, you do not throw Berra any fastballs for strikes—show him the fastball, but not for strikes.'

"So Berra comes to bat the first time with that rocking motion of his and he dumped a single into left field. Second time up, he dumped another single into left field. So I guess Bill said, 'To hell with this. I'm going to blow a fastball by him.' Berra teed off. I just stood there and watched it land in the upper deck. Needless to say, when we got to the dugout our manager was a little pissed off."

Carl Erskine used a line to describe Berra that briefly but accurately summed up his uniqueness: "Yogi was Yogi. There was nobody like Yogi. He never tried to be funny, but he'd say these things. Like when the Yankees played somewhere and the crowd was real thin and the players in the dugout were saying, 'Look at this terrible crowd. These people don't support their team.' And Yogi supposedly said, 'Look, if these people don't want to come to the game, who's going to stop them.'"

In a 2018 interview Erskine added, "Yogi was misunderstood. They had Yogi on a talk show and the host wants him to be funny. He's *not* funny. He's not a comedian, but he comes up with these unusual responses like, 'When you come to the fork in the road, take it.' But I would not put Yogi in a category of being a prankster—he wasn't, he was a serious guy."

Marty Appel believed that "Yogi enjoyed the evolution of his characterization. The thing about Yogi-isms is he began to realize people would make them up and attribute them to him, and he didn't resent that. He thought it was all fine. He wasn't crazy about being ripped off, like the Yogi Bear cartoon character which obviously took his name and ran with it." All in all, though, "He was just an affable, easy-to-be-with guy, and the stories that happened around him, he could just chuckle at whether they were true or not. He found amusement in them."

Some say that the typical Berra tale portrayed him as not being too bright. "Here's the important thing on that," said Appel. "When he came up in '46, long before the days of being politically correct, the writers were having fun at his expense, telling the readers that he was dumb and that he read comic books and they had fun with his appearance, which was not like an ordinary ballplayer.

"Casey Stengel deserves *a ton* of credit for changing that—he put a stop to that. He would always talk about Mister Berra, his assistant manager, and he never made fun of Yogi or ridiculed him. In his daily conversations with his writers—he called them 'my writers'—he would always sing the praises of Yogi Berra, putting a stop to the ridicule that was going on before Casey got there in 1949. That's an important thing to note about Yogi—and about Casey."

Berra didn't mind writers taking poetic license to epic proportions. He even said, "Most of the time, I don't even know what I said until I read about it. But I really didn't say everything I said." Author David Nathan noted, "The sportswriters don't mean anything by it, and it makes them famous." Plus, the lines were great. "I always tell anybody making a speech to an audience of a certain age, if you just start out by saying, 'Yogi Berra once said . . .' then the audience is already primed to laugh. They know it's going to be something kind of absurd, a little off kilter— something that you should laugh at, whatever the next line is."

Erskine related a story about the normally mild-mannered Berra. Before one of his starts in the 1953 World Series versus the Yankees, Brooklyn skipper Charlie Dressen called him into his office. Erskine said, "He told me, 'I know you don't do this, so I'm not going to ask you, I'm going to order you to throw at him. Yogi is dug in—he's trying to hit the ball over that short, 297-foot fence at Ebbets Field. I want you to knock him down and loosen him up because he's dug in so you can't see the back of his shoe. Get a strike on him then I want you to flatten him.'

"I didn't do that—I thought the knockdown pitch was just crazy. You're not going to scare a major league hitter; you're going to make him mad. If he's a .280 hitter, he'll be a .400 hitter the next couple of pitches.

"The first time Yogi's up, I get a strike on him and I threw an inside pitch, but not a good one—I hit him in the ribs. When I went back to the bench, Dressen says, 'That's the lousiest knockdown pitch I've seen. I want you to get a strike on him and do it right.' Well, sure enough, the next time Yogi's up, I got a strike on him then I threw a high, inside pitch. He should've gone down, but he didn't. He just turned away from the pitch and it hit him in the back of the elbow."

The next inning Erskine was due up versus the hard-throwing Vic Raschi. "I figured Yogi would be pretty mad. He's looking up through his mask. He had a real deep voice, and he said in surprise, 'Carl, are you *throwing at me*?' He wasn't mad at all. He was looking at me [innocently] like, 'You wouldn't throw at me, would you?'" That quaint, naive attitude is one reason Berra was so loved.

Another obscure Berra story comes from the time Steve Barber fanned Berra looking on a pitch right down the heart of the plate. When Berra spun around to confront the ump, Barber said, "What are you griping about? It was right down the pipe." Berra replied, "I know. But there's 60,000 people out there. I got to say something."[7]

Yet another seldom repeated line, and actually a very astute one, came when Berra considered Sandy Koufax's 1963 season, in which he went 25–5 with a minuscule ERA of 1.88. In awe, Berra mused, "I can see how he won 25 games. What I don't understand is how he lost five." He could have wondered the same about Koufax's record in World Series play. The untouchable Koufax had an ERA of 0.95, yet somehow lost three and won only four.

One quote that may not be true, given the way Berra's life was chronicled by reporters, has it that a mutual friend introduced Berra to a famous author, saying "Yogi, I want you to meet Ernest Hemingway, the writer." Berra asked, "What paper does he write for?" Another time, when asked if a player had exceeded his expectations, Berra said, "I'd say he's done more than that."

One Berra line not mentioned quite as much as others came when he met Robert Briscoe, then mayor of Dublin, Ireland. Upon learning that Briscoe was the city's first Jewish mayor, Berra beamed, "Isn't that great. It could only happen in America."

Once, when presented a check made out to "Bearer" by broadcaster Jack Buck, Yogi said, "How long have you known me, Jack? And you still don't know how to spell my name." It's also been written that Berra was asked what he'd do if he found $1 million, and he said, "If the guy was real poor, I'd give it back to him."

Then there's the time Berra was reading a comic book while his roomie, Bobby Brown, was studying his medical textbook. When Brown shut the book, Berra supposedly asked, "How did yours come out?"

Mike Gibbons said he once had the chance to work with Yogi Berra and his museum staff on a project. Even though it didn't come to fruition, Gibbons said he came away from his dealings with Berra with three observations: "First, he really talked like that. Second, when we went to dinner at his favorite Montclair, New Jersey, Italian restaurant, he brought his own bottle of vodka, a ritual welcomed by the maître d'. Third, over dinner he told the story of serving in the Navy during World War II and spending hours on D-Day in a small craft as a spotter, hundreds of yards off of Omaha Beach. Witnessing that carnage took a toll on Yogi, as he was obviously still shaken in recalling that day more than 50 years later." Obviously, despite writers' efforts to portray Berra superficially, there was a serious side to him.

On an anniversary of D-Day, a French government delegation visited the Yogi Berra Museum to thank Berra for his service at Normandy. Mike Vaccaro stated, "He was on a supporting ship in the rear and he got wounded, hit by a small piece of shrapnel which barely made a dent, but he could say that he was wounded on D-Day." Berra told Vaccaro about the delegation's visit, saying, "One of the French guys came over and gave me a kiss. He gave me one of those French kisses." Of course, he meant the traditional kissing of the cheeks.

Vernon Law remembered how Berra fooled around with hitters. "Yeah, he was pretty good at distracting you while you were up to bat. I'd walk up there and then, 'Hey, Deacon, how are you?' I'd say, 'What?' He'd say, 'What are you doing after you get through with baseball—get another job?' Oh, he'd talk. Ask you where you're from and so forth to distract you from the game. I remember that like it was yesterday, there in Yankee Stadium. That was Yogi Berra. I had to say, 'Wait a minute, wait a minute. Yogi, just be quiet. I'm up here hitting. I'm not here to visit.'"

When Berra's name came up with Dick Groat, he broke into a spontaneously laugh. "I remember Yogi never shut up when he was catching. I told him to shut the [expletive] up. He just laughed."

Berra normally was the one on the giving end of humorous stories, but not always. He was the Yankees manager in 1964, and after a tough 5–0 defeat the normally placid Berra blew his top. Erskine picked up the story. "Phil Linz got on the bus one time right after a road loss. He's sitting in the back and Yogi hadn't gotten on yet. But when he got on the bus, he heard a harmonica being played so he yelled out, 'Put that thing away.' Linz said, 'What did he say?' And Mantle says, 'He wants to hear it again.'" In fact, the mischievous Mantle is said to have told Linz that Berra wanted him to play his amateurish rendition of *Mary Had a Little Lamb* even *louder*. Linz obliged. Infuriated, Berra stormed back to Linz and either slapped the harmonica out of his hands or took it and threw it, accidentally striking Joe Pepitone. Linz got so much publicity for the incident, a harmonica company gave him a $10,000 fee for his endorsement. Years later the two posed for a newspaper photo with Berra plugging his ears while Linz played his harmonica.

Asked what makes a good manager, Berra sagely said, "A good ball club." Many of Berra's comical lines were terse, like when he addressed the topic of his appearance by noting, "So what if I'm ugly? I never saw anyone hit with his face." When told by a photographer to look directly into his camera, Berra supposedly said, "I can't. That's my bad side."

Roy Blount Jr. wrote of the time some reporters invited Berra to go to a dirty movie. He refused, saying he was going to see the movie *Airport*. They insisted several times, but Berra declined. A final appeal was made: "You can see *Airport* anytime. Let's go see this dirty picture." To which Berra replied, "Well, who's in it?"[8]

Berra himself said it was true that when Mary Lindsay, the wife of New York City mayor John Lindsay, told him he looked nice and cool, he replied, "You don't look so hot yourself." And when he listened to a discussion on how to pitch to Stan Musial prior to an All-Star Game, Berra made the observation: "You guys are trying to stop Musial in 15 minutes when the National League ain't stopped him in 15 years."

Berra even touched on the usually morbid subject of death, commenting that actor Steve McQueen looked good in an old movie Berra had watched on television—"He must have made it before he died." In one game Whitey Ford was getting rocked, so Stengel conferred with Berra, asking how Ford's stuff was looking. Berra replied, "How should I know? I haven't caught [a pitch] yet."

He was asked what he thought about Joe DiMaggio's marriage to actress Marilyn Monroe: "I don't know if it's good for baseball, but it sure beats the hell out of rooming with Phil Rizzuto."

Once, long after his rookie season, Yogi Berra spoke with longtime Yankee coach Frank Crosetti, asking him if he could remember the first time he had ever seen Berra. Crosetti replied, "Sure. You were just coming out of the Navy and were wearing a sailor suit." The squat 5-feet, 7-inch, 190-pound Berra remarked, "I bet you didn't think I looked like a ballplayer." Crosetti shot back, "You didn't even look like a sailor."[9] Speaking of appearances, when Berra was 45 years old a fan asked how he kept his youthful looks. Berra answered, "Well, I used to look like this when I was young and now I still do."[10]

When Joe Torre managed the Yankees and Berra was one of his coaches, Berra became an unwitting accomplice in a great practical joke. A visitor dropped in on Torre, who was in his clubhouse office. Torre heard Berra go sauntering by and, knowing the uninhibited Berra paraded around the locker room naked as he went to and from the shower, Torre mischievously asked his guest if he'd like to meet Berra. The man readily said yes.

Picture Berra in the buff. Better yet—don't. He was a far cry from personifying the body beautiful; there would never be a Greek statue carved of a nude Berra. When Berra entered Torre's office, he stood directly in front of the visitor to shake his hand. The seated guest was at eye level with Berra's privates, forcing him to grapple with the problem of how to be polite without gazing directly at what was staring him right in the face.

To make things worse, and funnier, Torre purposely prolonged the conversation as his friend grew more and more ill at ease. In the book *Driving Mr. Yogi*, Harvey Araton wrote, "The guy was continuing to look this way and that, anywhere but straight in front of him. Torre knew one thing: Berra was not going to excuse himself out of embarrassment."[11] One can almost imagine Torre keeping the encounter going by saying, "Yogi, show my friend here how you used to get down in your catcher's squat, then show him how you'd quickly bounce back up again."

JOE GARAGIOLA (1946–1954)

Garagiola acted as if his bat was as effective as a nostrum, but he hit .257 lifetime. This childhood friend of Berra's played nine big league seasons, proving he was better than he gave himself credit for. Still, he played in 100+ games only twice, and his single-season high for homers was 11 and his best RBI total was only 54. In the end, he made far more money by being clever than he did by wearing the tools of ignorance.

* * *

If pitchers, especially relievers, produce an inordinate number of colorful characters, then next in line are those who have a lot of time on their hands, typically benchwarmers and bullpen catchers. Carl Erskine said that many of baseball's most colorful characters were, to use a term in baseball, "scrub-beanies. They weren't great in the lineup, they were bench guys. To spend the time on the bench, they had to do something to keep their sanity."

Garagiola, a witty bench jockey, was that type of player. He could spin a lengthy amusing story or toss off a quick one-liner with the best of them. Like fellow catcher Bob Uecker who followed him years later, Garagiola joked about his status as not exactly being a superstar. He said, "The highlight of your season is taking the team picture, knowing that the trading deadline has passed and you're a part of the club." He also claimed that when a scout wrote up a report on him it read, "Deceiving runner. He's slower than he looks." As a marginal player, Garagiola never became famous—kids never clamored for his autograph. His lack of fame is why he said, "I went through baseball as a 'player to be named later.'"

When his Cubs finished one rung above the cellar the two years he was with them, he observed, "One thing you learn as a Cubs fan: when you bought your ticket, you could bank on seeing the bottom of the ninth."

He was with the 1952 Pirates, a pathetic team that went 42–112. He quipped that his Pirates were the first team to wear protective helmets, but they were unnecessary—with all the weak hitters on the team, opposing pitchers never felt they had to throw at them.

Pirate teammate Johnny O'Brien recalled a time just before a game began when his team announced a trade. "We were playing the Cubs and Fred Haney called us all off the field to say we just made a trade with the Cubs effective immediately. He said, 'Meat—that was Ralph Kiner— you're involved. You, too, Dago—Garagiola—you're going over to the Cubs.' Joe said, 'I ain't going. I just put a down payment on a house.' We practically had to throw him and his equipment out of the locker room.

"Toby Atwell was traded to us in that deal so he asked Haney, 'What are the new signs?' Haney said, 'Ah, we'll keep our old signs. Those birds who left didn't know them anyway.' And we found out the Cubs never changed their signs that day, either. That's why those teams were always fighting for last place.

"Oh, Garagiola. Now there was a character. One time we were playing the Phillies in Pittsburgh and Danny O'Connell was playing third base for us and he was 5-foot-8. And my brother Ed was playing shortstop at 5-foot-8. I was playing second base at 5-foot-9 and Paul Smith at 5-foot-8 was at first base. Just before the game starts, Garagiola calls time-out and talks to the umpires. Finally, they broke it up and Dusty Boggess says to me, 'You know what that buzzard wants? He wanted us to cut the infield grass so he could see his infielders.'"

O'Brien went on, "We were in spring training in Fort Myers and we had all signed. In those days, nobody had an agent. But Garagiola came to camp unsigned. He said, 'I'm going to get more money out of that buzzard,' referring to Branch Rickey. He said he was going to go head-to-head with him. If you want to think about a mismatch, that was it. He went in to see Rickey and with that gravelly voice Rickey said, 'Joseph, why are you here?' Joe said, 'I had a career year last year, Mr. Rickey, and you didn't offer me enough money. I want more.'"

Rickey read off Garagiola's statistics, then said, "I admit for you that was a career year, but look at it from my standpoint. We finished last with your career year. So I'm sure we could finish last without you this year."

At that point Garagiola barked, "Give me the goddamn pen." O'Brien said Rickey wasn't done with Garagiola. "Rickey handed him the pen and said, 'Sign legibly and watch your language.' Joe told us, 'I told that old goat off,' but we found out the true story later on."

Joe Cunningham, who hit .345 in 1959, second-best in the National League behind only the great Hank Aaron, knew an intense side of Garagiola. "I remember when he hit a ground ball to me at first base and he tried to elbow me, but we became good friends."

When players batted while Garagiola was hunkered down behind the plate, he tried to distract them, just as his childhood pal Berra did. "Yeah, he did try to talk to you," said Cunningham. "He and Harry Walker were the same like that, even when Harry was coaching third base. Eventually, I had to tell them to shut up so I could concentrate on my hitting."

Ron Necciai, who struck out 27 batters in a minor league game and pitched briefly for the Pirates, said, "I loved Joe, loved him. He was very witty and upbeat, a fabulous, fabulous guy. He was fantastic to me." Nevertheless, he said that like other catchers such as Berra, Garagiola would "look up at the batter and say, 'Get ready because this guy's going to throw you a fastball.' They're trying to get your mind off what you're doing and thinking, 'Is it going to be a fastball?' A lot of times he'd call a fastball and he told the truth, but the next time he'd [have the pitcher] throw something different. Oh, yeah, they play mind games with you all the time."

Vernon Law called Garagiola "an interesting player. There are a lot of things that he said that were funny. I will say one thing about Joe when he came over to the Pirates, I don't know how he could get so dirty in one game. I mean, his uniform would just be covered with dirt, all over. He was a good player, though." A good defensive catcher who bore a resemblance to the comic strip character Pigpen, that is.

"He was a fun guy to have on the team," continued Law. "He could make you laugh. He said a player heard his phone ring so he woke up and the guy calling said, 'I'm sorry to awaken you.' The player said, 'That's OK, I had to get up to answer the phone anyway.' He always joked about our ball club at that time [1951–1953]. He called us the Rickey Dinks [or Rickey's Rinky Dinks] and said, 'It's a good thing that we never got in a fight with another team because we'd surely lose.' I think we had a first baseman about 5 feet, 9 inches and the O'Brien twins who were about 5 feet, 8 inches. We didn't have any big, strong guys on the team."

Garagiola was a spellbinding storyteller, and one of his gems involved his manager, Fred Haney, who gave the steal sign to one of his Pirates. Brooklyn catcher Roy Campanella, sensing a steal attempt, called for a pitchout but the runner didn't break from first. This happened two more times, causing Haney to later ask the runner if he had seen the sign. When told yes, Haney asked why he hadn't run then. The reply was, "I didn't think you meant it."[12]

Garagiola said once when he was anchored at third base, a teammate took off from second base and slid into the bag as if to share it with Garagiola. So he asked the disoriented, misguided base thief where he thought he was going. The reply was basically, "Back to second base if I can make it."

As a broadcaster, Garagiola worked many Yankees games, but not during that team's great seasons. "When I covered the Yankees they had players like Horace Clarke, Ross Moschitto, Jake Gibbs, and Dooley Womack. It was like the first team missed the bus."[13]

Garagiola loved to tell the story about the time Smead Jolley was batting with men aboard first and third. The runner from first took off with the pitch on a stolen base attempt and when the catcher threw to his shortstop, the runner from third dashed for the plate to pull off a double steal. As the return throw from the shortstop neared the plate, Jolley took a mighty cut and ripped the ball to the outfield in a clear case of interference. Jolley then turned to the home plate umpire and explained that he simply couldn't resist illegally taking a hack at the ball because, "That's the first fastball I've seen in weeks."[14]

Erskine summed up Garagiola: "He saw the funny side of baseball. He wrote a [fittingly titled] book, *Baseball Is a Funny Game*, and he became a clever broadcaster." Erskine said that years after Garagiola's playing days ended, he was earning more money for delivering a speech than he made for playing a full season back in the 1940s.

CHUCK CONNORS (1949–1951)

Kevin Connors went by the name Chuck because as a kid playing first base he'd yell to teammates, "Chuck it to me."

Connors once led the Piedmont League in homers, and his best minor league season came in 1949 when he hit 20 home runs, drove in 108 runs, and hit .319 for Montreal of the International League. He did play 67 games in the majors, hitting an anemic .238 lifetime with two home runs.

* * *

After he left baseball, Connors became famous as an actor, mainly portraying television's Lucas McCain, the lead in *The Rifleman*. However, he honed his skills as a marksman when he was a major leaguer, in his role as the Squirt Gun Man. He occasionally sat in his hotel lobby with his face hidden behind a newspaper, one that he had cut a small hole into. Waiting in ambush for an unsuspecting person to walk by, Connors aimed and fired his squirt gun through the hole. His moist victims were left wondering if the roof had sprung a leak, or what.

The 6-feet, 5-inch Connors is one of the rare men to play in the majors and in the NBA. He played in 53 pro hoop games from 1946 to 1948, but his aim must have been better with squirt guns than with a basketball as his field goal percentage was .252 and he averaged just 4.5 points per game with the Celtics over their first two seasons of existence. He is also said to be the first pro basketball player to break a backboard, doing so when he hurled a 40-foot shot at the conclusion of warmups before a 1946 contest.

"I played with Chuck in the minors," said Carl Erskine. "He was considered a little flaky—he'd do things that a serious player would never consider doing. He tried to make our [Brooklyn] club a number of years, but Gil Hodges was so entrenched at first base that he couldn't make it.

But Chuck was a showman, and way before he got into movies he was always doing something bizarre." He did cartwheels during some of his home run trots, for example.

Erskine went on, "Playing first base there are a lot of close calls. If we got one against us, one of his gimmicks was this—the umpire would be down the line a little bit and back of first base, and if the wind happened to be blowing right, Connors would get in position and kick up the dust on the field and send clouds of dust blowing right over the umpire. On the road, he would antagonize the crowd by a lot of bizarre things. One thing he used to do was take 10 bats, or as many as he could hold, up to the plate. He'd take them one at a time and try them out. And he'd throw one out, then take another one, try it out, and throw it away. In the meantime, the crowd is booing him like crazy. He was always on stage."

Connors liked to perform card tricks, like the time he had teammate Toby Atwell secretly stationed in a phone booth as his accomplice. He had another teammate choose a playing card then say he would then call a swami on the phone to divine that card. Atwell answered the phone and began naming the suits. When he got to the correct one, Connors pretended Atwell had just picked up the phone, saying, "Hello, Swami." Atwell then rattled off the names of the cards, "King. Queen. Jack . . ." until he mentioned the correct card. At that point, Connors, always the entertainer, would stop Atwell by using a discreet code, then dramatically hand the phone to his mark. He who would hear Atwell say in an ethereal voice, "This is the Swami," then recite the name of the correct card.

When Connors was about to negotiate a contract with the frugal Branch Rickey, he heard that a teammate was refused a raise when he admitted to Rickey that he took an occasional drink. So when Rickey asked Connors if he was a drinking man, Connors feigned indignation, saying that if he had to drink to be on Rickey's team, he didn't want to be a part of the club. Rickey, pleased with Connors' response, granted him a raise.

Erskine remembered another minor league incident from a game in Syracuse, New York. "A guy was getting on Connors big time. He came right down over the dugout and just kept getting on his back. Chuck went to the plate, took a third strike, and when he was coming back to the dugout, this guy's really on him. So Connors, who was a tall guy, comes toward the bat rack, but instead of going into the dugout, he took a leap over the dugout into the stands and he chased this guy up the aisle. With his spikes on, he was slipping and falling—he never did catch the guy, but he was a target of the fans because he asked for it. He always created some kind of a scene."

When Connors was traded to the Cubs, he was shipped to their Triple A club in Hollywood. "Now, Chuck did all kinds of goofy stuff," said Erskine. "He'd run the bases backwards. He'd hit a ball that was an obvious out and run to third base and he'd slide. He hit a ball back to the pitcher and he ran and slid into the mound. Somehow, doing that crazy stuff in Hollywood, he made contact with somebody who saw him as an entertainer, and that's how he ended up being the Rifleman."

Actually, his first role came in a movie. He earned $500 for one week of work, prompting him to say that organized baseball now had one fewer first baseman.

JIMMY PIERSALL (1950–1967)

Outfielder Piersall may have been to his era what Garry Maddox was to his, as described in the line, "Two-thirds of the world is covered by water. The other third is covered by Garry Maddox." Casey Stengel said Piersall, who won two Gold Gloves, was the best defensive outfielder he had ever seen—placing him ahead of his own Joe DiMaggio. Of course, he also said Piersall was "great, but you have to play him in a cage."[15]

Piersall wasn't exactly a power hitter, but he was no joke at the plate—he hit .322 in 1961 for a personal best and he once led the league in doubles, with 40. Quite the athlete, he led his high school basketball team to a championship, drilling 29 of their 51 points in the title game. He was even offered a baseball and basketball scholarship to Duke.

Joe Cunningham, who cracked the top 10 in his league for doubles twice, played against Piersall a few years. His view of Piersall was concise: "He was a good ballplayer, a good center fielder, and a pretty good hitter. He had some funny mannerisms. He was a jokester and did some funny and crazy things on the bases."

* * *

Carl Erskine said, "Jim Piersall was, by reputation, the name I think of as being somewhat off the wall during my days." Piersall's actions were off the wall for *any* time period. He could have come directly out of the Marlon Brando movie *The Wild One*. It's easy to imagine someone earnestly asking, "Jimmy, what are you rebelling against?" and the high-strung outfielder replying tersely, "Whaddya got?" To be fair, instead of being branded solely as a rebel, consider the fact that Piersall did have serious mental problems.

This one-man circus sideshow played 56 games in his rookie season through June 27, 1952, then was sent packing to the minors in Birmingham. Later that summer he went to a mental hospital after suffering a breakdown while under the pressure of playing pro ball. He was diagnosed as having a bipolar disorder. He underwent electroshock treatments and later said he had no memory of that season or of his time in the hospital.

His stay in Birmingham had lasted 20 days. Over that span he was ejected from six games and suspended four times. In several plate appearances he let his bat drop, then mimicked the pitcher when he wound up, forcing delays in the game. Other times he interrupted game play by bolting from the batter's box to the first or third base coach ostensibly to give them, or a base runner, instructions.

He also said that when he was in the majors, every year he'd say to himself, "This is the new Piersall." Then he lamented, "He never showed up."[16] One season he set a record by being ejected from seven games. His emotional problems were chronicled in his book *Fear Strikes Out*, but problems aside, he was also considered to be a bona fide baseball kook. In 1960, about eight years after he had recovered from his mental problems, he got into trouble with his team's front office. It seems the Indians brass had leaked word to the media that Piersall should again see a psychiatrist.

Angered at what he saw as an unfair allegation, he went to a psychiatrist and demanded that a then stiff rate of $100 per hour be charged—"I won't talk to you unless you do. Charge the most you can," he gloated, "because the Indians are paying for it . . ." That type of logic almost seemed to prove that he was quite lucid and *didn't* need additional psychiatric help.

Marty Appel said that in Piersall's era, "people would happily say, 'Oh, that guy's nuts.' We're a little more word sensitive now. He did have issues and he was institutionalized, so you wouldn't say that about a player today, even Piersall. But he did some erratic things on the field which were attention-getting.

"The first time I ever met him, he was working for the Texas Rangers. I shook hands with him and said, 'Hi, I'm Marty Appel. Nice to meet you.' And he said, 'Hi, Marty. Let me ask you, are you sane?' I said, 'I'd like to think so.' He said, 'Well, do you have the papers to prove it?' And he took a xeroxed copy of his discharge papers from the institution out of his pocket. So he could prove it, but I had nothing to prove it."

Former manager Mike Hargrove had a similar tale. "Jimmy told me one time when we were at a party, 'Mike, you see all these people here? They all think I'm crazy.' I said, 'Is that right?' And he said, 'Yeah, but I'm the only sane person here because I'm the only one with papers to prove it.'"

Piersall later became a broadcaster and Dick Groat, a Duke standout in baseball and basketball, related a story from that time period. "I remember vividly him telling me, 'Everybody thinks I'm wacky, and I get paid good money to speak because they think that, but I'm not really.'"

Piersall actually said that the best thing that ever happened to him was "going nuts." That label allowed him to get away with outrageous behavior. For example, when umpire Bill McKinley ejected Piersall from a game, the free spirit commented, "They shot the wrong McKinley." Back then, nobody pondered, "Too soon?"

At times he'd run to first base, arms outstretched like a child pretending to be an airplane. When the bullpen cart drove by him to deliver a pitcher to the mound, Piersall stuck out his thumb as if he were hitchhiking. He batted lefty and righty in a single at bat even though he was not a switch hitter—and he struck out. He threw a baseball and an orange at Bill Veeck's exploding scoreboard, and he often took a dramatic bow after making a catch. He once made pig-like noises at Satchel Paige. In a way, it got to where nothing he did was unexpected.

In the minors, he asked an umpire to clear the dust off home plate. The ump refused. The next time Piersall settled into the batter's box, he pulled a water pistol out, and squirted home plate. One game, after being called out on strikes, he blew up, got thumbed, then whipped his water pistol from his pocket and drenched the ump's face. Furthermore, between innings in a minor league game he squirted the opposing right fielder, Frank Thomas (not the Hall of Famer), when they exchanged positions. After about three times, Thomas picked him up and shook him, letting him know he should desist.

Once after getting kicked out of a minor league game, Piersall joined a group of kids in the stands, becoming the oldest member of their knothole gang. The childlike Piersall then led the kids in a chant of, "We want Piersall. We want Piersall!" Another time after an ejection, he heckled the ump from high atop the grandstand roof.

Clearly, Piersall craved attention. Milt Bolling, a minor league teammate, said he would stand on street corners passing out autographed publicity pictures of himself just so the pedestrians would know who he was. It was as if Piersall wanted his every action to be punctuated by the opening drum roll and the final cymbal clash in our national anthem.

Piersall's antics live on forever in baseball lore. Like the time he slid into home plate dramatically and quite unnecessarily after hitting an over-the-fence home run. He liked to switch the contents of players' aftershave lotion with their mouthwash. He intentionally crashed a motorcycle into a brick wall. When he was told he must wear a batting helmet in the on-deck circle, he later came to the plate wearing a football helmet. Another time when a pitch was on its way to the plate, Piersall tried to soak the baseball using a can of insect spray. There's also a picture of him positioned in center field, squirting a large can of bug spray into the air above his head.

The list of Piersall's antisocial baseball behavior is almost endless. In 1960, he jumped up and down and danced around, waving his arms from his position in center field in order to distract Ted Williams at the plate. He was ejected for that loose cannon act. On another occasion, doing his best imitation of a National Football League punter, he kicked a fan's butt after he had come onto the field to harass him. Fans would heckle him, saying the men in their white coats were on their way to get him, but he had quick comebacks other than his swift kick.

Playing in Yankee Stadium, he once trotted out to second base, did some jumping jacks, then sprinted to Ruth's monument in the outfield and sat on it. Yet another time he came in from his normal position, sat on second base, and defied a weak hitter to crack the ball beyond his reach. Once he broke out into a hula dance while in the outfield. In Cleveland, he sometimes sat on top of the outfield fence. During pitching changes at Yankee Stadium he was known to rest against a monument in center field, simulating a nap.

He performed a disappearing act, which preceded that of Manny Ramirez by decades. Yankee second baseman Bobby Richardson, who was close with Piersall, added, "One time Piersall came from center field to sit on second base. The manager made him go back out. When I came up, he was hiding behind a monument that was 447 feet away in center field. The manager took him out of the game then. I talked to him later and he said, 'Everybody thinks I'm crazy, but I'm making $45,000. I'm not as crazy as they think I am.'"

Former big leaguer Bob Hale said some of Piersall's ways were calculated, merely histrionic outbursts. "When there were 40,000 in the stands or the game was on TV, you could expect Jimmy to make something happen."[17] Sometimes during batting practice Piersall would walk across Fenway's Green Monster, acting like he was a high-wire artist.

Erskine's Dodgers met Piersall's Red Sox in a spring game in Miami. "He came to bat and hit a double. Don Zimmer, just a rookie, was playing shortstop. After Piersall slid into second base and called time, he walked over to Zimmer and said, 'You know who I am? I thought maybe you might want my autograph'—in the middle of a ball game!"

In a 1957 game against the Yankees, Piersall was in the throes of a slump. Yankee pitchers had thrown at two straight batters, so when Piersall entered the batter's box he muttered to Berra that if the Yankees threw a knockdown pitch at him, Berra would regret it. He said that he would get away with an attack on Berra by claiming temporary insanity. Unperturbed, Berra said, "We don't throw at .200 hitters."

Piersall had a large family, so in order to spend more time with them, he had a clause put in his contract permitting him to travel home when his Indians had an off Monday. He then sometimes purposely got kicked out of Sunday games to get a head start on his trips. Vernon Law said, "I was pitching against him and had gotten him out three times in a row. He hollers out to me, 'Deacon, give me one right down here where I can hit it. I got eight kids to support.'"

After taking Jim Bunning deep, Piersall stood at the plate and took a bow. He completed his journey around the bases by sliding into home plate, then stayed there pretending to snooze. Once he scored from third on a deep drive by crawling home on all fours. When he heard the Athletics were trying to book the Beatles to play in their park, Piersall went to the plate wearing a Beatles wig.

Asked to name a flake, Cubs great Billy Williams said, "Certainly one of the first guys who comes to my mind is Jim Piersall. A lot of people talk about him when he hit his 100th home run, he ran around the bases backwards." Here's how that scenario played out: the date is June 23, 1963. Dallas Green is on the hill for the Phillies at the Polo Grounds. He's facing Jim Piersall of the New York Mets, then managed by Casey Stengel, making quite a duo. It's an auspicious occasion, with Piersall sitting on 99 career homers. Green jams him, but he makes contact and the ball carries 248 feet down the right field line into the seats for a not atypical cheap Polo Grounds home run. And then it happens—Piersall takes a few strides toward first base, then turns around and runs the bases backwards.

Hungry for publicity, he prepared for this moment by practicing his running, backpedaling all the way. He also said his original intention was to run to third base, then on to second, first, and back home, but he learned that action would result in him being called out.

He later explained his backward style of running, "That way I can see where I've been. I always know where I'm going." He also proudly spoke of his backward running ability, saying he was even able to shake hands with his third-base coach. Moe Drabowsky's wife Liz said Piersall didn't face her husband often, but "Piersall told Moe that if he ever hit a home run off him, he would run the bases backwards."

Piersall also said that when he returned from his trip around the bases, and passed Stengel in the dugout, Casey didn't even crack a smile. Some wondered if it was a case of the elder clown being speechless for once. Later, Stengel basically echoed to Piersall the words he had used to chastise the colorful Frenchy Bordagaray: "If there's gonna be a clown on this team, it's gonna be me."

As a postscript to this misadventure, Piersall was released by the Mets about a month after his base running caper. He signed as a free agent that same day with Los Angeles. There, writers had a field day scrawling headlines such as: "BASEBALL'S BAD BOY IS NOW AN ANGEL!" Not long after joining his new team, he unashamedly and humorously alluded to his condition, saying, "The Angels are the first team I've ever been on where I feel I belong. They're all nuts, too."

ROCKY BRIDGES (1951–1961)

Infielder Bridges was a typical benchwarming colorful character, one with plenty of time to kill. He hit .247 over 11 seasons, playing in 100 or more games just five times. His best RBI total was 47, and he never hit more than five homers in a season. When he was hired to manage a California League team, he joked that he was back where he had started his batting slump, one that lasted 17 years.

* * *

Carl Erskine said, "Rocky was my teammate for three or four seasons. He was a utility player, and they had to have a mentality that fit their role because otherwise they're always unhappy because they never get to play, or very little. So Rocky was a bit of a comedian and a funny guy who pulled little tricks. One was to take a spoon and cut off the bowl and just have the handle. He'd go in, order a cup of coffee, and he'd say, 'This coffee looks really strong.' The girl would say, 'We just made it this morning.' In the meantime, he's stirring the spoon. He pulls it out and there's nothing on the end.

"Chico Carrasquel was one of the early Latin players coming into the league in the '50s, and he couldn't speak English. So the guys would help him order in the hotel dining room, and they'd have him saying some terrible things. Bridges might have Chico say to the waitress, 'You're a nice-looking S-O-B.' Finally Chico got burned so many times that he learned to say ham and eggs, and that's all he'd ever order."

Erskine continued, "Bridges was not what you'd call a handsome guy. He had kind of a pockmarked face a little bit, so he took a lot of kidding about being handsome. Rocky had an annual event—he would make up an All-Ugly team and post it in the clubhouse. Don Newcombe used to help him, giving some suggestions. Everybody was anxious to see whether they made the list or not. He'd kid guys like Buddy Kerr, who played for the Giants. He was in a similar role to them as Bridges was for the Dodgers—he was a second-level player who didn't play a lot. Kerr was not the most handsome guy in the world. Bridges would yell, 'Hey, Buddy, you selling that handsome cream you've been using on your face?'

"But probably the most bizarre thing Bridges did involved golf. He never owned any golf clubs but he would go to pro shops and get clubs that had been lost or left, used clubs that were sitting around. Rocky would beg or buy a five iron—he didn't have anything in his bag but five irons. Somebody would say, 'What club are you using, Rocky,' and it was always a five iron. He'd hit on a par three over the water—and he was a real high handicapper—if he hit the ball in the water, he'd throw the club in after it. He was a cut-up guy."

When he was managing in the minors, one of his players, Johnnie LeMaster, told umpire Billy Lawson that he had been hit with a tight pitch. Lawson disagreed. Bridges, well aware that LeMaster had lost the tip of his pinky finger when he was a child, told Lawson to check out his hand. When Lawson saw the little finger, he was taken aback, but then got the better of Bridges: "Tell you what, Rocky. You find the rest of that finger and I'll give him first base."[18]

Bridges came up with a famous line about being the skipper of a poor club when he said, "I managed good, but, boy, did they play bad." He once told his troops after another bad showing, "We may lose again tomorrow, but not with the same guys." He also scolded, "If you don't catch the ball, you catch the bus." He was not exactly a great glove man himself, noting, "I got a big charge out of seeing Ted Williams hit. Once in a while they let me try to field some of them, which sort of dimmed my enthusiasm."

Bridges was asked why he wouldn't eat snails. He cleverly replied, "I prefer fast food." He joked that he played for so many teams, he had more numbers on his back than a bingo card. One time he finished second in a pre-game cow milking contest then explained, "I didn't try too hard. I was afraid I'd get emotionally involved with the cow."

Perhaps his funniest line came when he spoke about shortstop José Gonzalez, who was traded in 1985. Between the time the deal was consummated and the time he reported to his new team, he changed his name to José Uribe because he said there were too many Gonzalezes in the majors. Hearing that, Bridges commented, "José truly was the player to be named later."

MARV THRONEBERRY (1955–1963)

The New York Mets were born in 1962, and Throneberry, whose initials were M. E. T., was a big part of their growing pains. In 1956 and 1957 he hit 42 and 40 homers respectively in the minors. Expected to give the Mets power when they acquired him in a May 1962 trade, Throneberry hit 16 homers with 49 RBI over 116 games to go with a .244 batting average. He may also have given up as many runs as he scored (29) due to his leaky glove. He would last only 14 more games in 1963 before forever vanishing from the big league scene.

* * *

One eyewitness said Throneberry's strangest plays unfolded when the all-time flake was at the plate with Gene Woodling on second and Frank Thomas leading off first. Throneberry hit a shot to the gap and legged out a triple. However, the visiting Cubs, thinking he had missed second base, made an appeal play. The umpire at second called him out, a ruling that catapulted Mets manager Casey Stengel out of his dugout, ready to chew out the ump. He didn't get far. His third-base coach told him, "Save your breath, Casey. He missed first, too."

New York coach Solly Hemus tells a slightly different version of the story, saying one of the umpires told Stengel that after they had called Throneberry out, Woodling's run counted, but if Chicago had appealed at first base, no run would have counted. After the mess had cleared, Stengel, never at a loss for a bon mot, said, "I know damn well he didn't miss third because he's standing on it." Newspaper writer Jack Lang stated, "How could he be expected to remember where the bases were? He gets on so infrequently."

Throneberry's glove didn't exactly glisten like gold, either. One year he was guilty of 17 errors at first base in just 97 games. Sportswriter Jimmy Breslin said, "Having Marv Throneberry play for your team is like having [famous safecracker] Willie Sutton guard your bank." When teammate Frank Thomas committed two errors on the same play, Throneberry teased, "What are you trying to do, take my fans away from me?"

Carl Erskine recalled an Old Timers' Game at Shea Stadium featuring many Mets from their futile years and other New York/Brooklyn players. "We were all lined up down the foul line. It was Casey's 80th birthday so they wheeled out a big cake at home plate. Marv Throneberry, who was a good hitter but didn't have much of a glove, says, 'Hey, Casey, I just had a birthday last week. Nobody brought me a cake like that.' Casey said, 'We were going to get you a cake, but we were afraid you'd drop it.'"

Marty Appel said Throneberry "was a Casey favorite. He had him with the Yankees when nobody knew he was a colorful character. Then when he went to the Mets under Casey again, he just found himself in situations where his ineptness on the field shone through on a team that was quickly gathering a reputation for all-time ineptness."

One pundit said that Marv never made the same mistake more than once because he always made different mistakes. Another line, though written about Harmon Killebrew originally, fit Throneberry perfectly: "He hasn't got much range, but what he can get to, he'll drop." Marvelous Marv wasn't happy about how he was portrayed, especially when the entire team was bumbling, not just him. Regardless, more than anyone, Throneberry's misfortunes and his misadventures came to serve as a symbol for the expansion Mets.

A baseball adage has it that *every* team will win at least one-third of its games and lose at least one-third, but that it's what a team does with the other third that will determine whether it will be a pretender or a contender. But these Mets defied the odds, unable to win even a lousy one-third of their games. Their final record stood at 40–120, meaning they had a miserable .250 winning percentage that translates into winning one-fourth, not one-third or more, of their games. The not-so-amazin' Mets finished the season in the cloud of dust the pennant-winning Giants left behind, a whopping 60½ games out of first.

No doubt about it, this team was a joke, but a horde of New York fans who missed having a National League team in their city since their Giants and Dodgers fled to the West Coast in 1958 took to the Mets. Plus, some New Yorkers, accustomed to the Yankees with their "rooting for the Yankees is like rooting for U.S. Steel" robotic winning ways, found the sad Mets to somehow be charming, endearing. Spectators by the thousands made their way to the old Polo Grounds to root on their favorites, mainly men like Stengel and Throneberry.

DICK STUART (1958–1969)

Big Stu played for six different clubs during his 10 seasons in the majors. In the minors, he put up some huge numbers. In his five most potent seasons there he hit 31 homers in 1954, then 32, and the next season he more than doubled that output, smacking a phenomenal 66 in Class A ball for the Lincoln, Nebraska, team. Then he added 45 and 31 shots. His 66 homers set a record for the Western League that was never shattered, but it wasn't enough for him to earn a call up to the majors, as his porous defense and his 171 strikeouts stymied that.

Never shy, Stuart took to signing autographs "Big Stu—66—No. 7," indicating his home run high and his jersey number. He sometimes dotted the "i" in Dick with, not an image of a heart or a flower like a teenage girl might do, but with similar affectation—a star. At the age of 23 he was the youngest man ever to top the 60 home run level.

His apex in the majors was his 1963 showing with the Red Sox when he won the Comeback Player of the Year Award after belting 42 home runs, leading his league in total bases, and driving in a league-leading 118 runs, one of three 100+ ribbie seasons. He was the first player to hit 30+ home runs with 100 or more RBI in both leagues. The two-time All-Star also finished in his league's top 10 four times for runs driven in and five times for home runs. Of course, he also was in the top 10 six different times for most times striking out in a season.

* * *

A defensive butcher, with about as much range as a flagpole sitter or a traffic pylon, Stuart earned the nickname Dr. Strangeglove and the Man with the Iron Glove. Twice he wound up in the top five in his league for the most errors committed. What makes that so unbelievable is the fact that he played first base, while the men who committed the most errors during those two seasons played much more demanding infield positions. In theory, no first baseman should finish high on the errors committed list.

Stuart, though, was no ordinary first baseman—he made more misplays at his position than any other first sacker in 7 of his 10 seasons, and ranked second another time. The only two times he didn't crack the top 10 were in 1966 when he played in just 69 games, and in 1969 when he saw action in just 22 contests. Thus there was only one full season in which he didn't lead his league in errors. In fact, he managed to lead the National League in errors as a rookie (with 16) despite playing in fewer than half of his team's games (only 64)—one misplay per four games. Only a handful of recognizable first basemen and/or men who were not from the early days of the game made more errors than Stuart's 169.

His highest season total of errors was 29 in 1963, even though he played errorless ball until the 27th game of the year. Those errors represented 12 more than the next worst fielder at, again, a position where low error totals are the norm. His nadir of 29 misplays were the most at first base since 1919 when Harry Heilmann committed 31 errors. Finally, his 1959 fielding percentage of .976 was the worst at first base since 1914—in short, Stuart was historically horrible.

Once when he was manning first base, a bat slipped out of the hands of a batter. It whirled through the air, touched down briefly on the turf, then ricocheted up to Stuart. The first sacker fielded the bat cleanly. For that he was showered with good-natured cheers.

During a blustery game in Pittsburgh's Forbes Field, a hot dog wrapper blew onto the field. When it flew near Stuart, he stabbed it cleanly, reportedly prompting the crowd of around 30,000 to erupt into a standing ovation. Not bad, they thought, for a man who owned a stranglehold for topping his league in errors. Some first basemen have gone an entire season while committing zero (Steve Garvey) to, say, four errors. Still, to his credit, his lifetime fielding percentage for handling hot dog wrappers was 1.000.

Cleveland Plain Dealer writer Bill Livingston wrote about a time when the PA system at Forbes Field blared out its usual message: "Anyone who interferes with the ball in play will be ejected from the ballpark." Pirate manager Danny Murtaugh joked, "I hope Stuart doesn't think that means him."

Stuart played in the infield next to Gold Glover Bill Mazeroski. Pirate pitcher Steve Blass remembered, "Any time a ball went up in the air on his side of the infield, Stuart would say, 'Plenty of room, Maz,' no matter where the ball was." One day word got around that Stuart had been out late on the town the night before and, said Blass, "when he came back home his wife tried to throw a bowling ball at him. He said, 'You shouldn't have done that, you know I couldn't catch it.'"

One newspaperman wrote, "He's a Williams type player. He bats like Ted and fields like Esther." When he was with the Red Sox some called him the Boston Strangler. Mickey Mantle said that his Yankees called him Steel Fingers, but Stuart didn't seem to care one bit. "I know I'm the world's worst fielder," he stated, "but who gets paid for fielding? There isn't a great fielder in baseball getting paid the kind of dough I get for hitting." Former Pirate teammate Dick Groat summed up Stuart's situation: "Dick's biggest problem was his lack of concentration—thinking about hitting instead of playing defense."

Former Pirate Johnny O'Brien agreed. "We used to call him Stone Hands, but he was a fellow who was interested in distance and home runs. I think he could have been even a better player if he'd have concentrated on some other aspects of the game, but he had it in his head that distance and home runs were his career—that was his bag." Bob Oldis, who was on the 1960 Pirates team, said that "Stuart took great pride in hitting home runs, but you had to make perfect throws to first base otherwise there was a chance he'd drop it or miss it."

When Stuart played ball in Japan, he joked that his fielding improved, saying he once went four straight games without botching a play. He also said he won two Triple Crowns in Japan, leading his league "in errors, strikeouts, and quotes." He refashioned an old baseball line about a Cubs double play combination: "When I'm at first, it's like Tinker to Evers to take a Chance." [19]

He seemed unfazed about his weak glove work. He said at some home games thick with fans he purposely butchered plays during pre-game infield practice just to incite the crowd and to see if fans' eyes were on him. He claimed the spectators got so riled up, they'd shower the field with pop bottles and cushions. When Dick Radatz suggested Stuart's license plate should read E-3, he purchased that vanity plate.

Pirates teammate Dick Schofield said, "We called him the Big Donkey and all kinds of stuff, and sometimes he didn't catch the ball, but he made fun of himself a lot of times. He had a fielding disability, I guess you might call it. One time there was a man on first base and Elroy Face came in to pitch. Stuart went to the mound and said, 'Now don't go throwing the ball over here real hard cause I might miss it.' He warned Face because he threw hard and he was quick over to first base. Stuart wanted no part of it."

Vernon Law said there was one game when Stuart had been jawing with the Dodgers in their first-base dugout throughout the game. Later, Stuart thought a ball was a sure hit, but shortstop Dick Groat came up with the ball. He fired the ball to first, but Stuart "was still yelling at the Dodgers and the ball whizzed by his head." That error went to Groat even though it should have been another "E" added to Stuart's long column of errors. Despite fielding flaws, Law said Stuart was likable. "He was just a big kid that never grew up. We had a lot of fun with him."

When Hal Smith was asked if he remembered anything about his former Pirates teammate, he laughed then said, "Oh, yeah! The first time I met him, when I was traded to Pittsburgh, he hit one out of the park the first day. He said, 'Smitty, if you want to go see where I hit that last home run, let's get a golf cart and we'll drive out there—it's too far to walk.' He was so full of shit. He said he didn't like to go in the field, he liked to just hit. One day he said, 'I wonder if they'd let me play and just hit and not have to go out there and try to field the ball.'" Clearly, the designated hitter position came too late for Stuart, who could really slug a baseball.

Anytime that he wasn't wearing his mitt, Stuart was flashy, choosing, for example, to drive a gold Cadillac. Due to his power, he was a Pirates fan favorite as they tended to—or at least *tried to*—overlook his short-comings with the leather. Law said it seems like every team had at least one player who was a real card. "We had Dick Stuart." Stuart's attention-getting behavior sometimes resulted in negative results. Law related, "He had a habit of walking between the umpire and the catcher [as he went to bat]. When he'd get there, he had a certain habit—he'd be chewing gum and he'd take a little piece of it out of his mouth, roll it, throw it across the plate, and then he'd have to take his helmet off and put it back on again. He had lots of things that he would do before the pitcher threw the ball. When he was traded to the Dodgers, he pulled that stuff on me. He used to ask the umpire to have the pitcher throw the ball in and have the umpire look at it—that always happened, too. So my first pitch was up, kind of under his chin a little bit. I said, 'Take a good look at *that*, Stuart.'"

Oldis shared a story about baseball's most dramatic home run ever: "Stuart did not start that seventh game of the 1960 World Series, and Maz batted eighth. Haddix was due up in the bottom of the ninth after Maz, and Danny Murtaugh said, 'Stuart, grab a bat.' So he was on deck when

Maz hit the home run. He told Maz later, 'People came to see me hit the home run, not you.'"

Another Pirate, Bill Virdon, said, "I remember he was probably the only Pirate that wasn't happy when Maz hit his home run. He was a home run hitter so he wanted a chance to try to do that. He wasn't unhappy that we won, but he was unhappy he didn't get to hit." Stuart never lacked confidence with the bat.

He had a good sense of humor, too. After he was hit by a pitch he appeared to be groggy, so the trainer asked him if he felt dizzy. Stuart responded, "No more than usual." All the jokes about Stuart aside, Schofield said, "First of all, Dick Stuart was a *good guy*. He hit home runs, but he was a pretty good hitter also. He was no fluke. He was a pretty good player."

Former scout George Zuraw summed Stuart up: "He was a likable guy because he was so up-front about his ability, and he did a lot of good things with the bat. He was just a real likable teammate."

Groat said, "I really liked Stuart. He's the best. We were close friends. I've never been able to figure out why he was so well loved by the Pirates but he wasn't with the Red Sox and the Phillies. Everything about Stuart was funny. His first home run in spring training, the guys decided while he was circling the bases that he had talked so much about his 66 home runs that there was going to be dead silence in the dugout. He came across home plate, came in the dugout, and nobody said a word. He walked up and down the dugout and finally said, 'No worry, boys, there's plenty more where that came from.'"

BOB UECKER (1962–1967)

Although Uecker joked about his ability, experts knew he had talent. Bob Skinner was a teammate of Uecker. "The one thing about him is he was a jolly guy and he was very steady as far as relaxing and joking went. He had a good approach to the game and was a real good catcher."

In 1967, he caught just 76 games, yet was charged with a league-leading 27 passed balls, 19 more than his previous season high. The reason? He was assigned to catch Phil Niekro's darting knuckleball. He got that job because he was actually one of the best in the business at handling that elusive pitch.

* * *

When Charlie Dressen sent Uecker to the minors in 1961, he told him there was "no room in baseball for a clown." Boy, was he wrong. Without clowns in the game, laughter would be greatly diminished. Uecker not only made it back to the majors, he has clowned around for decades.

Berra, Garagiola, and Uecker are easily the three funniest catchers ever. Former teammate Carl Warwick told two stories about the self-deprecating Uecker. "Every time we'd be on the road and get on the bus, he would mimic Harry Caray like nobody's business. Bob would be on the back and he'd sound just like Caray and that ticked him off." Caray would storm back to Uecker, tell him off, then swivel to head back to the front of the bus. "As soon as he started back, Bob would talk just like him again."

Tim McCarver was also on the Cardinals when they brought up pitcher Barney Schultz, who frequently threw knuckleballs. "One game," said Warwick, "Schultz started and McCarver gets hit twice. He cannot catch that knuckleball. So after about four innings, Timmy had been hit all over—the ball went by him, through him." Manager Johnny Keane then inserted Uecker into the catching spot. "Uecker goes in and the ball never gets by him. He never drops one. He played a heckuva game. After the game Harry Caray said, 'Tell everybody that's listening to this [interview] what your secret about catching the knuckleball is.' Uecker looked at him and said, 'I just wait until it quits rolling and pick it up.'"

Quite often his audience was made up of teammates, and his humor, said Groat, "kept that [1964] Cardinals team very loose coming down the stretch when we were chasing Philadelphia and finally caught them and won the World Championship. Everything he did was funny—he was the most entertaining person and great to have on a ball club." One of Uecker's main platforms back then was a seat on the back of the team bus, a typical berth for team funnymen, said Groat.

Former teammate Ed Spiezio visited Uecker in his broadcasting booth in Milwaukee County Stadium. Later, when Spiezio got home, he realized he had lost his sunglasses. To make things worse, the glasses were an expensive and sentimental gift from his son, Scott. Although he returned to the ball yard the next day searching for the glasses, he had no luck.

Then, said Ed, "A year later I'm watching TV and there's Ueck with my sunglasses. He probably wondered where the hell they came from."

So much of Uecker's best material was at his own expense, and it was true that his bat seemed about as effective as a soggy rolled-up newspaper. When asked to name his biggest baseball thrill, the man nicknamed Mr. Baseball and who jokingly boasted about his lifetime batting average of .200 said, "I walked with the bases loaded to drive in the winning run in an intrasquad game in spring training." He said another thrill was when he once escaped from a rundown, and he said his manager sent him to the plate without a bat, instructing him to try for a walk.

In jest, Uecker once revealed, "My best year was 1965 when I made about $21,000; $17,000 of that came from selling other players' equipment." He said that anyone with talent could play in the majors, but to be able to fool everyone and stick around the game as he did took real talent.

Uecker claimed his father once bought him a football even though, coming from Europe, he knew nothing about the sport. Uecker said they tried to kick and throw it around, but they couldn't, which upset them. Finally, he joked, a neighbor was kind enough to pump some air into the ball for them.

Uecker said there were signs that his teams didn't regard him highly, like the time they sent him to spring training in Bradenton, Florida, while the rest of his team was in Clearwater. He claimed the Braves let him know he was no longer on the team by approaching him as he was suiting up to inform him that no visitors were permitted in the clubhouse.

Uecker appeared over 100 times on Johnny Carson's show, tossing out stories like the time he was told his team's next contest was a night game, but when he showed up he discovered game time had been 1:00 p.m. Another favorite was his story about coming to bat in the last half of the ninth with his team trailing by one with the bases loaded, but with two men out and a full count on him. He said he then glanced over to his dugout and saw his teammates had already put on their street clothes.

He also joked that when he took a glimpse at his third-base coach for a sign one day, the coach dismissively turned his back on him. He said that in his first game in his hometown of Milwaukee, he heard fans cheering for no apparent reason, which he found perplexing. In the third inning his manager told him he was doing fine, "but up here in the big leagues most of us wear our athletic supporter on the inside of our uniforms." He also stated, "In 1962, I was voted Minor League Player of the Year. Unfortunately, that was my second year in the majors."

Carl Erskine observed, "He had a lot of fresh material. He was self-effacing, he made fun of his own career. He said a scout came over to talk to his dad when he was a teenager and they wanted to sign him. The scout said, 'Mr. Uecker, we're thinking about signing your son. How does $3,000 sound?' Uecker said, 'My dad said we don't have that kind of money.'"

Uecker stated that he made a big impact on the Cardinals as they fought for the pennant in 1964. How? By coming down with hepatitis and *not* playing. When asked how he contracted the disease, Uecker replied that the team's trainer injected him with it. He also said one of his managers, Gene Mauch, told him to pinch hit, instructing him to "grab a bat and stop this rally." He said his hitting was so pitiful, opposing catchers didn't bother giving signals to their pitchers, they simply shouted out what pitch they wanted, unafraid of tipping off what was coming.

One of Uecker's St. Louis teammates when they won it all in 1964 was outfielder Charlie James, one of just a few men to smash a grand slam off Sandy Koufax. James said there was more to Uecker than his joking about his weak stick. "Uecker was quite a character. He kept everybody real loose. He was a darn good catcher, by the way, but Timmy McCarver won the number one catching position that year. If McCarver had gotten hurt, I think we would have had a very good replacement for him. I don't know if he would have hit as well as Timmy, but catching-wise he was excellent. I think if he'd have had a chance to play some, he probably would have hit pretty well, too." Perhaps, but McCarver hit .288 in 1964 to Uecker's .198.

One classic moment from that season was related by James. "When we were getting ready to play the first game of the 1964 World Series in St. Louis, we were taking batting practice and Uecker took his catcher's mitt to the outfield to shag a few balls. There was a band that was coming on the field to practice in dead center field. He went over to one of the tuba players and said, 'Hey, let me have your tuba and I'll let you hold my glove and catch a few fly balls.' The guy let him borrow his tuba [Uecker's version has him borrowing it without permission] and Uecker ran around catching fly balls in the tuba. He didn't fare too well with the management on that one—when those balls come down with some force, they kinda leave some dents in metal. He dented the tuba and Uecker had to come up with $250 to cover the damage that was done. Can you imagine a ballplayer running around the outfield with a tuba around his neck and shoulders?"

Milwaukee pitcher Brent Suter said Uecker told him he did it to keep the team loose. He also did a bit of marching around in the outfield that day, putting on a show and hitting all the wrong notes. Uecker also told Suter how his hitting a home run off Koufax "almost kept him out of the Hall of Fame. He's so self-deprecating. It's refreshing because not everyone at his level of fame and celebrity could rip on himself, but he does it time and time again with hilarity."

Other great lines from Uecker include: "Philly fans are so mean that one Easter Sunday when the players staged an Easter egg hunt for their kids, the fans booed the kids who didn't find any eggs." He saw a fan fall from the upper deck in Philadelphia and later said, "When he got up and walked away, the crowd booed."

On a team flight, he spoke over the intercom, "This is your captain speaking. Please remain seated and keep your seat belts fastened until the plane has hit the side of the terminal building and come to a complete stop."[20]

Moe Drabowsky's wife Liz said Uecker and her husband "would pretend that they were Allen Funt and his *Candid Camera* crew. Bob would go up and say, 'You're not supposed to know this, but up there in that corner—no, no, don't look—is a camera, and you're on *Candid Camera*.' Some people would say to him, 'Oh, let me comb my hair.' He did quirky little things."

Uecker said he once promised to homer for a kid in the hospital. He said he went 0-for-4, including two strikeouts, causing the boy to suffer a relapse. The kicker, Uecker joked, was that the kid was just an outpatient.

Suter said, "He's one of the guys. He's 85 years old, but in spirit he's right with us in the low, mid-20s. On one trip we all dressed up in his [style]—funny colored jacket or some kind of outfit similar to what he had worn on talk shows. We knew he'd appreciate it, but, man, the level of appreciation that he had for us having fun with him was incredible—he was almost in tears, really thankful that we include him. He's a better human being than an announcer, and that's saying a lot."

Uecker's popularity led to his having his own television show, *Mr. Belvedere*, and he became a well-known broadcaster for the Brewers and a pitchman for Miller Lite beer. Vernon Law said, "There are a lot of things about Uecker that brought a lot of laughs. In commercials he was always in the 'front rooooow.'" Another Uecker line that caught on big was his, "*Just* a bit outside, " from the movie *Major League*. He even wrote the book with the clever title *Catcher in the Wry*.

JOE PEPITONE (1962–1973)

As colorful as they come, Pepitone, who realized many people viewed him as a Brooklyn playboy, lasted 12 seasons and swatted 219 homers, many as a teammate of huge Yankee stars such as Mickey Mantle and Whitey Ford. He had 100 ribbies in his second full season, but never again cracked the 90-RBI mark.

* * *

Pepi fit in with the era of the hippies, what with his long locks. He is said to have been the player who introduced hair dryers to the clubhouse. When he joined the Cubs, old-school manager Leo Durocher was aghast to learn that Pepitone was using a blow-dryer in the locker room, but he was unquestionably vain, overly concerned about primping. When Pepitone began to lose his hair, he purchased several wigs, one he wore out in public and the other during games. Once when he took off his cap for the playing of the national anthem, he was mortified when his wig became dislodged.

His hair dryer had earlier became the target of Yankee pranksters Fritz Peterson and Jim Bouton. They loaded the appliance up with talcum powder, which blew all over Pepitone when he turned it on, giving Pepi a ghostly pallor. His puffed-up white hair made him resemble a geriatric Bozo the Clown. When he was with the Astros, Pepitone once stood naked in the clubhouse with two gun holsters on his hips. Each holster held a hair dryer. Dick Schofield said, "Pepitone was different. He was always combing and fixing his hair, and he even had hair spray on it."

Pepitone carried an attaché case with a label on it reading, "I'm humble. It's just tough being so great." A career average of .258 is great? Bobby Richardson had a Pepitone story involving his ego and the man who was the Nolan Ryan of softball, Eddie Feigner, a super fast and talented pitcher. "His team, called 'The King and His Court,' came to town and wanted Mantle to bat against him. Mantle was too smart to do that. Pepitone said, 'I will,' and [Feigner] made him look silly, striking him out."

Durocher wasn't happy about Pepitone's tendency to rack up cumbersome bills, especially for a large wardrobe, while expecting the Cubs to bail him out of debt. Pepitone once said he rarely refused to give autographs except for when the fan looked old enough to be a bill collector.

"You had certain guys, Leo used to call them 'buffoons,' and we had one of them here when Pepitone came to the ball club," said Billy Williams. "He had ways to get the team to laugh. He did some things that were out of the ordinary from what a baseball player does. Pepi used to do a lot of those things when he first came here. Leo had his office upstairs in the old clubhouse, and Pepi used to have this chopper, this motorcycle, and he drove it up the steps, right next to Leo. Leo would be doing an interview or trying to make up a lineup and all he could hear was this Harley-Davidson sound coming in." He barged through Durocher's office, then through the clubhouse before exiting. He also arrived at the ballpark in a limo and insisted the driver roll out a red carpet for him to walk on.

Williams added, "You had a lot of guys like that in baseball. On every team, it seemed like you had one individual who every manager loved because when the team would go bad, this guy would maybe get in the clubhouse and do a joke or something to keep the team loose."

However, baseball is a business, and being a beloved clown doesn't always help. If two men were fighting for a spot on the roster and one helped keep the team loose, would a manager select that one? Denny Walling says no. "I don't think it would have anything to do with it. You're doing the job or you're not. I don't think if you're a colorful character it's going to keep you in the big leagues. It's tough to get here and it's tough to stay here. And when you go through a down period if you're the guy on the bubble and you're not doing the job, it doesn't matter if you're one of those fun-loving, colorful characters or not, you're going to get sent down to get your stroke together."

Dick Mackey wrote of the time Pepitone was being given the "steal" sign from his third-base coach. The signal was a wink, which Pepitone saw, but he had forgotten the sign so he stayed glued to first base. Before the next pitch, another wink, and another missed sign. The final time the wink was directed his way, Pepitone finally reacted, blowing a kiss to his coach.[21]

While Pepitone did win three Gold Glove awards, he shied away from pitchers' pickoff throws to his bag. This may seem inexplicable, but slick-fielding Todd Helton once disclosed that his weakness was catching pop-ups. Now Pepitone did Helton and Dick Stuart one better, as Jim Bouton related in his book, *Ball Four*.

It began when Pepitone botched a throw from Yankee third baseman Clete Boyer in the 1963 World Series finale, claiming he lost sight of the ball against a background of many white shirts worn by spectators behind third base. The throw struck him in the chest, and his miscue led to the winning run to give the Dodgers the championship. After that, wrote Bouton, "He didn't want to handle the ball any more than he had to." When told this story, Billy Williams grinned, then said, "Knowing Pepitone, that could have happened."

It did. In the following World Series, Pepitone was stationed at first base holding on St. Louis speedster Lou Brock. Bouton wanted to keep the mercurial Brock close to the bag, so he signaled to Pepitone that he was going to throw over. To his astonishment, Bouton peeked at Pepitone, who was "standing there shaking his head, tiny shakes because he didn't want anybody to see. It was the first time I ever saw anybody shake off a pick-off sign."[22] A few pitches later, the bemused and amused Bouton again flashed the pick-off sign. Would Pepi again shake him off, he wondered mischievously. You bet. Once more, fearful of having to cope with a hard throw over, Pepitone did indeed shake his pitcher off, not unlike a pitcher sometimes does to his catcher.

Sportswriter Ralph Wimbish recounted a typical Pepitone tale: "At the end of a road trip, when we arrived at La Guardia airport, we used to place bets on whose luggage would come out of the shoot first. The usual bets were between five and 10 dollars. As we were standing there in anticipation, all of the sudden we see Pepi come from behind the plastic flaps, riding his way around on the conveyor belt with a giant smug look on his face. Needless to say Pepi won the bet."

LOU PINIELLA (1964–1984; MANAGED 1986–2010)

The 1969 A.L. Rookie of the Year was a professional hitter (.291 life-time). While not a prototypical power-hitting outfielder, he had some clout. He led his league with 33 doubles in 1972 and he hit 305 two-base hits. His zenith for RBI was 88 and he hit .300+ six times.

* * *

Ken Griffey Sr. said the main thing he recalled about Sweet Lou was "his arguing. Lou argued all the time. I played with him for two years with the Yankees, then he became our hitting coach, then he became the manager. And I got involved with him when I went back to Cincinnati. He would try to stir up the clubhouse a lot. I mean, he was that type who would just try to get everybody fired up and ready to go. A lot of times I would watch Lou argue, and he'd argue for 25, 30 minutes for nothing sometimes. But he was funny.

"When I went to Cincinnati, he picked at Rob Dibble and he told him he was going to beat him up one day. Lou looked at me and he said, 'Man, I think I'm going to take an ass kicking with this big dude.' Lou went over and started messing with Dibble, and Dibble had him all hung up in the locker. It was nuts that day." Griffey said that later Piniella commented, "Well, I got him fired up." Sounds like a funny line, but Griffey said he believed that "Lou's intention was to get him fired up. He got him fired up, all right. He got everybody fired up—Norm Charlton, and the main pitching staff. He stayed on the pitching staff. He didn't worry about the lineup with Barry Larkin and those guys."

Griffey continued with a story his son, Ken Griffey Jr., told him. "Lou traded Jay Buhner to Seattle and told him he couldn't play, that he'd never break into his lineup. Then, when Jay was in Seattle, he was one of the stars, one of the big-time stars. So, Junior and Jay were talking junk one day about hitting a home run or something, and Lou [now managing the Mariners] said, 'If you don't do that, you guys have to buy me a steak dinner.' It just so happens that one of them didn't hit the home run. So what they did was they bought him a whole cow, a live cow and stuck it in his office. It [defecated] all over his desk and everywhere in his office, and Lou came in and he threw up everywhere. Junior and Jay said, 'You got enough steak to last a year.'"

Orioles star Merv Rettenmund said that while he didn't know Piniella personally, "I have a feeling that he's a lot like Doug Rader. I mean, he seemed to be a good manager and the players seemed to play hard for him. I know that Doug's teams, especially the ones he had in California, played real hardball—they played very good for him." As a player Piniella was a "hardball" kind of guy, so it fit that he'd demand an aggressive, go-all-out brand of ball from his players. Further, the Rader comparison was apt in that both men were quite colorful. (More on Rader later.)

Ralph Wimbish stated, "You could go through Lou's whole career from player to manager and he was always animated at the plate, particularly his arguments with umpires—he would kick [dirt]. He kind of came out of the Billy Martin mold a little bit."

Bucky Dent was a Yankee teammate of Piniella and thought of him as being a wild guy when his temper took over. "He'd do things when he was mad that made the guys laugh, like when he was trying to tear his uniform off."

In 1999, Orioles coach Sam Perlozzo said the most colorful character he could remember was Lou Piniella. "He was pretty animated out on the field when there were questionable calls. I was with Cincinnati when he [uprooted a base from its moorings then] threw the base, and with him in Seattle for three years. He was a pretty amazing guy, intense. I mean, he wasn't afraid to say or do anything. He was a man I never thought would be embarrassed. He just did what he thought and laughed about it."

One vivid example was the time in 1998 when Piniella's Mariners were in Cleveland and the fiery manager became livid over a call. He put on an Earl Weaver–like show, kicking his hat all over the field. Commentators compared him to an inept NFL field goal kicker. As he stomped off the diamond, having been ejected, he wound up hurling the cap into the crowd. A spectator got it, then threw it right back toward Piniella.

Perlozzo said, "He tried to get it off the field. I talked to him about that recently, as a matter of fact. The last kick went in the other direction. I asked him, 'You debated about whether to go get that one more time or walk off the field, didn't you?' He started laughing and said, 'Yeah, I was going to go off, but I went back after it.'"

In "honor" of his actions, Cincinnati staged a base-throwing contest for fans. Reportedly, more people turned out that day than had been at the game when Piniella went wild.

JAY JOHNSTONE (1966–1985)

Johnstone led the league in errors by a center fielder one year, but also was first for assists as a center fielder one season. His .318 batting average in 1976 placed him in the top 10 in National League play.

* * *

Johnstone was no superstar, but some years he was as pesky as a "dehydrated," bloodthirsty mosquito, working his way on base one way or another. He was also funny. Asked to name the most colorful player he knew, Larry Bowa responded, "Probably Jay Johnstone. He stands out big time." Pitching ace Don Gullett concisely observed, "Jay was a little crazy." He paused then added, "Still is, I guess. He played all kinds of practical jokes on guys and did a lot of crazy things." Johnstone's minor league skipper Rocky Bridges called him, "a real box of chocolates,"[23] and another manager called him a goofball.

One of Johnstone's managers, Tommy Lasorda, said that some people are funny, "but Jay is more than funny. He's crazy. There are a lot more people in asylums who are saner than Jay Johnstone."[24] For that matter, Johnstone did author a book titled *Temporary Insanity*. All-Star Steve Blass said, "I thought I was clever and funny, but he was way above my level. I was very impressed with how quick he was and how good his stories were."

Lasorda saw Johnstone as devious, envisioning his nemesis sitting up late at night conjuring up ways to drive him wild, and that would include slathering boiling hot ointments such as Capsolin in people's underpants, tossing firecrackers under players' feet, pitching cream pies at others, and brandishing and emptying fire extinguishers where there was no flame.

One day Johnstone tied a rope around the door handle of Lasorda's hotel room, ran the rope through a hallway window and secured it to a palm tree opposite the door which opened inward. Lasorda was trapped inside the room. Johnstone also had the foresight to disable Lasorda's phone so he was unable to call for help.

Johnstone and some teammates surreptitiously spray-painted the letters GH in green paint, for Green Hornet, his mischief persona, on players' equipment and even on Lasorda's shoes. During a rain delay,

Johnstone stuffed his uniform until it appeared as if he had a fat gut and a big butt, mocking Lasorda.

Lasorda was proud of the many autographed pictures he had of Hollywood stars, which decorated his office. One day he discovered the pictures were missing. In their place were signed pictures of the three perpetrators of the petty larceny, Johnstone, Jerry Reuss, and Don Stanhouse. Later Johnstone defended the prank, saying the three pitchers involved had won more games for him than his celebrity friends such as Don Rickles.

Johnstone slipped into the shower area behind Fernando Valenzuela one day, and every time Valenzuela, eyes firmly shut, tried to rinse his hair of shampoo, Johnstone poured gobs more on his head without him catching on.

Danny Ozark, who also managed "Moon Man" Johnstone, noted, "What makes him unusual is that he thinks he's normal and everyone else is nuts." Another of his managers, Bill Rigney, said, "I plead guilty to assigning Jay Johnstone and Jim Piersall as roommates. It was an easy decision. I didn't want to screw up two rooms." Johnstone claimed he had never been a jokester until he met Piersall, but Piersall countered, "Don't blame me for Johnstone. He was crazy before I met him."

Another revealing anecdote comes from Dodger executive Fred Claire, who stated that "the darndest thing I ever saw related to a time when I had been down on the field [pre-game] at Dodger Stadium, and in those days you could leave the field and walk to what's called the dugout level, and there was a concession stand to the right. Now, the game had actually just started, just minutes old. I look into the concession stand as I'm walking to get to the elevator and there's a player in uniform at the hot dog stand—and that would be, of course, Jay Johnstone. He was known for his unusual antics, but one thing was very important to the Dodgers and that's Tommy Lasorda appreciated Jay so much because, in addition to providing some good moments for us, he clearly kept the clubhouse loose—so that was Jay. I mean, he was a fun-loving player, but never before and never again did I see a player in line to buy a hot dog when the game was starting."

Larry Bowa spoke of another wild and crazy time when Johnstone should have been on the field but wasn't. "In Chicago, right before infield [practice], I look up in the stand and he's got his hat out, and he's getting donations [from the fans] for a charity, but it was strange. He's got his uniform on walking up and down the aisles. Every time we had infield, he would never take it. Danny Ozark, who was our [Phillies] manager, asked him, 'What's the story?' He says, 'Well, when we don't take it, that's when I feel like taking it, and when you do take it, I don't feel like taking it.'"

Bowa continued, "One day he pinch hit in the eighth inning of the game and got a base hit, ended up scoring a run and we batted around. He was [due up as] the hitter, he's inside, in the sauna, eating a pizza with his shorts on."

Johnstone created an official-looking letter which he then mailed to a rookie, instructing him to report to a local television station on a certain date and time to do a live interview. When the raw rookie, beaming and with visions of fame dancing in his head, showed up, the studio's personnel had no idea what he was talking about.

When Dodger teammate Steve Howe got tagged one game, Johnstone procured a gasoline can and hung it up in Howe's locker, teasing the reliever for, on this occasion, being an arsonist rather than a bullpen fireman. He ran a pair of Howe's underwear up a flagpole, and on a scorching hot day Johnstone placed a brownie in Steve Garvey's mitt then wiped some chocolate onto Jerry Reuss's pants so he would take the fall.

GRAIG NETTLES (1967–1988)

One thing Nettles took seriously was hitting. Chris Chambliss spoke of men with great bat speed. "There was Graig Nettles, who I played with, who could hit the fastest fastball out." Of course, it didn't hurt his power production that, at least once, he doctored his bat, packing it with Super Balls. His lifetime homer total was 390, and he drove home 1,314 runs.

* * *

Former Yankees PR executive Marty Appel said Nettles fit into the category of a clever, witty guy rather than an elaborate practical jokester. Yankee teammate Bucky Dent said, "Nettles had great one-liners. He was really quick and really witty." As a member of the chaotic Bronx Zoo Yankees of the 1970s, Nettles often grumbled about things team owner

George Steinbrenner did and how he ran the team. For example, Nettles mused, "When I was a little boy, I wanted to be a baseball player and also join the circus. With the Yankees, I've accomplished both."

That line brings to mind something humorist Oscar Levant said about another Yankee, Joe DiMaggio. When the Yankee Clipper got divorced from sex symbol Marilyn Monroe, Levant philosophized, "It proved no man can be a success in two national pastimes."

Appel said, "Nettles was outspoken and he didn't pull back if he had criticism of Mr. Steinbrenner." Mike Vaccaro said Nettles was "like most Yankee veterans; he had a falling out with Steinbrenner. They always had a back-and-forth going. Steinbrenner had been very critical about Nettles gaining weight. One day after a game Nettles was coming out of the shower and he noticed a crowd around his locker. Steinbrenner was there, holding court." Nettles joined the group saying, "You know what? George is right, Nettles is getting fat," and then walked away.

Nettles ripped Steinbrenner's propensity for interfering with his managers and for actually believing at times that he was a better tactician than the many skippers he hired. "It's a good thing Babe Ruth still isn't here," Nettles began. "If he was, George would have him hit seventh and say he's overweight."

Nettles sometimes employed gallows humor, like the time he was able to be optimistic about a Yankees losing streak. "The more we lose," he said, "the more [Steinbrenner] will fly in. And the more he flies in, the better the chance there'll be a plane crash."

During a team flight Nettles remarked, "We've got a problem. [Cuban pitcher] Luis Tiant wants to use the bathroom, and it says no foreign objects in the toilet."

When the spring of 1994 rolled around, the Dodgers faced an odd situation. They had acquired rookie pitcher Chan Ho Park from Korea. There was a language barrier because Park spoke no English. Baseball officials ruled Park's interpreter would not be permitted to make a trip to the mound, so communicating with Park was a real concern. Upon learning this, Nettles joked, "I don't know what all this concern about the interpreter is all about. George Scott played 15 years and he never had an interpreter." Scott, not the most articulate player in the majors, didn't appreciate the humor.

Nettles earned the nickname Puff because, says former teammate Sean Berry, he was like a puff of smoke, "an instigator who disappears after stirring things up. Those are the kinds of guys you have to really watch out for." However, Appel said there was another explanation for Nettles' nickname. "No, it was really more for the fact that he would just disappear when you thought he was part of the crowd—in a bar together or even in the Yankee clubhouse, you'd look up and he was gone. People would say, 'Where'd Puff go?' That's where the nickname came from." But, Appel conceded, "the two [theories of the nickname's origin] could converge." Nettles's license plate read PUFF E5, for "error by third baseman," and he wrote E5 on his gloves.

Ken Griffey Sr. said his Yankee teammate Nettles "did a lot of pranks. I didn't see too many of them. I thought Nettles was one of the better guys on the team because he took care of a lot of the guys. When I first got to the Yankees, he was all over me for a while, but after he found out I was there and serious and was ready to play baseball and I [accomplished] some things, I became one of the guys on the team.

"It was the same way with Goose Gossage, Dave Righetti, and Lightning, Ron Guidry. But Nettles did play his pranks on some of the guys, the guys who were in his clique. Like Goose. He loved Goose. He always played tricks on him. He was one of his main targets."

Nettles wasn't immune to tricks, though. Fritz Peterson got Nettles good by having his wife steam the labels off a can of hair spray and a can of deodorant, then, using glue, switching the labels around. Nettles applied deodorant to his hair, then soaked his underarms with sticky hair spray.

DOUG RADER (1967–1977; MANAGED 1983–1991)

Rader won five consecutive Gold Gloves at third base from 1970 to 1974, but he also carried a pretty big stick. Four times he had 80+ RBI, three times he hit 20 or more homers, and he compiled 20+ doubles nine years running.

* * *

Ex-teammate Larry Dierker summed up Rader: "He was crazy. The thing about him that was probably the most disconcerting was he is extremely intelligent, strong, and powerful—and absolutely, totally crazy. When you put that combination together, sometimes people get hurt. He hit a golf ball around the clubhouse a few times. That had guys diving into their lockers, covering up."

Merv Rettenmund said, "I coached for Rader for a couple of years, and I made it—it was a miracle. Oh, my God. He would go deeper for a prank than anyone. He's lucky no one was ever hurt because he would get serious about it. Like we had a coach, Glenn Ezell, and he would take immaculate care of his equipment. We slept a lot of nights in the locker room in Texas and one night Doug gets Ezell's glove. Glenn took great care of his glove because he was in the minor leagues his whole career and never got free gloves. Rader got a razor blade and cut the lacing, but not all the way through. The next day, Glenn would play catch. The next night Doug would cut a little more. Now, if that glove's in front of Glenn's face when it gives, he's going to be smoked.

"Another time Wayne Terwilliger, another coach, had this beautiful hickory fungo bat. He did most of the fungo hitting because it was great exercise and he was an exercise nut. Well, Rader took the bat and dragged a piece of wire back and forth across it. He did that [nightly, gradually] until there wasn't much bat left. When Terwilliger hit some fungos, the barrel snapped off."

Another Ezell story from Rettenmund: "He used to chew Copenhagen tobacco. Rader got a razor blade and a full can of Copenhagen. He peeled the paper off the can and packed the Copenhagen down. He caught a big cucaracha and put it in the can, closed it, and glued the paper back on so the can looked new. The Copenhagen burned that cucaracha to death. Eventually, Ezell reached in the can and pulled that thing out."

Rettenmund went on, "I don't know how Rader could ever think of all of his pranks, but he had an IQ that was off the board. He had a vocabulary that was fantastic. The thing that I liked about him was there was never a dull day with him and *definitely* never a dull night. He'd get crab claws and pop someone's hubcap and put them inside. He was creative, different than other people. He was always rolling and boy, oh boy, he would tell you what he was thinking. Maybe you didn't want to hear it, but, look out, he's going to tell you."

One cold night in Montreal, Rader used baseballs as fuel for a gas heater in the dugout. He recommended that youngsters eat their baseball cards in order to digest all the stats and data on the back of them. He also advised that negative statistics were difficult to digest, so kids should only eat the cards of star players. He was known to greet unwanted visitors to his home by opening the door wearing only a smile. Rader once took his team's starting lineup to the umpires, serving it up in a skillet.

Blass said that when Joe Pepitone joined the Astros, Rader "introduced him to the team when a birthday cake came—let's just say Rader 'decorated' it when it was still in the box, put the lid back on the box, and left it out on the clubhouse table." At first teammates believed Rader had placed a realistic plastic piece of fake poo on the cake. That is until the odor hit them. Rader boasted of his technique saying he simply squatted over the cake and had impeccable aim. Repulsive, but much of baseball humor in the majors is.

Likewise, he once picked his nose and wiped what he extracted on the bare arm of a teammate. To disgust others, he'd wedge some gum up his nose, extract it, then plop it in his mouth and chew.

Rader once organized a naked swimming race at the pool in the team hotel. He videotaped it and later televised it through the hotel's closed-circuit system.

Although Jim Bouton wrote that Rader was baseball's number-one flake, Rader resented that label, contending he joked around simply to release tension. Blass said, "I just thought the world of him. He was a great professional. I hit a triple against the Astros and, being a pitcher, I had no idea what I was doing. It was a long trip from home plate to first to second. It wasn't a slide into third base where Doug was playing, it was a surrender. I was safe, but he had the ball. I was so out of breath, he kept touching me all over with the ball, asking, 'Does this tickle? Does that tickle?' I couldn't even answer him. I tried to laugh, but I didn't have any breath left, and he knew I was out of gas."

Larry Parrish, a veteran of 15 seasons, said that unlike some players who become managers, Rader was colorful and crazy even as a manager, "always known for off-the-wall things." A prime example occurred when players had to submit a urine sample for drug testing. "He put some Cepacol in as his sample, so his urine sample was mouthwash."

MICKEY HATCHER (1979–1990)

This fun-loving guy hit a very respectable .280 over his 12 big league seasons. His 35 doubles in 1984 put him in the number seven slot in American League play, and he was instrumental in the Dodgers winning the 1988 World Series.

* * *

Minnesota Twins shortstop Roy Smalley gave his take on Hatcher, saying, "He's the first guy ever to make the major leagues on one brain cell." After all, Hatcher once chased a young bear so he could capture a better picture of it. The bear went into a cave and Hatcher threw a rock into the cave to flush it out. Instead, the mother bear lumbered out, chasing Hatcher to his car. He later took flak from a woman who admonished him for being a bad influence on kids. Hatcher responded, "I never knew I was getting into this! Kids all over, wondering, 'Should I chase a bear?' And then they read about me and decide, 'I guess I should.' That never *occurred* to me!"[25] Even his style of play in high school basketball was frenetic. He set state records in Arizona for committing the most fouls in a season and lifetime. He played in 21 games as a senior. Had he fouled out of every game, he would have amassed 105 personal fouls. His actual total? 104. Hatcher went on to become a wide receiver for the Oklahoma Sooners and appeared in the 1976 Fiesta Bowl.

He once talked to a teammate, Rudy Law, about flying saucers and later hid in Law's darkened room, ready to frighten him with strange flashing lights and an even stranger appearance—Hatcher wore glowing glasses, pretending to be a Martian. Before a game on St. Patrick's Day, he painted his arms, hands, neck, and face green. Soon he felt a burning sensation on his skin, and a trip to a hospital was required to remedy his condition.

Former Dodger catcher Mike Scioscia said before a spring training game, "Hatcher had been traded to the Twins from the Dodgers, so while we were hitting he went into our clubhouse and cut Tommy Lasorda's pants up. They looked like sleeves. Tommy was not too happy." He was, in fact, almost apoplectic. Hatcher was also part of a group of players who threw a live pig into Lasorda's office, then slammed the door shut.

When the Twins released Hatcher in 1987, Fred Claire, on just his second day as the Dodger general manager, obtained him for his second stint with the Dodgers. "He was instrumental to our 1988 World Series. When I thought of Mickey, I thought of what he could add to a team, not that just that he was a colorful player. He *loved* the game. He loved to play the game and had ability. And clearly, as the record shows, he fit in great with us."

Everyone knew he was very entertaining, but when Hatcher became a coach for the Angels, he was asked to relate some of his funniest acts. Feigning ignorance, he said, "What do you mean? I didn't do anything funny." He refused to waver from that stance even though one magazine labeled him as the flakiest player in baseball.

One of his more colorful creations came during spring training of 1988 when he and a group of fellow Dodger bench players, including Rick Dempsey, formed a group he called the Stunt Men. On one hand, they played a serious role in prodding the starters to excel, but it's also true that in Game 5 of the World Series that fall, he and three other stunt men were inserted into the starting lineup.

In the Series opener, Hatcher homered, matching his home run total from the entire season. As soon as he realized the baseball had cleared the fence, he enthusiastically jetted around the bases. He joked with the media that, no, he had never practiced a home run trot.

Twice Hatcher posed for baseball cards while holding an oversized baseball glove, one that was nearly as large as his torso. He joked that he really needed the glove because his defense needed every bit of help it could get.

He put smoke bombs in paper planes, then glided them out his hotel window. One lit on a nearby roof and a small fire broke out. Despite his protestations, he obviously was quite the character.

RICKEY HENDERSON (1979–2003)

Having Henderson on your team was equivalent to owning a sleek Bugatti. Unchallenged as the greatest leadoff hitter ever, he was the ultimate run producer. All-Star Johnny Damon said Henderson often teed off on the first pitch of the game, frequently a fastball, "because pitchers definitely did not want to fall behind Rickey and possibly walk him, so they would try to get that first pitch over and Rickey would be ready for it. That's why he has that record [81] for career leadoff homers."

If he didn't get a juicy pitch, he might patiently draw one of his record-setting (since broken) 2,190 career walks or lace a line-drive single or beat out an infield hit. Then, with jet vapor trailing behind his spikes, Henderson would steal a base or two and score on, say, a ground-out or sacrifice fly. One way or another, this speed merchant, this "Man of Steal," crossed home plate a record 2,295 times.

Henderson, a 2009 Hall of Fame inductee with a gaudy 94.8 percent of the votes cast, four times led his league in walks, five times in runs scored, and twelve seasons in stolen bases, in almost half of his 25 big league campaigns. He finished in the top 10 for steals in an unfathomable 22 seasons. It seemed as if he could outrun a ray of sunlight.

In 1998, this catalyst led his league in steals, 18 years after the first time he had done that, a sensational case of domination and longevity. He established the single season record in 1982 when, in just his third full season, he pilfered 130 bases. That was one of three times he topped the 100 steals plateau, something done only eight times in the modern era. Henderson even took to wearing a gold necklace which bore the number "130" on a disc. Merv Rettenmund said Henderson was so quick out of the gate: "For the first 10 yards, he was the fastest man that ever played."

A member of the exclusive 3,000 hit club, he also played a great left field. Billy Williams, also a Hall of Famer left fielder, said Henderson "was one of the best ever at that position" and called him one of the quickest at getting to the left-field line to prevent singles from becoming doubles.

Henderson loved playing so much that when his big league days were through, he willingly dropped down and played in much lower leagues. In 2005, for example, he was with the San Diego Surf Dawgs in the Golden Baseball League at the age of 46.

* * *

Michael Brantley, an All-Star outfielder, said he enjoyed "hearing him talk—how he speaks in the third person so many times. That just brings a smile to my face every time he did it."

Joe Charboneau also got a kick out of Henderson, the all-time leader in stolen bases with a staggering total of 1,406. "I love him and the way he talks, 'Rickey-this and Rickey-that.'" Adapting a line used in connection with Manny Ramirez, Charboneau observed, "Rickey was just Rickey. He loved to steal bases, worked on it hard, studied it, robbed me of a few home runs up over the fence. He was a character—the whole A's [Oakland team] were flaky in the '80s with Billy Martin and Billy Ball."

Charboneau turned raconteur, saying, "One of the funniest stories I heard from one of the A's came when I was at a banquet with him. He told me the radio station, which won the team [broadcasting rights] because they weren't supposed to do well that year, was such a small station that his wife couldn't get it where they lived. So after a game he'd stop, get a couple of beers, and she wouldn't know what time he [should have been able to get home]. He could get home any time and say, 'Ah, we went extra innings.'"

Henderson had a notoriously bad memory when it came to recalling men he had played with or against. One story, probably based on that fact but manufactured, occurred when he was with the Mets in 1999. He spotted John Olerud playing the field while wearing a batting helmet, a practice he did under doctor's orders after he had an aneurysm removed from the base of his brain. Henderson approached Olerud and said that he had once had another teammate who wore a protective helmet on defense. Olerud patiently explained that the player Henderson was remembering was none other than himself. They had been with Toronto six years earlier.

Like Ramirez, Henderson wasn't too quick when it came to cashing his paychecks, regardless of how large they were. As a matter of fact, it's said that he framed the first check he ever earned that hit the $1,000,000 mark. He finally cashed it when the team said that he had to do so. He is also said to have once held onto a check for a big pile of money because he thought it best to wait for interest rates to rise before he redeemed it. And when he was seeking a lucrative new contract, he said, not realizing how obvious his words were, "All I'm asking for is what I want."

He had a flair when hauling in routine fly balls. After settling under the baseball, he made initial contact with it up near the top of his head, then quickly snapped his arm downward and to the side with a flourish. Some called it "the Snatch."

One ex-teammate, Ken Griffey Sr., said, "Rickey was good people to be around—he was funny, fun to be with. We were out one night in Milwaukee and we were going to have dinner. He was looking at one thing on the menu. He said, 'Wow, I can't pronounce that. What is that, Griff?' I said it was chateaubriand and he said, 'What the hell is chateaubriand?'" When told it was a steak large enough for two people, Henderson said, "Man, I ain't gonna eat nothing I can't pronounce."

When Tony Gwynn was discussing Henderson's veteran status on the Padres, he told him he was a long-standing veteran, that he had tenure. Feeling cheated, Henderson stated his case, "Rickey don't have ten year. Rickey have eighteen."

Henderson stole a base in one game when his team was winning so comfortably, his opponents got angry. After the game he blamed it on his third-base coach, saying if it had been up to him, he would not have been running, but Tim Flannery had flashed the steal sign. Flannery refuted that, saying, "Rickey said I gave him the sign? Rickey didn't even *know* the sign."[26]

JOE CHARBONEAU (1980–1982)

Charboneau, a consummate king of flakiness who enjoyed one shining season for the Indians, displayed great power pretty much right away. As a rookie capable of bench pressing 410 pounds, he jolted a ball so hard, it jumped off his bat and flew with rocket speed into the third deck at Yankee Stadium. It was the first homer hit there after the park had been remodeled in 1976.

Back issues led to him undergoing surgery after the 1981 season. He said he had parts, or all, of five or six discs taken out. He was never again the same. He played in just 48 games in 1981 and only 22 more after his first operation. After hitting 23 homers as the 1980 American League Rookie of the Year, he hit just six more. He drove in 87 runs as a rookie, then just 27 more. He went from being a 25-year-old whiz to a man out of the majors before turning 28. Seemingly all that remained was some degree of fame, but little money to show for it. His signing bonus was just $5,000, he earned $21,000 as a rookie (back when he was delighted to make $34 per diem), and his biggest salary was $75,000, but almost half of that was lost when the players went on strike.

His last-ever professional trip to the plate was unique. In 2000 the Canton Crocodiles, who played in the Frontier League, signed Charboneau, their hitting coach, to a one-day player's contract. They held a special promotion in which a deal was struck: if, during his only at bat, Charboneau whiffed, the opposing pitcher for the London Werewolves earned a $500 check; if Charboneau homered, one lucky fan would receive $25,000. For the record, the 45-year-old pinch hitter rapped a single in that final at bat. The league's commissioner, who had to grant special permission for this promotion because the league had an age limit of 27 for players, was none other than Bill Lee.

When Charboneau's daughter was born, he named her Dannon, because that's the name of his favorite yogurt.

* * *

Charboneau knew from the start the type of baseball player he wanted to be. He elaborated, "The flaky guys, the quirky guys, the guys known for stuff like that were, to me, even growing up, the players I identified with. I thought the game should be enjoyed like that, so that's kind of the type of player I wanted to be." He succeeded.

Charboneau said that big league players fit into several categories. There were the men who were "just all business. Some guys turn it on and off—mess around in the dugout, happy-go-lucky, but business on the field. I was impressed with how fun the big leagues were—the interaction with other teams—but how professional they still were despite all that." Players could act like kids yet show "professionalism on the field," realizing there was a time for fun and a time to get to work. Charboneau fit into that last group.

The Charboneau saga is Paul Bunyan–esque, with tales that border on the mythical. Naturally, some of the stories may be apocryphal and/or hyperbolic, as happens with baseball's *very* colorful characters. So yes, some aspects of the Charboneau story may have been embellished (he once said that was the case), but probably not too much because his life definitely was wild. He contends he opened a beer bottle with his eye socket just once, but people believe he did that often.

He once bought himself a birthday present, an alligator he named Chopper, which was prophetic as his pet bit his thumb down to the bone. His wife finally made him get rid of the exotic pet after it nearly took a chomp out of a kitten.

Even as a youth he was wild. In high school he gave himself a homemade tattoo, but when later told to get rid of it, he scraped it off using a razor blade. He won $5 by eating 10 filter-tipped cigarettes, and once tried to eat a shot glass, giving up only when blood flowed too much—even for his liking. He fought between 30 and 50 illegal bare-fisted boxing matches as a teenager to earn money. Further, at the age of 17 he began to fight in boxcars and warehouses. Backed by local gamblers, his top purse was a paltry $30. Charboneau said fighters continued until one dropped, and nobody followed any of the Marquess of Queensberry Rules—kicking, grabbing, and bare-knuckle punching were the staples of the sport.

While in the minors, Charboneau pretended to be the Incredible Hulk by holding a rock in front of his chest awaiting a teammate who would crash into him while holding another large rock. On the receiving end of a figurative pile driver, Charboneau's rock would soon crumble. Other times he'd lie down with a large rock on his chest and allow a teammate to act as if he were a prisoner busting up rocks with a sledgehammer. The only difference was the teammate would repeatedly hit Charboneau's mini-boulder with a small rock.

Charboneau may never have killed him a bear, but Cleveland fans were regaled by a song extolling his early adventures. In the middle of the 1980 season, not very long after Charboneau burst onto the baseball scene, a musical group cashed in on his fame and Indians fans' craving for a hero by releasing a song (some said it was more of a chant than a tune) titled "Go Joe Charboneau." The song peaked at number three on local radio charts. The recording group's name was Section 36, after the ballpark's seating area near where Charboneau roamed left field.

Even though he had only one big league season under his belt, a biography was rushed into print in 1981 to appease fans hungry to hear more about the man nicknamed Super Joe. The book's subtitle was *The Life and Legend of Joe Charboneau*, something of a peculiar title for a man whose life was still in its early stages and whose legend had barely begun. Nevertheless, his whirlwind days of glory even featured him as a guest on the *Today* show before baseball's most virulent career-killer aside from the aging process caught up to him—injuries. In his case, health issues with his back did him in. He played in fewer career games, 201, than any other Rookie of the Year winner, and he was the first man to win that honor only to be sent to the minors the following season.

According to Charboneau, most of the stories are true. Which ones? Well, that would ruin the magic. He stated, "A lot of them are true, but as the [1980] season progressed and we went from city to city and played different teams in the American League, some stories came out that I'd never heard of. Like football, everybody started piling on."

Some of his craziest actions were results of a dare, while others were executed to win wagers, like the time he got inspired watching a nature show that featured a snake swallowing an egg. Not to be outdone, Charboneau replicated the feat, swallowing a raw egg whole, shell and all. The egg got lodged in his throat, choking him until a friend punched his throat allowing the then smashed up egg to smoothly go down.

One time his roommate, Toby Harrah, was sitting in their Detroit hotel room when he heard Charboneau calling out for his attention. Harrah looked around the room for a moment or two before spotting Charboneau hanging on the ledge outside their 30th floor window.

Some might argue that Charboneau's offbeat behavior served as a magnet for strange events. However, that doesn't seem to be true of one of the oddest incidents in his life. This one was a crazy incident *not* performed by himself. It came on March 8, 1980, when the Indians were taking part in an exhibition game in Mexico City. That's when a crazed fan stabbed Charboneau. His weapon? A ballpoint pen.

Here's how it all unfolded. A man named Oscar Martinez approached Charboneau, requesting his autograph. Martinez then asked him where he was from, and when Charboneau replied, "California," the man attacked him, thrusting a Bic pen into Charboneau's left side, striking a rib and leaving behind a four-inch wound. Charboneau believed he was targeted because "I was American, because he asked me where I was from." It turned out Martinez was, in fact, known as an anti-American. Charboneau reportedly wasn't too concerned about the cut—after all, he had intentionally done more damaging things to himself. He did, however, say he wondered if the pen could still write. That thought prompted him to consider asking someone in the marketing department of the company which produced Bic pens to hire him to advertise their product by saying it could write under blood.

Charboneau had also been stabbed three times in fights with migrant workers which, no doubt, means he leads Major League Baseball in one unenviable stat—Most Knife Wounds, Lifetime (4).

During a 2010 interview, Charboneau stated that the fan who had stabbed him was punished—barely. "Fined," said an incredulous Charboneau, "2 dollars and 20-some cents." The police stated that a pen was not a deadly weapon. "He had attacked a French consulate before that and seriously hurt him, and he had escaped from a mental institution. He said he had announced he was going to do this attack—it was really a bizarre situation; but that's just the type of crazy stuff that seems to happen to you." To you, that is, if your name is Joe Charboneau.

The attack didn't last long, said Charboneau. "Our whole team kicked the crap out of him. I felt bad for the guy. They beat the hell out of the guy—half his hair was pulled out, his eyes were swollen shut. It was bizarre, crazy—kind of like my career." Well spoken. Ironically, four years after the pen-is-mightier-than-the-sword attack on Charboneau, he was used as an extra in *The Natural*, a Robert Redford movie about a baseball player who was shot by a fan.

Charboneau was once a teammate of infielder Jim Morrison, so when they later played against each other and Charboneau reached second base, the two would engage in banter. Chicago's maverick owner, Bill Veeck, made his team wear shorts as part of their uniforms one year. "I used to kid Jim about the White Sox wearing those shorts," said Charboneau. "I was always on him about that, or I'd flip some rocks at him, at his legs, and ask him what his knee pads were for, stuff like that."

He said his crazy actions "were all fun, and like a snowball rolling down a hill, they got going and going [in the media]. The stories all had a little mystique of their own—people would ask, 'Are they true?' To this day," he said during a 2010 interview, "I don't say anything about it, but I do think it makes you more approachable to fans because it kind of takes you off a pedestal." Then, taking a pause from the interview held near the field of a Great Lakes League team, he put his own stamp on his colorful ways. "I think it's apropos that we're doing the interview by the port-a-potties. You can better relate stuff to your career—some people say it went down the shitter, flash in the pan, but injuries are a part of baseball." He fully realized how meteoric a baseball career can be.

Kevin Rhomberg, one of Charboneau's close friends and former teammates, noted, "He had two or three back operations. They were ignored because he dyed his head and drank beer through his nose [usually using a straw]." Therefore, Rhomberg felt that people considered Charboneau's colorful ways rather than his accomplishments. "I think later on people started realizing that, but he's just a lot of fun." He was able to pull off the sipping beer through the nose stunt because a doctor had removed all the cartilage from his nose.

Charboneau was also rather serious when he pointed out that his color-ful ways were confined to "off-the-field [activities] and a lot of it was in college. I just enjoyed myself, but on the field it was business. One of the greatest compliments I got was when I went down to Triple-A to play for Doc Edwards on a rehab assignment and he goes, 'You know, every time you take the field you play 100 percent all out—run through fences, dive for balls.' Sometimes I believe the stories about me might have got in the way of that."

Despite his refusal to disclose which stories about him are true and which are exaggerations or come with media embellishments, during a 2010 interview Rhomberg said, "Joe's stories are not exaggerated. He likes to believe they are, but he's done more things than I think most of us ever think we could do. Joe's stories—many of them I can't tell you about—are all good. I saw the beer through the nose, I saw the eye socket [opening beer bottle caps]. He's still a kid. He's still trying to figure out what he wants to be in life.

"But one thing about Joe, he's a very dedicated guy. He's very loyal and he's hard working and he does stick up for his teammates no matter what. He's a good guy to have in your corner. I look at Joe's career, the way it went up and down—and I played with him when he was on the way down and when he was on the way up because we crossed paths in the minor leagues.

"One year when I was playing with Joe we were playing Memphis, a Montreal Expos club, and they had Bill Gullickson, a number-one draft pick going through their organization throwing hard. The first time up Joe hits a home run off of him, second time up hits another one, third time he hits another one, and they're [Charboneau and Gullickson] going around the base paths, they're mouthing back and forth, they're flipping each other off. It was a sight to see with Joe taking on Gullickson, and Gullick-son ended up throwing a ball at the PA announcer."

As for more colorful tales of Charboneau, he performed amateur den-tistry, a phrase that is in itself enough to make most human beings cringe. When he was netting $500 a month, he faced a root canal procedure that would cost $250, so he elected to extract the tooth himself.

The next sentences are not intended for the squeamish. His anesthesia was the type used in old Western movies, a half of a fifth of whiskey. He cut the gum near the targeted tooth with a razor blade, loosened it with the pliers, then yanked it out with the vice grips, capping off a grueling two-and-a-half-hour procedure. His post-op treatment consisted of a chaser, killing off the remaining whiskey. He also became an amateur surgeon, setting his broken nose with his ever-handy vice grips, and once he used a fishing line to weave 20 sutures to close up a wound.

Philadelphia scout Lou Kahn called Charboneau "a kooky guy," but said some "kooky guys make good ballplayers." His logic—they don't worry about anything. As for Charboneau's wild antics such as his unlicensed acts of dentistry, no big deal: "I figure as long as he don't go pullin' someone else's teeth more power to him."[27]

When it was suggested to Charboneau that the determination he displayed in operating on himself, that rugged, fearless spirit, was typical of what he took onto baseball diamonds, he replied, "I hope so, yeah, I hope so."

KEVIN RHOMBERG (1982–1984)

Rhomberg, a native of Dubuque, Iowa, is an interesting man in many ways. As a major leaguer he played in three seasons, batting only 47 times. Over those at bats he collected 18 hits, all singles save a home run during his first big league start. His lifetime batting average stands at .383, yet he played in only 41 big league games (many as a pinch runner).

He looked back on his biggest minor league highlight: "In '79, Joe Charboneau won the batting title in the Southern League [at .352] for the Chattanooga Double-A Lookouts. In '81, I won it; I hit .368 to beat Joe's record."

* * *

As for Rhomberg's colorful ways, he was well known for a most unusual habit/superstition—some say it was because he had OCD (obsessive-compulsive disorder). Charboneau was a teammate of Rhomberg on the Cleveland Indians in 1982 and earlier in the minors, and recalled, "He drove me crazy. If someone touched him, he had to touch him back. He had to make all left turns driving to the ballpark, so he'd go down extra streets to make his turns."

Charboneau wasn't exaggerating. Any time someone touched Rhomberg, he was compelled to get in the last tag. He simply *had* to. "It was a lot of fun," said Rhomberg, "and everybody got involved in that. In fact, one time in Triple-A [ball] at Pawtucket—Wade Boggs was on that team and they did the hidden ball trick. I was on second base and I thought they were just messing with me, touching me, so I reacted and touched them back—I knocked the ball out of the glove. By the time the umpire turned around [to rule on the play], he called me safe. I was out, though." Thus, his quirk saved him from a humiliating moment.

Rhomberg doesn't like to dwell on his superstitions, but said that, "At the end of the day when you get into that business, you need a form of concentration. And my family was into it, my kids are into it, everybody was into it. When you play and go to the ballpark as much as we do, you need to have a good routine—it's no different than your everyday life when people get up and go to work. They do their coffee, they shower, they shave, they do this every morning. They go a certain route, if they don't stop off at this place and get their coffee, they think their whole day is messed up. So you had a good focus and good concentration on how you prepared yourself and it was helpful. But when it got into a game in fun, then all of a sudden, 'This guy's sick. He's neurotic.' Then it wasn't as fun anymore."

One story has it that a player touched Rhomberg then took off, never to be retouched, but Rhomberg mailed him a letter in which he stated that the act of opening his piece of mail, meaning the recipient had touched the letter, counted as being tagged. Rhomberg laughed, "You should remember, it's my rules, my game, my mind—I win, that's all that matters.

"All I can tell you is Rod Carew touched me in Municipal Stadium [Cleveland's old park] during BP [batting practice]. And I had whole teams come over. I had guys do it while I was in the shower, while I was in the bathroom, reaching underneath the stalls and all that stuff. But when Carew touched me, I said to myself, 'You know what? My kids are starting to read about me being a little crazy and being the most superstitious guy in the American League.' And the knuckleballer in Texas [Charlie Hough] said, 'Oh, Rhomberg's nuts,' So I said Rod's a good one to quit on. He still ran pretty good. I was chasing him in the outfield and I thought, 'Damn, I got to go after this guy—he's older than I am, he's toward the end of his career and I'm starting my career.' So I quit on Rod Carew."

When Rhomberg was in the bathroom one day, Rick Sutcliffe reached under the stall and touched Rhomberg's toe. Not knowing the identity of his assailant, Rhomberg had to rush through the clubhouse touching everyone. Teammate Brook Jacoby touched him with a ball and then flung it out of the park, causing Rhomberg to waste two hours tracking the ball down. And Dan Rohn tagged him, hid for two hours, and escaped to his hotel, convinced he had outmaneuvered Rhomberg. At 3:00 a.m., Rohn was awakened by a loud knock on his door. He stumbled over, opened the door, and immediately got touched by Rhomberg, who then fled.

Eventually, though, enough was enough. Rhomberg said, "We had the *Star* magazine calling the locker room wanting to do a story on it, but like I said, it just got [blown up] to a higher level where it wasn't as fun anymore."

Author Mike Blake wrote that Rhomberg did "things in multiples of four. Four squirts of water at the water cooler before he left the dugout, four taps of the bat on the ground, four taps of the bat on his helmet, four taps of his cleats with his bat, a left turn into the batter's box, and four practice swings." [28]

"Kevin's a bizarre guy, a fun guy," concluded Charboneau. "We've been great friends and he's a great humanitarian."

ANDY VAN SLYKE (1983–1995)

Baseball history could have been changed if the recalcitrant Barry Bonds had listened to the advice of Van Slyke when they were Pirates teammates in 1992. During the seventh game of the National League Championship Series, center fielder Van Slyke cautioned Bonds to play more shallow in left field. His warning came after pinch hitter Francisco Cabrera, just 3-for-10 on the regular season, had just hammered a foul ball to left field. A sneering Bonds responded by reportedly shooting back an obscene gesture, dismissing the advice and refusing to budge.

His stubbornness cost the Pirates a trip to the World Series when Cabrera's two-out line drive on the next pitch fell in front of the out-of-position Bonds, who had a long run to get to the ball. Furthermore, Bonds's throw was off target, up the first-base line, allowing the slow-footed Sid Bream to score from second. Van Slyke's reaction told the tale as he plopped to the ground in center for a few minutes, disgusted and powerless.

The gregarious Van Slyke was a fine outfielder who won five Gold Gloves, two Silver Slugger awards, and was a three-time All-Star.

* * *

A true baseball wit, a veritable court jester who combined clever observations with practical jokes, Van Slyke is another player who believes baseball produces a greater wealth of humor and creative hijinks than any other sport because there is so much down time. He also addressed the subject of the connotations of the word "flake" in baseball—and the evolution of the word's very definition. He said that the term flake "once was not negative. I guess it was, in some ways, a colorful way of saying a guy's got a sense of humor and he has fun at what he's doing. But as far as being a flake, I think that terminology in today's game is considered in a derogatory way, whereas when I first came up it wasn't."

In the late 1990s, Pat Borders was asked to name some of the top flakes in baseball. He bristled at the question and implied the writer was trying to bait him, to get him in trouble with his peers. When the writer explained he was using the term flake as a synonym for colorful, Borders politely but adamantly refused to cooperate and the interview skidded to a halt. Harry Walker said he felt flakes are usually thought of as being silly, even goofy. Meanwhile, Jay Johnstone said he never minded people calling him a flake.

It's a case of a rose by any other name, and Van Slyke, label him what you may, is a very interesting, funny, colorful man. For example, he spoke fondly about an old tradition carried out "in Chicago where there's a statue of General Sheridan on the way to the ballpark and we used to paint the groin area of the horse in black and gold [the colors of his Pittsburgh Pirates]. Well, we would make the rookies go out and paint the horse. We got a couple of local cops in the precinct near Wrigley Field to come in and the two detectives arrested the rookies in the clubhouse.

"They fell for it, but the great thing about it was the cops, as they were interrogating one of the kids, kept pushing, 'We want to know who the other suspects were.' And he said, 'Well, I'm not giving up my teammates. You're going to have to find somebody else.'" The trick was so effective because the officers were not only real Chicago policemen, but "they had handcuffs and guns, and they handcuffed the kid right in the manager's office. That was one of the best ones of all time."

Former Pirates pitcher Denny Neagle said Van Slyke was deft at "comparing something that he was going through, maybe it was a slump, to, say, the national debt." Neagle called Van Slyke a "laid-back kind of guy, the guy who had the one-liners and quotes for the media. He was good at that, coming up with something quick and witty, responding fast. He wasn't so much of a crack-up, telling a joke [guy], but he was very witty."

One such example came when the Baltimore Orioles signed Van Slyke to a contract in 1995. Upon arriving at his new club, he was informed that the Orioles had a policy stating that players couldn't have any hair below the lip. Although that really didn't apply to the beardless Van Slyke, he saw the opportunity to flash his sense of humor. With a straight, and clean-shaven face, he asked with apparent innocence, "Does that mean I have to shave my legs?"

Steve Blass said, "Andy was a great outfielder—did a great job for the Pirates. One of the funniest things was when he tried to be a weather forecaster. He thought he could be a television meteorologist. They put him on one night. You talk about the concern about tsunamis, watching him was like waiting for the weather apocalypse of all time." In other words, as a weatherman, he made a great ballplayer.

When Van Slyke was asked to select a few of his personal favorite one-liners or anecdotes, he gladly complied. "When people do some individual pieces on you, they come up with some unusual questions, and one of them was if I could be anybody for one day, who would I like to be. I said, 'I'd like to be my wife because I want to know how wonderful it is to live with me.' At one point I was in Pittsburgh and I was kind of in a slump, and I kept leaving a lot of men on base. The summer hit that year was Morgan Freeman in *Driving Miss Daisy*. After a game when I left five or six guys on base, I said, 'Well right now I couldn't drive Miss Daisy home.'"

He teased reporters saying, "Ballplayers shouldn't complain about writers. They should . . . say nice things. Admire his clothes. Compliment him on his T-shirt." He said such clever comments are spontaneous— "It's not something I think about." While some Yogi-isms, colorful quotes from Yogi Berra, are said to be manufactured by the media, Van Slyke said his are actually his own, that writers have not begun to attribute things to him which he has not said. Then, however, using a Berra line, Van Slyke joked, "No, I never said all the things I really said. My favorite story about Yogi is they asked him why he kept going to all his ex-teammates' funerals and he said, 'If I don't go to theirs, they won't come to mine.'"

Van Slyke may actually be baseball's version of Milton Berle, but when he was with the Cardinals he once broke up a pre-game meeting with an exchange he had with his manager, one that seems like another homage to Berra. It started when his manager, Whitey Herzog, mentioned a new player whom he felt might see action against St. Louis that night. Going over opposing batters is a routine, as is asking for intel about new players. So Herzog addressed his men, "Anybody know anything about him?"

"Yeah," said Van Slyke, "I played against him in winter ball."

"So how should we pitch to him?" asked the Redbirds manager.

"I don't know, he was on the disabled list," was Van Slyke's exasperating reply.

Turning serious, Van Slyke stated, "The thing about baseball is when you deal with the media every day, it's hard to come up with new stuff because it's not like football or basketball, you're out there every day and you're being asked questions every day. I took the attitude, I always tried to have fun with it. I never had animosity toward the media; I always thought that they had a tough job, too, because they have to come up with new questions. Therefore, I tried to make their job easier and come up with some colorful answers for them."

In 1993 the Pirates struggled at 75 victories against 87 losses. The prospects for 1994 were none too bright, and players also knew that a strike seemed imminent. So when Van Slyke was asked to assess the upcoming season, he said, "If it's anything like last year, it will be a long year. If it's anything like last year, I'll be looking forward to the strike."

When he was with the Pirates, the PA system pumped out a song for each player as he walked toward the batter's box. Van Slyke smiled, recalling his song was the theme to the old Dick Van Dyke show—fittingly, a comedy.

STEVE LYONS (1985–1993)

Lyons's versatility made him quite valuable. In an exhibition game he played all nine positions, and in a 1990 blowout he handled mop-up pitching duties. Additionally, during the 1991 season, at one time or another he played every position but catcher. Only 229 of his 808 games were played at the hot corner, yet he led all third basemen in turning double plays in 1988.

* * *

Any mention of Lyons must start with the time in 1990 when he nearly "mooned" an entire stadium. He laid down a drag bunt, slid headfirst into the bag on a close play, and barely beat the throw. He then wanted to rid himself of the dirt that had gone inside his pants. So he yanked down the pants which fell to his knees. When it dawned on him, with apparent stunned mortification, that all he had on under the pants was his sliding shorts, it was as if a cartoon light bulb illuminated. Like snapping out of a dream, he realized, "Hey, thousands of people are gawking at me." So, with a grin, he quickly hoisted his pants up.

Alan Trammell was asked to name a colorful character. He responded, "There's Steve Lyons, Psycho. He was a little bit different, but in a good way. He dropped his drawers trying to wipe his pants off. He accidentally—whether or not that was a put-on or not, he made it look like it was accidental—dropped his trousers right there." Former manager Jim Leyland said, "That was the funniest thing I ever saw. He dropped his pants like he didn't know where he was. That was hard for me to believe." Since Lyons was both a showboat and a fan favorite, Leyland may well be correct that, like the classic line from the movie *Cool Hand Luke*, Lyons knew *exactly* what he was doing.

When Lyons was traded for Tom Seaver, someone said Psy-cho was exchanged for Cy Young. The fan club for Lyons was called the Psycho Ward.

During a minor league contest, Lyons sneaked away from the team and managed to borrow a vendor's outfit. He then hawked popcorn through the stands, occasionally being asked for an autograph.

The durable Carlton Fisk was still doing some squatting behind the plate when he was 45, a tribute to his ability to handle arduous catching chores. Before Ivan Rodriguez, who shared the nickname Pudge, came along, Fisk caught more games than any other player ever (2,226). That didn't prevent Lyons from joking, "He's so old they didn't have history class when he went to school."

One of Lyons's favorite pranks was to place shaving cream on telephones, then inform a teammate that he had a call. And when he played first base, he sometimes drew a tic-tac-toe grid in the infield dirt. He then scrawled an "X" in a square with his cleats, inviting the opposing first baseman to take his turn to play the game out. He played hangman with Kent Hrbek and left messages for opposing players in the dirt, too.

Lyons began his career with the Red Sox, then was peddled to the White Sox where he spent five seasons before being traded back to Boston. He observed, "I find that every five years a man has to change his Sox."

JOHN KRUK (1986–1995)

Kruk, one of 200 lifetime .300 hitters, was named to three All-Star teams. He hit exactly 100 homers and 199 doubles. Three times his batting average was in his league's top 10, and his .397 career on-base percentage is number 72 all-time.

* * *

When Kruk was a rookie, he was hardly a sophisticated world traveler. On his first bus ride to Wrigley Field as a visiting player, he glanced out the window and saw Lake Michigan. He (supposedly) inquired naively, "What ocean is that?"

Teammates teased the West Virginia native, calling him a hillbilly. When 50 of his relatives and friends made the trip from his hometown to Pittsburgh to see him play, a Pirates official said, "I looked at his pass list and asked him if it was the cast from *Deliverance*." Before he was a star, a security guard wouldn't let him in the park, refusing to believe Kruk was a player. Kruk wasn't offended, saying, "If I didn't know me and I saw me, I wouldn't think I was a ballplayer either."[29] Kruk agreed with Andy Van Slyke, who said that he looked like a beer delivery man who managed to sneak by security, borrowed a player's uniform, and went on the field.

On a road trip to play the Rockies in the Mile High City, the lofty altitude led to his having difficulty breathing. Huffing and puffing, Kruk griped, "I don't think I'd like to play here. I'd die. It's a nice city, but what would I see of it if I was dead?"

In 1993, Kruk made the All-Star team and made baseball humor history when he batted against fireballing Randy Johnson, a very intimidating figure at 6 feet, 10 inches. "It's one of those things you laugh at every time you see it," said baseball researcher Bill Deane. "Johnson had about a hundred-mile-an-hour heater and his control was still a little bit suspect at that point. He was the kind of pitcher that a lot of batters would have stomachaches on the day he pitched. It was bad enough for Kruk to face him, but it was lefty against lefty, so the ball looks like it's coming right at you with his three-quarter delivery." Johnson began by intentionally whistling a 98-miles-per-hour fastball four feet over Kruk's head, behind him and to the backstop. Kruk reacted to the heartstopping pitch by fluttering his hand over his chest, as if to indicate a need for a quick shot of epinephrine.

Kruk swung feebly at the next three throws, futilely flailing away and comically bailing out badly. "They were two feet outside by the time he stepped into the bucket. He was glad to sit down," said Deane. On one cut at a breaking ball, he pirouetted so much that when he was done with his swing, his right foot was a good yard outside of the box. Strike three was way, *way* off the plate, but Kruk swung. He later stated, "When I stepped in the box I said, 'All I want to do is make contact,' and after the first pitch I said, 'All I want to do is live,' and I lived, so I had a good at bat." He also said he figured if Johnson was going to hit him, he'd force him to hit a moving target. For that matter, even when he first stepped into the batter's box versus Johnson, Kruk stood way off the plate, leading writers to tease that he might as well have batted from the dugout.

It was very much like what occurred later in the 1997 All-Star Game when Larry Walker, like Kruk a left-handed hitter, saw a Johnson fastball fly way over his head. In mock(?) fear of Johnson, Walker turned his batting helmet backward and moved to the other batter's box to bat righty instead of his normal lefty.

When Mitch Williams was acquired by the Phillies, he wanted to wear his old jersey number, which Kruk was wearing. Williams wanted the number mainly because his wife had a lot of jewelry adorned with that number. Kruk had heard that after being traded, Rickey Henderson once paid $25,000 to a player to get his uniform number. Kruk wasn't as demanding, agreeing to surrender his number for two cases of beer. He said Williams later divorced his wife and, almost worse for Kruk, his beer was long gone, making this a sad tale.

When the clean-living Dale Murphy joined Kruk with the wild Phillies, Kruk quipped, "We were 24 morons and a Mormon." When he heard Canadian customs officials were going to detain any suspicious-looking Phillies at the border, Kruk said he hoped Murphy could play all nine positions that day. One day he got on Murphy again and again until Murphy confronted him. Kruk said that after backing down, he did the only thing left for him to do—start ripping on someone else.

Kruk was a willing target of humor, too, often due to his physical appearance. He was listed at 5 feet, 10 inches, and 214 pounds. That caused pitcher Don Sutton to comment, "He looks like a guy who went to fantasy camp and decided to stay." A fan hollered at Kruk, "If you hauled ass, you'd have to make two trips."[30] One player said Kruk's wearing jersey number 8 meant he was wearing his silhouette on his uniform.

Kruk agreed. "Before the game they told me I looked like Babe Ruth. Then, in my [ugly] at bat against Don Carmen, I looked like Dr. Ruth." Kruk was asked if people mistook him for a player, and he joked, "Me, no! John Goodman, maybe."[31] One day he was walking ahead of another short and dumpy character, manager Tommy Lasorda, who shouted, "Wait up, I want to walk with you so I can look real thin." Kruk replied, "You're still gonna be real short."[32]

CASEY CANDAELE (1986–1997)

Candaele's mother, Helen St. Aubin, taught her son how to play baseball, and she was quite qualified, having played five seasons in the All-American Girls Professional Baseball League, the organization featured in the movie *A League of Their Own*. When it came time for Casey and his mother to play in a Little League mother and son game, she was banned from playing for fear she'd hurt someone. His father played semi-pro hockey in Canada.

* * *

Besides Casey Stengel, baseball had another colorful man who went by that same first name, Casey Candaele. Mike Hargrove, who managed him, said that Candaele was "loosey-goosey and turned on all the time."

Cy Young Award–winner Doug Drabek said Candaele had "a lot of Steve Martin in him. He'd act wild to make people laugh. He was very animated. He had a knack of keeping everybody loose no matter how the team was doing. He had a way of bringing a smile to your face, and he was always the judge during our kangaroo courts. He kept things going, put it that way." Candaele called himself "kind of an improv guy, not so much a prankster."

Candaele's former manager, Larry Dierker, concurred: "He's maybe the craziest guy of anyone that I've ever been around." Dierker told of the time Candaele's over-the-top theatrics calmed chaotic teammates. "He did a routine in the clubhouse at Riverfront Stadium one night. We had a hurricane coming through the Gulf of Mexico and it was bearing down on Houston. We were on the road and there was some concern about whether we'd be able to fly in after our game in Cincinnati.

"All the guys were on the phone with their wives telling them to go get tape and tape up the windows, get extra water, batteries, and supplies because of the hurricane. Most of the guys looked a little nervous before the game, and here comes Casey. He went all across the clubhouse talking about how the end of the world was near and this hurricane was going to blow through Houston and wipe the Astrodome down and knock all the buildings down and take all our families. By the time he got finished with that, everybody was howling. It really broke the ice and the guys weren't so nervous anymore." They later were relieved when the storm missed Houston entirely.

Teammate Craig Biggio said Candaele was the best Astro for "singling everybody out and ripping everyone. The better you did, the more he got on people." It was his way of maintaining the team's concept of unity. Candaele even said, "If somebody's not ragging on you, it means you're not accepted. And I know who to stay away from and who you can mess with."

Another Houston great, Jeff Bagwell, agreed. "He'd have a couple of beers then he'd go up and down the bus ripping on every single person. And Casey wasn't the so-called star of the team, but he didn't care who you were, he had something funny to say about you and he kept every-body humble." Factoring in everybody, counting himself. Candaele de-cided the American League was the better league because when he was in the National League, he got to play a lot, but in the American League he rarely saw action.

On a serious note, Bagwell said it was Candaele who taught him how to conduct himself as a pro. "He taught me how to act, and the things I should and shouldn't do. The biggest thing I remember with him was in 1991, when the Braves clinched against us. I remember sitting there [in Atlanta's ballpark] and that place was rocking—you could actually feel the ground shaking. It was my rookie year and I just wanted to prove myself. Anyway, I was sitting there and I go, 'Man, this is awesome.' He said, 'Dude, this is what it's [expletive] all about.' And I learned from him that *is* what it's all about. It's about winning. We're not here to make money, we're here to go out and win baseball games and Casey helped me do that."

Former reliever Paul Shuey smiled, remembering Candaele, the man he called the craziest player he ever knew. "I saw Candaele taking batting practice with peanut butter on his butt while being butt-naked. He started doing that in Houston to get out of a slump. He'd hit until the peanut butter would melt off his butt, then he'd go play."

Candaele freely admitted, "Probably what I was best known for was my naked batting practice. One Sunday after playing an extra-inning game the night before, we came in for a day game that started around 1:00. I was just sitting in my locker [having] just taken my clothes off and we were about to start batting practice. So I said, 'I don't even feel like putting on clothes. I'm just going to put on my spikes and go out and hit.' So I put on my batting gloves, grabbed my bat, had my shoes on, and went into the batting cage and started hitting naked. It made me concen-trate a lot more because I couldn't foul any balls off because that was dangerous. But everyone got a kick out of it and I think we won that game and I got a couple of hits so it became a ritual. Unfortunately, I couldn't get any of my teammates to do it, but it was a lot of fun."

Candaele surprised his teammates anywhere, such as the time players were standing around the luggage carousel in an airport. "When the bags came out [on the conveyor belt], he'd be riding around on it," said Shuey. Once, at an airport years before 9/11, Candaele said he spotted "some security guards standing by the luggage area. So I put on some glasses and walked around real slow, and I began hiding, trying to get their attention. Then the bags came out and I saw mine so I sprinted from behind a pillar, grabbed my bags and ran out the door. They chased me and as I got to our van, they stopped me. 'You took some bags,' one of them said. I said they were mine." They checked the bags and found everything was okay, but, concluded Candaele, "They weren't too happy, but I told them, 'I stole my own bags. Is there anything wrong about that?'"

Yet another airport prank Shuey recalled was when Candaele "would cry on people's legs." Basically, he'd walk up to people and more or less put his head down on their laps and begin to sob. Shuey said that behavior scared people, "They didn't know what to do."

Denny Walling called Candaele "a high-energy guy. He has a tendency to pick a team up and keep them from getting in a deep sleep. If you're not doing so well, it livens the atmosphere up and keeps you loose."

Major league outfielder Scott Pose said Candaele's forte is "he's just got a spin on everything to make you laugh. I've seen the guy describe a play at a team meeting. I asked him how he got this play done, and he threw a base down and did a headfirst slide right in front of everybody. He's real bubbly."

BILLY RIPKEN (1987–1998)

Ripken was never the hitter his brother Cal was, but he carved out a solid career. He was the Orioles 11th-round draft pick in 1982. Four years later he led the Southern League in total chances and double plays turned by a second baseman.

His offensive highlights included a .308 batting average as a rookie and his 28 doubles in 1991. Billy, another fun-loving guy who was serious on the diamond, was described by Cleveland manager Mike Hargrove as possessing the work ethic handed down from Cal Sr., "a hard, blue-collar work guy that put in a lot of time and energy and loved what he did."

Elrod Hendricks, who was with the Orioles seemingly all his life, opined, "Billy was in the shadow of his brother. He tried to live up to that, which was unfair to him because he was always being compared to Cal. He had good abilities; he was good at second base, but everyone expected him to hit like his brother, which was not fair at all. At times, he'd try to match Cal, and he became very frustrated. I think if Billy had an injury-free career, you'd have seen some numbers put up. Defensively, he was outstanding. He could turn the double play and he was a very smart player."

Billy and Cal Jr. played together 5½ seasons from July 11, 1987, through the 1992 season. Their father was the first man to manage two sons simultaneously in the majors. The Ripken boys became the fifth set of brothers to play up the middle at second and short. In 1990 they combined for a mere 11 errors, the fewest in major league history by a double play duo. No other brother act at the keystone positions ever played in more games together than the Ripkens.

A few more such notes: in one contest the brothers homered in the same inning, only the 15th time brothers hit home runs in the same game, and just the fifth time that occurred in the same inning. The last two men to achieve that were the two brothers who combined for more homers than any other pair of brothers ever, Hank (755) and Tommie Aaron (13). Finally, when the Ripken brothers and their father wore Orioles uniforms together, it was just the fourth time three men from a given family were all on a big league roster. One of those times featured three brothers playing in the same outfield at the same time: Matty, Felipe, and Jesus Alou. So, in many ways, the Ripkens were special, but when it came to being colorful, Billy was the main man.

* * *

Ripken sees himself as a Casey Candaele type, who Ripken said provided comic relief but was "not a prankster." The comparison to Candaele is quite a self-tribute because, as Ripken stated of his 1995 Buffalo Bisons teammate, "I'll go down on record as saying Casey is *the* funniest human that I have ever met. There are a lot of 'seconds,' but they're not even close."

Ripken was both literally and figuratively in that same ballpark with Candaele. Under the heading of it takes one to know one, Candaele said, "Now that guy's a character. He's *good* out of control, a good flake. It's hard to explain. He's a true flame. He's great. He's funny, a character." He felt that Ripken had to be seen on a daily basis to fully appreciate "the joy you get to come to the park and see that guy and the things he's going to say [and do]."

Ripken's take on baseball was as interesting as it was one-of-a-kind. For instance, he joked, "Errors are part of the game, but Abner Doubleday was a jerk for inventing them." He believes it is crucial for a team to stay loose during the long, demanding major league season. "I think that everybody who plays this game has their moments. There are very few people that I would go out and say are normal. When you're with everybody every day through the course of the season and you're playing 162 games in 180 days, I think it has a tendency to weigh on you a little bit."

Pitcher Dave Burba added that, "It's tough to play on a club with no class clown, which makes for a long year. Playing jokes and goofing around helps out [because] day in and day out it can [otherwise] get old."

Mike Hargrove managed Ripken in Cleveland and stated, "He's just got a good sense of humor. Brian Giles and Bill were running buddies when they were playing Triple-A and Giles is about a half-bubble off sometimes."

Paul Shuey can't forget the time Ripken "threw firecrackers under Jeromy Burnitz when he was taking a crap. You'd see Jeromy come bustin' out of his stall pretty good."

Candaele appreciated Ripken because while it's good to be flighty, "you have to know when to stop, when it's time for business." Ripken, he says, always knew when it was time to play ball and when the team needed a jolt of humor.

Ripken's most famous incident took place when he posed for a photograph that was to be used on his baseball card. With a little innocent smile on his face, he rested his bat on his shoulder as the photo was snapped. It wasn't until the card came out that someone noticed the profanity written on the knob of his bat. He claimed he had grabbed a random bat out of the rack, which turned out to be his obscene practice bat. No wonder one of Ripken's coaches, Dick Bosman, shook his head and said, "He's unpredictable."

It seems that many people believe that Cal Jr. took after his father and tended to lack the strong sense of humor that Billy had. Hendricks dispelled that belief, saying, "It again goes back to [Billy] trying to live up to his brother, so he tried to get his own demeanor." But during a 2001 interview he divulged, "Cal Jr. was not always that calm as you see him. He was a little wild kid himself. As a matter of fact, he was, and still is, a prankster, but rather subtle, as opposed to Bill who's more vocal. Once Cal established himself, then he toned his act down." That may be, but it's Billy who belongs in the Flake Hall of Fame, not Cal.

MANNY RAMIREZ (1993–2011)

Word association—mention the name Manny Ramirez, and one subject often pops up. Sportswriter Bill Livingston said, "He was a juicer. He got real big, really muscular even here [in Cleveland], but you couldn't prove it at the time. He got busted after he left the Indians. It's definitely going to cost him the Hall of Fame although so many guys doped back then."

All negatives aside, such as his two violations of Major League Baseball's ban on performance-enhancing drugs and his zany misplays, Ramirez was a hitting machine. Former catcher Jason Varitek said, "He has the same consistent swing each time. Some guys pull off the ball, dive into the ball—he kinda stays in the same area. He has good fundamentals. Fundamentals play a key role in our game. I think it's the ability to repeat fundamentals; when you get mistakes, you don't miss them."

Ramirez rarely missed them, and when he didn't, he was known to lose many pitchers' mistakes over distant fences. A career .312 hitter, he crushed 555 lifetime home runs. His RBI high-water mark was 165, but many of his stats definitely proved too good to be true.

* * *

Mo Vaughn said Ramirez also excelled at setting up and "working the pitcher. The offensive game is definitely a cat-and-mouse game." Vaughn elaborated that a batter such as Ramirez might take a pitch early in a game "when you know you can drive it, to set the pitcher up. Later, in a more important [at bat], you'll get that pitch again." Plus, Hall of Famer Lee Smith said Ramirez was one of the top five two-strike hitters he knew.

Cleveland teammate Travis Fryman said Ramirez took a smart approach to hitting, and that he wasn't pull happy. "He prepares himself every day to hit. If you watch Manny in batting practice, 70 to 80 percent of the balls he hits go to right field. That's the thing I've really taken from Manny." Livingston chipped in, "In batting practice he would hit to the opposite field, then pull and hit straight away. He didn't pull that much. When he was at bat, Ramirez didn't do a Mark McGwire thing or put on home run derby displays. He was all business when he was in the batting cage. He put in his work in baseball, you got to give him that."

Gold Glove outfielder Jeff Francoeur noted, "I'll tell you what, when you talk about a pure hitter. You can talk to all those guys on the '95 Braves when Manny was a rookie with Cleveland and they all said this guy was destined to be one of the best hitters in baseball. He was. He could *hit*." In short, Ramirez was a baseball rain man, a hitting savant.

Ramirez didn't graduate from high school, and both a former teacher of his and an Indians beat writer believed he suffered from attention deficit disorder, which would help account for some of his behavior. However, the Indians psychologist said that is not the case.

Certainly, though, odd things did happen to Ramirez, far beyond what might be considered to be his fair share. On July 1, 1997, the Astrodome was the venue of one of his crazy plays. Houston hosted the Indians, which used to be a regular season impossibility, but that was the first season featuring interleague play.

Every ballpark has its own ground rules and players must be fully aware of these, but Ramirez, often accused of blithely playing the game, of having a short attention span, was either not acquainted with a specific rule, or had forgotten it. Because of that, his actions resulted in a cheap home run. Ramirez was in right field when Tim Bogar hit a bouncer that rolled down the first-base line. Ramirez charged the ball, but when he noticed it had come to rest under the Astros bullpen bench, he waved to an umpire to indicate that the ball was out of play.

The only problem was, it was *in* play. First-base umpire Charlie Relif-ord gestured that the ball was live, but Ramirez's hesitation gave Bogar plenty of time to take his round trip for an uncontested inside-the-park home run.

As Indians television announcer Matt Underwood once said, "*Nobody* knows what's going on in Manny's head. He's very enigmatic." He was even known to treat other player's lockers like a personal sartorial smorgasbord, helping himself and wearing teammates' socks, T-shirts, and even underwear. Naturally, somebody coined a blanket phrase to describe such behavior by Ramirez, and soon everyone, from teammates to the media, would observe him doing something way out of the ordinary, shake their collective heads, and mutter it was just another case of "Manny being Manny."

Francoeur said, "You hear [that phrase], but at the end of the day, he was who he was. And I give him credit: whether he was 0-for-15 or 15-for-15, that guy played the game the same way *every single day*. And I don't know if there's ever going to be a better play than when he cut that ball off from Johnny Damon in the outfield. I still think that is one of the greatest plays that you'll ever see. You want to ask him, 'What was going through your mind that you said I got to cut this ball off from a guy who just threw it 20 yards away?'"

That outlandish act came in 2004 when Ramirez was playing left field and inexplicably decided it was perfectly appropriate to cut off a throw made from center fielder Damon. The throw was targeted for third base to make a play on a runner headed there. The ball had been driven off the wall in straight-away center and ricocheted away from Damon, who chased it down on the warning track as a run scored. It was then that Ramirez, instead of getting out of the way, chose to make an awkward leaping (then falling) catch of the ball to cut off Damon's throw, one intended, and on line, for his true cutoff man. Ramirez then became baseball's most unusual relay man, throwing the ball from his knees to second baseman Mark Bellhorn. All of these events provided enough time to allow David Newhan to easily leg out an inside-the-park homer.

Quick aside: George Brett said he once fielded a slow grounder and got off a throw to first base. His throw never got there. Pitcher Marty Pattin cut it off, and this was years before Ramirez's gaffe.

On May 28, 2014, the Red Sox invited Ramirez back to Fenway to throw out the game's first pitch. Sporting a mohawk haircut, he made the throw, but it never reached catcher Jason Varitek. Instead, as had been planned, Damon streaked from a spot just off the diamond to intercept the throw before tumbling to the turf. Manny embraced Damon, grabbed a microphone and chanted to the crowd in a singsong style that the Sox were going to Disneyland because that's what you say when you're champions. Some teammates laughed while some merely scratched their heads.

Once Ramirez fell while pursuing a fly ball. After several moments he realized that he was sitting on top of the ball. His reaction, the opposite of the reaction of club officials, was to laugh as if it were a big joke—and, of course, to him, it was.

Then there was the time in 2005 when he ducked inside Fenway's Green Monster, vanishing during a lull in the game due to a mound visit by coach Dave Wallace. The problem was that when the game was ready to resume, Manny was still missing. He only returned to the field as the game's next pitch was being made. Manny, it turns out, was relieving himself inside the Monster.

He's also made a phone call during a pitching change, took his iPod into the outfield, and after making a fine catch near the outfield wall, did a high-five with a fan, then spun and rifled the ball in to complete a double play.

Twice he didn't show up when his world champion Red Sox were invited to the White House. The first time Damon told President George W. Bush that Manny's grandmother was sick. Three years later in 2007, Boston accepted another Bush invitation to visit, but Ramirez again was a no-show (and not for political reasons). Bush joked that he guessed Manny's grandmother had died once more.

According to an excellent article by Nick Underhill for Mass Live, Ramirez was stopped by a police officer for several traffic violations in 1997. After accepting the tickets, he returned to his car and began to drive away from the officer, making a U-turn in the process. So the policeman again stopped and ticketed him. When the cop told him that he was about to give him a ticket, Ramirez replied, "I don't need any tickets. I can give you tickets."[33] Knowing Ramirez, he wasn't being sarcastic—he meant he could get free game tickets for the officer. But the cop had to give him yet another ticket when the oblivious slugger made yet another illegal U-turn. To borrow a Bill James line about another player, Ramirez gave people the feeling that he wasn't even able to read a Superman comic book and figure out who Clark Kent really was.

There was no placating his 1997 Indians manager, Mike Hargrove, when Ramirez stole second base. Standing safely on the base, he then decided he should trot back to first. He was *not* trying to emulate the famous move of Germany Schaefer; instead, he explained that he somehow thought the pitch had been fouled off.

Ramirez and Jim Thome made perfect dupes back in their early years with Cleveland. During spring training at Winter Haven, Florida, veterans arranged for two local policemen to barge into the Indians clubhouse. In their finest official tones, they asked for the whereabouts of Thome and Ramirez. When the culprits were discovered, they were placed under arrest for creating a disturbance at the team's hotel. They fell for the practical joke like a Mike Tyson victim keeling over from his mighty uppercut blows. It wasn't until they were being led out to the police cruiser that they caught on, because their teammates could no longer stifle their laughter.

After a game in 1994, some Cleveland players clustered around the television to watch the drama of the O. J. Simpson white Bronco chase unfold. One Indian, Chad Ogea, who pronounces his name like the letters O and J, was not on hand. Ramirez joined the crowd in time to hear the name O. J. used frequently, so he asked, "Why are the police after Chad?"

Ramirez fell for another traditional prank when he broke in with Cleveland. Thome explained how the Indians performed a trick known as the three-man lift on him. "The older guys tricked Manny and Julian Tavares into laying down for the 'lift.' One of the guys said to Manny and Julian, 'I bet I can lift you two guys up,'" said Thome. Expressing disbelief, the two players went along with the premise, getting down on the floor, one on either side of the veteran who was bragging of his strongman status. Thome continued, "The three guys interlock hands, and usually the middle guy is the one who knows what's going on. So, when he's interlocked, the other two guys are trapped. That's when everybody else comes up and lifts their shirts over their heads and puts baby powder and shaving cream on them. They even dumped trash on them. They can't go anywhere. That was the funniest thing I ever saw in baseball." Like the old shaving cream shoved in a player's face, such tricks are a case of the Three Stooges meet big league baseball.

Being as wealthy as Croesus didn't stop Ramirez from trying to borrow money. Bill Livingston said, "He's just a flaky guy, but Charlie Manuel, who was a hitting guru, said Manny was the best right-handed hitter he had ever seen, and the ball just sounded different coming off his bat—it just had more velocity. Manny was kind of a naive guy. Anyway, he went up to a couple of the beat writers and asked, 'Can you loan me some money?' They said, 'How much do you need,' thinking he didn't have any cash on him for lunch. And he said, '$10,000.' He wanted a motorcycle [one source says he asked for $60,000 for a motorcycle for himself and one for a teammate]. He left his paychecks in the glove compartment of his car and didn't cash them. He was just a different guy." In Boston, he continued to treat his hefty paychecks the way someone might flick off detritus, tossing them in his locker and then forgetting them.

Ramirez would engage in puzzling behavior, then flash a goofy grin in an attempt to charm and disarm the media and the public, an act that had surely worn thin by 2009, when he was suspended for 50 games for a failed drug test. That was also the year in which he left a vital playoff game and hit the shower rather than sticking with, and supporting, his teammates.

Eventually he was basically exiled from baseball after a short stay with Tampa Bay in 2011. But in 2014, he was hired as a Cubs minor league coach. Ironically, his message to the young players was to follow the rules. A case of do as I say, and not as I did.

In April 2019 he still didn't seem to grasp reality very well. He said that despite his suspensions he still hoped to make the Hall of Fame. His reasoning was basically that all humans make mistakes and that nobody's perfect. Experts believe that just as he seemed to sleepwalk through life at times, he should now dream on. It takes 75 percent of the votes cast for the Hall to get in, and Ramirez hasn't even broken the 24 percent mark.

ADRIAN BELTRE (1998–2018)

Beltre retired after the 2018 season with his 3,166 hits earning him the number 16 slot on the all-time list. In 2018, he also became just the fifth player to have 30+ extra base hits over 20 consecutive seasons. Upon his retirement, just 23 players had driven in more runs than his 1,707. His 477 homers place him 30th all-time. A five-time Gold Glove winner, he is first among all third basemen for hits and RBI, and third for homers. Most fans would not come close to guessing his career totals for doubles (636), nor do they recall that his single-season best output for home runs was 48. He even once led the American League with 199 hits.

Jeff Francoeur believes that Beltre "is one of the most underrated players in the last 40 years. You go look at his stats. He reminds me of Paul Goldschmidt who is so good and no one ever really gets a chance to see it. That's a shame." Under-publicized, Beltre's approaching, then topping, the 3,000 hit strata crept up on Francoeur and many others. He quietly did his job year in and year out.

In a 2018 interview, Marty Appel mirrored Francoeur's observations: "Now I see him mentioned for the Hall of Fame all the time and that sort of snuck up on me. I haven't been thinking of him as a Hall of Famer all these years, but now that's part of the conversation about Beltre. I've been educated."

* * *

Beltre has been known, on more than a few occasions, to hit a home run with a wild swing that finished with his back knee dropping to the ground. Francoeur stated, "Andruw Jones would do that a couple of times, but who goes to their knee almost every time they hit a curveball for a home run? It's insane. That shows you how strong he is. He's perfected that swing—it's hilarious." Sportswriter Mike Vaccaro agreed, "I've never seen a guy who's hit home runs from his knees more than he has. The extreme follow-through on his bat—he winds up on one knee as the ball goes out of the park."

Francoeur continued, "And one thing I love about him is he had fun without showing other people up. You can have fun the way he had fun. If you go watch Adrian Beltre and the things he would do—and the same thing with Manny Ramirez—he had so much fun; and Adrian respected the game, he respected the other people."

Beltre did some outside-the-box thinking which got him tossed from a game. He strayed from the on-deck circle to get closer to home plate so he could get a better look at what and how the pitcher was throwing. Umpire Gerry Davis told him he had to stand in the on-deck circle, so Beltre did something logical that he felt would satisfy both Davis and himself. He pulled the mat serving as the on-deck circle over to where he had originally been, and stood on it. Davis, failing to see the logic or the humor in the situation, ejected Beltre. He later stated, "He told me to stand in the circle, so I said OK." He could innocently contend he was ejected for obeying an order.

Beltre has a sort of phobia: He can't stand it when someone touches his head. Knowing of Beltre's aversion, fun-loving teammate Elvis Andrus often teased him. Beltre's quirk is the opposite of Kevin Rhomberg's. In a 2017 contest, a committee meeting of six Rangers convened on the hill. As the confab was breaking up, Andrus seized on a lull in Beltre's attention to cup his head with his gloved hand. Beltre responded by kicking toward the rapidly retreating Andrus. Then, removing his glove, Beltre double clutched before firing it after his impish teammate—all this in the middle of a game and in front of thousands of spectators. Their teasing, says Francoeur, "is hilarious, but I've never heard him say why it [ticks him off]."

Tom Grieve, a Rangers broadcaster, says he has no idea, either. "I've seen it for eight years. We put the replay on TV every night, but I never heard an explanation of why that bothers him. I think it's genuine. I don't think he could react like that every single time if it wasn't. Who knows, maybe in some way it's like someone who hits their funny bone or if you tickle someone under the armpit or chin. I don't know what it feels like to him, but it's a genuine reaction, for sure.

"I think if people started doing it to him that he didn't know, like out on the street, he might not be that good-natured about it, but I think that he knows that in the context of a clubhouse and a dugout, with his teammates, that maybe he can't react like he feels like reacting. And he has to keep it as light as he can, but I've never seen him laugh when someone does it, let's put it that way. If Elvis does it to him, it's one thing, but guys that don't know him as well, young guys—they don't do it to him. I think you have to have reached a certain level on the pecking order before you feel comfortable that you might be able to, in some way, get away with it."

Francoeur pointed out that Beltre and Andrus had another running gag going. On pop flies, which either man could handle, the two men "called each other off," both insisting they would make the catch. "I saw one time he almost pushed Elvis away so he could catch the ball—little things like that, that you're laughing at through a 162-game season. If Beltre got one thrown up and in on him, he'd tiptoe back. He kept it lighthearted. To me, that's the guy who has fun playing the game."

Grieve said the two men are very close. "They're like brothers. I've never seen Elvis rub his head and have Adrian turn around, smiling and laughing. He does push back and take swings at him, but never punched anybody in the face or gotten into a fight. But his reaction is such that it would lead me to very confidently say that he absolutely doesn't like it at all. It's not funny to him and he wishes they wouldn't do it, but, again, he knows he has to deal with it. It's like anything else in the clubhouse, once people find that you have a little weakness, they're never going to let you up. He has to try to go along with it the best he can."

DEE GORDON (2011–)

Darvis "Dee" Gordon is the son of big league pitcher Tom "Flash" Gordon. In 2015, Flash Junior became the first second baseman since Jackie Robinson in 1949 to lead the league in batting and steals. He motors around the bases at times under 14 seconds, scalding the bags at around 21 miles per hour. He's a two-time All-Star, a Gold Glove winner, and a Silver Slugger winner as well.

When Dee was just six, a man shot and killed his mother, so Tom won custody of his son and he and his mother raised the boy. Dee didn't play baseball until high school, but he was so proficient at basketball he received a scholarship offer from Louisville. On June 1, 2012, he was one of five Dodgers in the lineup who had a father who had played in the majors. The other four were Tony Gwynn Jr., Ivan DeJesus Jr., Jerry Hairston Jr., and Scott Van Slyke. Excluding Gwynn, the others made up the Dodger infield.

* * *

Christian Yelich was a Miami teammate of Gordon, who found him to have a limitless supply of energy and a hilarious nature. The fun-loving Gordon was in charge of a group of his fellow Mariners who, in August 2018, embarked on an unusual road trip. After they had won the getaway game of their homestand, they returned to their lockers and donned incongruous clothing. Many dressed in the uniforms of the NBA team that once played in Seattle, the SuperSonics, while Nelson Cruz and Mitch Haniger took on the appearance of World Wrestling Entertainment stars.

Gordon's 2018 Mariners were trying to snap their streak of 17 seasons without making it to post-season play, the longest skein among the four major pro sports in North America. They failed, but Gordon tried his best to help keep the team relaxed. Even a sedate clubhouse became energized when Gordon entered. Seeing him dance in the dugout or while filming a video is not unusual. A few of his most illustrious moves come from the Schmoney Dance and his floss dancing. There's even a video of him dancing the Texas Two-Step while wearing cowboy boots.

Jeff Francoeur was also a Miami teammate of Gordon who noted a serious side of the man, "Dee always was talking trash about football and how he could outrun everybody, but when I remember him, I think of the home run he hit after José Fernandez's death, how cool that was. And the funny part was we gave him crap because he hadn't hit a ball over an outfielder's head all year. Then to hit one in the upper deck in Marlins Park!"

In Gordon's first at bat after his friend's demise, he wore a batting helmet marked with Fernandez's number. In addition, Gordon, a left-handed hitter, batted righty, as Fernandez did, on the first pitch. After that, he went back to batting lefty and hit a 2–0 pitch for his first home run in 306 at bats. Gordon, who cried as he circled the bases, said he had never hit a ball so far, not even in practice.

Mike Vaccaro went into more depth on Gordon's blast. "He was responsible for one of the most poignant moments I ever covered. That was the day after José Fernandez died, when he hit a home run, and he's not a home run hitter. There was talk Bartolo Colon may have grooved the ball, but, you know what, even if you groove it, you still got to hit it out, and he did. That was one of my more memorable moments, forgetting whatever the circumstances were around Fernandez's death. Certainly in the moment when people were just stunned that this young, incredible talent had been taken, to see Gordon perform the way he did was pretty amazing." In fact, Brewers pitcher Brent Suter said watching Gordon's homer in the clubhouse had the Brewers tearing up.

Gordon will always be remembered for his colorful, good-natured ways, but no one will ever forget his emotional tribute to a fallen teammate, either.

BRYCE HARPER (2012–)

At the age of 22 years and 353 days at the end of the 2015 season, Harper became the youngest player to win the MVP unanimously. Oddly, he was younger than that year's Rookie of the Year, his childhood friend Kris Bryant. In 2015 Harper led the league in runs scored, homers (42), on-base percentage, slugging percentage, and on-base plus slugging at 1.109.

He began the 2019 season as a 26-year-old, yet he's already won the MVP and the Rookie of the Year Award and been on six All-Star squads over his first seven seasons.

* * *

An anti-purist, Harper has made it clear he feels his style of play, which includes admiring his homers at times and having unrestrained emotions, should be the norm for today's game. He believes the stoical, conservative way of, say, running out a home run—modestly, with head down like Mickey Mantle—is passé. Hit a majestic homer? Nothing wrong with gazing at it until it disappeared over a distant fence.

The Washington Nats played their first seven seasons in the nation's capital without Harper—they never smelled post-season play. Five of those seasons saw them in the cellar, and in their worst season they won only 36 percent of their games. Even in their best season they came in third at a remote 21½ games back.

During their next six years with Harper, beginning when he was just 19 years old, the Nationals turned things around drastically, averaging 93 wins per season with four treks to the playoffs.

During the 2018 All-Star activities, it was Harper who stole the show in front of an adoring crowd in Washington, DC. He won the Home Run Derby and made the win more savory by drilling his titan blasts off his father. In the final minute of the event, Harper homered on eight straight swings. The moment he clinched winning the Derby he celebrated exuberantly—flipping his red, white, and blue bat high in air—and later said that he is serious when he's playing, "But off the field, that's the kid in me you saw tonight."

In late 2018, Jeff Francoeur stated, "If you like baseball at all, what a great Home Run Derby. I watched the whole thing this year because it was so entertaining with Harper being in Washington with that crowd. At the All-Star break, the fans pretty much knew they weren't going to the playoffs, so I thought it was just a cool thing. This is a guy that everybody had a blast watching."

At the time of Francoeur's comments, speculation was strong that Harper would leave the Nats in 2019 as a free agent. "If he doesn't come back to Washington, what a great way for him to go out. I've always enjoyed watching him play because talents like him just don't come around often." As expected, he took the free agent exit route and signed with the Phillies for $330 million. Shortly before Harper signed, Steve Blass joked, "It's nice to know that a baseball player is probably going to own a country in Europe with his next contract."

Much of Harper's Home Run Derby garb resembled the American flag, including a red-and-white headband and a sleeve on his right arm complete with red-and-white stripes next to a blue area dotted with white stars. His patriotic-themed spikes honored Washington, DC.

Previously, for MLB's Players' Weekend in 2017, when major leaguers were permitted to design their own spikes, socks, and bats, Harper wore colorful, tie-dyed cleats, some decorated with emojis he handpicked, and one of his bats had a picture of his face on it. For the same special weekend in 2018, he wore clothing and used bats featuring drawings done by kids who were part of his Harper's Heroes program for victims of childhood cancer.

Brent Suter said Harper is "definitely a great player with some great [lines]. The 'That's a clown question, bro,' comes to mind." Suter referred to the time a reporter asked Harper a rather foolish question and Harper dismissed it. Carl Erskine said, "I think any good, clean, unique personality that excites the fans some in the right way is good for baseball. There are a lot of personalities who don't necessarily say a lot, but on the field they are entertaining."

In 2018, Francoeur noted, "It's unbelievable. He just turned 26 the other day and look at his numbers. Mike Trout, to me, is the best player in baseball, hands down. I don't think it's close. He has huge years every year, but I'll say this about Bryce Harper, he runs his mouth and he'll pop off, but that guy hustles all the time. For the most part, I've never seen him not run or get after it. I respect the hell out of the way he posts [shows up] and plays every single day." In 2018, Harper missed just three games.

Cleveland sportswriter Bill Livingston seconded those thoughts: "He's a multi-tool player and one of the guys who fans are going to enjoy for years."

Every Harper plate appearance generates excitement. As John Vorperian, host and executive producer of TV's *Beyond the Game*, said, "He's a competitor extraordinaire. Hey, the Beltway Basher crushes the ball over the fence or the bat over his knee. You got to love this guy."

YASIEL PUIG (2013–)

During his first two seasons, Puig came in second in the balloting for the Rookie of the Year, made an All-Star team, and made a pretty big splash on the baseball world. Over a two-game stretch in 2018, one year after he hit a personal high of 28 homers, Puig tied the major league record with five total homers.

* * *

As touched on earlier, baseball people nowadays don't use the term flake, but at least two men who played in this century—both with the Dodgers—fit that description: Manny Ramirez and Puig. For the 2018 MLB Players' Weekend, where players select a nickname to be displayed on the back of their jerseys instead of their surname, Puig used his "Wild Horse" moniker. Critics preferred labels such as Loose Cannon.

"What a character he is," began Jeff Francoeur. "He's like a [Jonathan] Papelbon. The first time I ever laid eyes on this guy was spring training in his first year with the Dodgers. I was with the Royals and we had a night game in Camelback, Arizona. I came home after the game and told my wife, 'I think I just saw Bo Jackson reincarnated.' The things he was doing! He's built like a brick, you know what, he could run, he could throw."

As for his antics, after the 2018 season Francoeur said he felt Puig had tempered some of his displays. "He's learned. He's been better, you don't see the huge bat flips, but some of those things he did—he just did them and he didn't care. He was who he was. The one thing I always gave the guy a lot of respect and credit for, and I'm big on this, is you see the way he is and, listen—if he got hit [with a retaliation pitch], he wouldn't say anything, he'd run to first base. If you're going to pimp stuff and do the things he does, you have to be prepared to get hit."

However, Puig wasn't always on the same page with his teammates. For example, early in his career he often was late for meetings, and the Dodgers shipped him back to the minors for a month. That didn't prevent him from poking fun at his image, posing once to be photographed standing alone on the Dodgers plane, as if pondering the whereabouts of the rest of the traveling party—as if this time he was *way* too late. During an interview he wore a shirt with this message written on it: "#PUIG

NOTLATE."

Issues aside, before he was traded to the Reds there was a legion of Los Angeles fans who followed this man with the energy of a whirling dynamo—there was a roar each time he appeared at the plate in Dodger Stadium. He gave a straight-faced answer as to why the throng was chanting his name during one at bat, saying it was because he was the one at the plate at that particular time.

The interpretation of some actions of today's players is a matter of the eye of the beholder. Colorful, or egocentric? Animated, or guilty of showing up others? People debate that when they observe Puig tossing his bat in the air to show his displeasure over, say, fouling off rather than ripping a pitch he felt was delectable, then snatching the bat out of the air with a dramatic flair and sheer disgust. Some argue that he was degrading the pitcher's skills.

Then there's his kissing his bat while at the plate. Steve Blass pulled no punches. "In my opinion he's an embarrassment to the game." When asked if it was okay to use his quote in print, Blass replied, "Please do." Puig explained his smooching by saying he is, in effect, making love to the bat and that in return the appreciative bat gives him base hits.

Erskine also feels Puig is over the top in his actions. "He's a little bit on the showboat side. I've seen him lick his bat—that's a little gross for me, but he is one great outfielder, I'll tell you that. He can throw accurately."

In one contest, he licked his bat then comically recoiled at the nasty taste of pine tar. Another time after he had drawn three walks in a game, he said the reason he didn't coax a fourth base on balls was "because my tongue didn't work on the bat so I struck out."[34]

He doesn't restrict his kisses to inanimate objects. Grateful for the help his hitting coach Turner Ward gave him, in 2017 Puig started a tradition of giving Ward a kiss on his cheek or forehead when returning to the dugout after homering. Puig commented rather cryptically, "I don't really like him, but I love him so I have to kiss him." Then he added, "I give him more kisses than his wife."[35]

Fred Claire said Puig "is a player with incredible talent, and everyone recognizes that talent. The thing that I like most about what I see from Puig—and I don't know him personally—is his relationship with the batting coach. Obviously they've got a great connection. What's better than that? It doesn't get any better than that—a player acknowledging the coaching that he's received, and the relationship that they have is tremendous. No, he's a great, great talent."

Keith Hall, who was a worker at Pittsburgh's PNC Park, said Puig was "more interested in having fun than just about anything. He wants to do whatever he can do to have fun and interact with fans—he enjoys the fans. That's what he thinks Major League Baseball is all about. I saw him giving autographs like he was giving out lollipops. And I never saw a guy hit a ball like him. The only one who ever hit a ball as far as he did at PNC was Sammy Sosa."

In Game 2 of the 2018 National League Division Series versus Atlanta, Puig attempted to swipe second on an ill-advised delayed steal. The throw beat him so badly, he stopped short of the bag, conceding the out. He then hugged his former teammate, shortstop Charlie Culberson. Finally, this kissing bandit, still embracing the shortstop, planted a kiss on his neck. Unlike a woman offended by an unwanted advance, Culberson playfully tapped Puig on his helmet. All in all, it was a "Puig being Puig" moment, as if he were the successor to Manny Ramirez.

Earlier in that game he stuck his tongue out, seeming to aim it at left fielder Ronald Acuna Jr. Moments later, Puig hit a single to left field. It was enough to make one wonder if he had he just called his shot—with his tongue?

JAVIER BAEZ (2014–)

In 2016 Cubs second baseman Baez was instrumental in his team winning its first World Series in more than a century—since winning it all in 1908. He copped the National League Championship Series MVP award, hitting .318 with five RBI, which propelled Chicago into the World Series versus the Indians.

Despite that, 2018 was his breakout season. He established career highs in RBI with 111, leading the National League. When he hit his 23rd homer on August 3, he had already tied his career high—he wound up with 34 home runs that year. When necessary, he could help his team out by playing shortstop, third base, and in a pinch, first base and outfield. That versatility has earned him several Fielding Bible's Multi-Position awards. His deft and clever play also earned him the nickname "El Mago," Spanish for the Magician.

His manager, Joe Maddon, compared Baez's popularity to the Beatles, and in 2018 fans voted him in as the All-Star Game's starting second sacker. An aggressive hitter, Baez went from April 12 to May 31, 2018, without drawing a walk, and the free pass he did receive right before the streak began was intentional. Jeff Francoeur remarked, "He takes his hacks—he's not up there to walk. He wants to drive the ball somewhere, and I guarantee he drives some of the analytical people crazy, but as a baseball guy, I love it."

Baez is known for the creative and lightning-quick tags he applies to runners. Bill Livingston called him "the best tagger ever. Until he burst on the scene, I didn't know that there was an art to that and that it could be used as a weapon."

* * *

Baez clearly adds excitement to the game in many ways. Francoeur said, "I love watching this kid play ball. You talk about having flair. You can never, ever say Javier Baez does not play the game hard—the guy runs hard all the time, he plays every day. He might have a big swing sometimes and people might want him to shorten it up, but I think this is the guy that we need to be promoting in the game of baseball.

"He's not big, but he can play shortstop, second, and I guarantee he could play third. He could play the outfield [regularly], I bet, if he needed to. He's old-school out there on the field. That guy comes to play hard every day. That's why I would love to be able to coach a guy like him. I remember Bobby Cox used to say, 'I love it that with some of the guys I managed I never had to worry about them.' He said that about me one time, and that was the greatest compliment I ever got."

Francoeur said that also applies to Baez. But is he a colorful guy? "Absolutely. If you ask some of those Cubs for stories—you see Baez in the dugout, always messing around with people."

In 2018, the savvy and dynamic Baez even came up with a sort of signature strategy, stealing home several times to spark his team's offense. His steals of home came when he lured the defense to sleep or when a teammate intentionally wandered perilously far off first base, drawing a throw. It was then that Baez would spring with feline speed, taking off for the plate.

Brent Suter said Baez is not only colorful, but "he plays the game with a lot of emotion and energy. He seems like a down-to-earth guy and a good teammate. One funny thing he did in 2018 was he struck out on a changeup and he pointed at Zach Davies, said, 'Hey, good pitch,' and walked to the dugout. I've never seen that before, a super sign of respect."

When the peppy Baez came to the plate as the leadoff hitter in the 2018 All-Star Game, he greeted American League starting pitcher Chris Sale with a beaming grin and a respectful military-style salute.

FRANCISCO LINDOR (2015–)

Lindor stated that he was called up to his school's varsity baseball team when he was in eighth grade, still 12 years old. He hasn't slowed down, finishing twice in the top 10 for the MVP trophy. A slick shortstop, he was the recipient of the 2016 American League Platinum Glove, an honor given to the league's best fielder regardless of position played.

He seemingly can do it all, as he finished fourth and second for total bases in 2017 and 2018 respectively; the latter year he led the American League in double plays turned by a shortstop. No switch-hitting shortstop has ever hit more home runs in a season than Lindor's 38. Furthermore, he is the first shortstop to put together a season of 35+ home runs, 40 or more doubles, and 20+ stolen bases.

Briefly put, this is one dazzling player, a colorful guy who also has a future as glowing as his omnipresent grin. Livingston observed, "He's a terrific ballplayer, a wonderful player to watch. He's a franchise player, probably the best player in the division and a fan magnet with his infectious personality. He's not a big guy, but he's got a lot of sock for a shortstop—that position began to change from the days of Omar Vizquel, who was the best defensive shortstop I ever saw, to Nomar Garciaparra, A-Rod, and guys like that."

* * *

While recent players are not as clown-like as many players from the distant past, Lindor is colorful in a different way, a more joyful way. Lindor's nickname, "Mr. Smile," says it all.

Jeff Francoeur spent time with Lindor in spring training of 2014. "I think that was his first year in big league camp, and I remember thinking *who the heck is this guy*. He was smaller then than he is now, but he had such a sweet swing. He's always smiling. He's a guy who we should be [promoting], making commercials about him, telling people this is how you play baseball—say you have fun, you're exciting, you show emotion, but you don't show people up. I love the emotion. I think it's great. You should have emotion, and he does it the right way."

Brent Suter said, "He's a heckuva player and seems like a heckuva human being, always smiling, always positive, and he does a lot for Puerto Rico. He's someone I respect a lot and a colorful character who seems like he enjoys life to the fullest."

Reporter Ashley Bastock said, "He's super willing to talk to the media after a win or a loss. After Game 5 of the 2017 American League Division Series when they lost to the Yankees, he stood on a stool in the middle of the clubhouse surrounded by reporters, and answered every question."

His effervescent personality was vividly on display during the 2018 All-Star Game, when he wore a microphone to share his thoughts with the fans. Possessing joie de vivre, Lindor spoke of how he was having a blast being at baseball's Mid-Summer Classic, how he was enjoying the ride. That gleefully childlike attitude is what endears him to others. During the game, he smoked a ball in one at bat, only to have it stabbed for an out. At the start of the next half-inning he trotted out to his shortstop position, dropped to the turf, and did some push-ups. When the television announcers asked him why he had done that, he replied that he had hit the ball as hard as he could, but that it had traveled absolutely nowhere. Apparently, he felt he had to beef up before hitting again. He called himself a kid at heart, a 24-year-old kid, yes, but a delightful big kid to be sure. Cleveland's newspaper, the *Plain Dealer*, ran a picture of him exercising in its July 18, 2018, edition with the caption, "The Indians' Francisco Lindor does push-ups between innings at the All-Star Game on Tuesday because . . . he's Francisco Lindor."

Admittedly loquacious, Lindor said that even during games he constantly gabs with someone, including opponents who reach second base. He most frequently jabbers with teammate José Ramírez, who is stationed next to him at third base. Lindor confessed that when Ramírez ignores him he simply talks to himself.

During the 2018 All-Star Game, Eugenio Suarez reached second base not long after being awarded first base when he was hit in his thigh by a pitch, and Lindor yakked it up with him, then he kissed his own hand and playfully patted it on the spot where Suarez had been hit, not unlike a mother soothing a boo-boo of an injured child. It was not exactly like the time the Kissing Bandit made an All-Star Game appearance in 1979 and again in 1981, when she planted a smooch on pitcher Len Barker, but a crowd-pleasing moment, nevertheless.

Even during the 2016 World Series Lindor joked around at times while on the field. Old-school baseball people expect solemn expressions and grim determination to be on display in vital games, not grins. However, Lindor was just being his congenial self. Mike Vaccaro said of Lindor's behavior, "I think that explains why people love to watch him play so much because he clearly loves playing." He likened it to the Roy Campanella line, "You have to have a lot of little boy in you to play baseball for a living."

Vaccaro continued, "It's easy to forget sometimes that these guys are playing a game that's supposed to be fun [even though] they're playing for high stakes and high money. Yes, the World Series might be a very serious event, but there's no reason to take yourself too seriously, because that's probably the reason why you're playing in the World Series in the first place." Lindor is a prototypical example of a man who plays for the love of the game.

4

QUICK TAKES ON THE PRINCES OF PRANKS AND ZANINESS

Some colorful players didn't do enough funny, witty, or wacky things to merit their own lengthy sections but do deserve being mentioned in this book. That's what follows. Just as the pitchers and position players were separated earlier, this chapter also splits the two categories of players.

QUICK-PITCH ITEMS FOR PITCHERS

Early Wynn (1939–1963)

Joe Cunningham played with Wynn on the White Sox. "He was a pretty nice guy, a regular guy, but I'll tell you one thing about Early Wynn—he did not like you hitting the ball through the middle. If you did that, the next time up, he'd throw at you." Some say that even if you merely looked the wrong way at Wynn, he'd throw at you.

Cunningham pointed out that brushing back a batter for hitting the ball through the box was actually a bit foolish. "As a hitter, I have no control sometimes when I hit the ball—whether it goes through the middle or not. But, you know, if you're going to hit the ball, hit it through the middle because that's where the largest space is, between the shortstop and second baseman, and the ball goes into center field for a base hit. So for him to throw at you, I thought was kind of crappy."

Wynn, who won exactly 300 games, was a sort of baseball one-trick pony when it comes to being colorful, because most of his humorous comments gravitated to one topic, brushbacks. Erskine said somebody "called Wynn a headhunter, contending he'd throw at anybody. The person said, 'If your mother came up to bat, you'd knock her down.' And Wynn supposedly said, 'Mother was a helluva hitter.'" Wynn is also credited with saying he'd only hit her "if she was digging in," and that whether he'd hit her or not hinged on "how well she was hitting" at the time.

Bob Feller scoffed at some of Wynn's alleged lines, like his claims that he would knock down his own mother (or grandmother) if she was crowding the plate. Feller dismissed such talk: "It's kind of like other legends—it's hype." Another Cleveland player said he didn't believe Wynn made his grandmother hit the dirt, but only because "when I knew him I think his grandmother was dead, but his mother was another story." Hype or truth, Wynn perpetuated his legendary status: "I'm tired of hearing all those stories that I'd throw at my mother." He paused for effect, then concluded, "Unless she had a bat in her hand."

Now, if a player bunted on the not-too-mobile Wynn, there was a good chance he would get knocked down, even in an exhibition game. And he *did* say that if he pitched in an age where hitters showed him up, "I might knock down more of them today than when I pitched. I wouldn't waste a pitch hitting them either. I'd hit 'em in the dugout."

Wynn contended that home plate belonged to him, and he nailed many a hitter who was foolhardy enough to dispute that. An Indian minor leaguer once faced Wynn during spring training and made the mistake of smashing a hot groundball back at Wynn. He said he knew right away what would follow, so he walked away from the plate. Wynn insisted he return for more batting practice, promising he would not throw at him. The batter resumed his stance. Predictably, Wynn fired a knockdown pitch. He just could not let it go; he had to show his mettle and his vengeance—to prove once again that the space between the foul lines was *his* office.

It's said that when George Kell ripped a single up the middle, Wynn fumed. He decided to get his revenge immediately by throwing over to his first baseman—not to keep Kell close to the bag, but with the intention of drilling Kell. Wynn's old roomie, Jerry Walker, said, "He didn't like to lose—ever." Wynn even learned how to switch hit in order to help his cause.

Chet Johnson (1946)

Years before Fidrych, Johnson talked to baseballs and manicured the dirt. He'd pretend catchers' throws back to the mound hurt, then take his glove off, revealing a fake swollen thumb. He used blooper and hesitation pitches and sometimes pitched underhanded. He wore a Davy Crockett coonskin cap and a Groucho Marx–like fake mustache on the field. The Marx Brothers loved him, and often watched him pitch in the Pacific Coast League.

Johnson pretended he couldn't clearly see his catcher's signs, so he'd creep nearer and nearer to him, squinting all the way to the plate. Then, his brother told writer David Eskenazi, "He would get down on all fours and stare at the catcher's crotch for a couple seconds, then stand up and shout, 'Eureka! I got it!' and run back to the mound." When he got on the rubber, he peered in and shook off the sign.

He'd wave a red handkerchief at batters like a toreador, and if a player homered, Johnson would trot with him around the bases, fanning him off with the handkerchief. He kept a black notebook in a pocket, pretending it contained intel on hitters. If that hitter homered, Johnson would rip the page out, tear it apart, and throw it in the air. If he got a close call from an umpire, he'd bow to him.

Gene Conley (1952–1963)

Baseball writer Bob Buege said, "Conley had a strange incident with Pumpsie Green when they were stuck in traffic. They got off the bus and decided they were going to go to Israel." The two originally had left the bus to find a restroom. When they returned, the bus had left, so they began to drink—a lot. Eventually, Conley bought a ticket to visit Jerusalem, but his lack of a passport killed that plan.

The 6-feet, 8-inch Conley, who played on three NBA championship teams with the Boston Celtics, is the only man to win titles in two professional sports. When he was released by the Indians in 1964, the four-time All-Star sought solace in a church. Buege said that when Conley began to sob, a deacon tapped him on his shoulder and said, "What's the matter son, did you lose your mother?" He replied, "No, I lost my fastball."

Buege added, "I heard him tell this story: he was visiting a former ballplayer at a nursing home. He went to the front desk and was told to wait there. A woman in a wheelchair stared at him. He walked over and said to her, 'Do you know me?' She said, 'No, but if you go to the desk, they'll tell you who you are.'"

Tracy Stallard (1960–1966)

Long time Atlanta Braves coach Bobby Dews recalled, "One time there was a guy named Fritz Ackley, he pitched for the White Sox. We were in Triple-A in Jacksonville and we had a lot of older guys on our staff—Ackley, Tracy Stallard, Bob Radovich, and a couple of others. Stallard was a kind of happy-go-lucky guy, he was the guy who gave up the [1961 Roger Maris record-breaking] 61st home run.

"Managers used to sit in hotel lobbies and when someone would come in late, they would have him. Ackley was coming in kind of late one night in Syracuse and the manager was in the lobby. Ackley saw him before he came through the revolving doors, so he went back out and called Stallard [on a nearby phone]. He said, 'Call Skip on the house phone and when he goes over to answer, I'll slip in behind him and get in the elevator and up to my room.' But Ackley owed Stallard $200 or $300, and he hadn't paid him back, so Stallard was mad at him. The hotel manager paged, 'Mr. Ackley, please go to the house phone, you have an important call.' When Ackley went over there, Stallard told the manager, 'If you turn around right now, Skip, you'll see Ackley coming in breaking curfew.'"

Rollie Fingers (1968–1985)

Trivia item: Fingers's father once roomed with Stan Musial in the minors. Of course, Rollie went far beyond his father in baseball, saving 341 games, and as of 2018 still number 13 all-time.

NFL quarterback Joe Namath once took a razor to his mustache after a shaving cream company offered him $10,000 to do so for a commercial. The most famous baseball mustache of the modern day probably belongs to Fingers. When he was asked if he, like Namath, would shave off his handlebar mustache for such a chunk of cash, he replied, "For $10,000 I'd grow one on my butt."

Catfish Hunter said Fingers sometimes did things that weren't too swift (in the minors, he once headed toward the batter's box before he realized he had no bat). Hunter tells the story about Oakland third baseman Sal Bando providing Fingers with a baseball that had its cover hanging off a bit. Bando knew the ball would dance erratically, making for a difficult pitch to hit before the umpire could toss it out of play. Bando trotted back to his position only to see Fingers step off the rubber and shout to the umpire that he needed a new ball, that the one he held was flawed, thus defeating Bando's scheme.

Merv Rettenmund said, "Besides being a heckuva good ballplayer, Rollie was a smart guy. It's amazing how many of the [colorful characters] that I consider to be pretty smart." That was true when Fingers and his catcher, Gene Tenace, pulled off a great act of deception in the 1972 World Series. Reds star Johnny Bench was at the plate in a situation where an intentional walk made sense. At first Fingers pitched to Bench, but when the count ran full, A's manager Dick Williams said it was time to put Bench on. Tenace stood and went through the motions of signaling for Fingers to throw a wide pitch. Fingers nodded in agreement, then threw a slider and Bench, lulled into inactivity, took strike three looking.

Jim Kern (1974–1986)

Kern's build and his resemblance to a bird, especially when he pranced around the clubhouse flapping his arms, spawned his nickname Emu, and when he was with the Rangers, the bullpen came to be known as the Cuckoo's Nest.

Infielder Greg Pryor said, "Jim Kern threw about as hard as anybody could throw. He threw a ball under my chin and I never saw it until the catcher caught it." However, Kern's pitches often flew unpredictable courses. He said that to him, a no-hitter was *any* game in which he didn't hit someone. He told reporters that he was working on a new pitch that he called "a strike." He said he never had any trouble throwing a baseball "through a cement block wall. The only problem was, I could never hit the wall."[1]

One story attributed to Kern, who loved to slather Vaseline on doorknobs as a prank, has it that he was getting rocked in a game. When his manager made a trip to the mound to lift him, Kern protested. "I'm not tired," he insisted. "No," said the manager, "but your outfielders are."

Bill Caudill (1979–1987)

Although his nickname—"The Inspector"—sounds as if Caudill had a connection to top-notch detective work, he got it, says Seattle writer Larry Stone, because he inspected bats carefully, "trying to figure out which ones had hits in them." And, evoking images of Inspector Clouseau, Stone said, "They played the Pink Panther theme over the loudspeaker when he came into games." On the other hand, his other nickname—"Cuffs"—pertained directly to crime. "There was a car theft and he matched the description of the suspect, so he was detained and the team started calling him Cuffs." After Richie Zisk bought Caudill his own set of handcuffs, he took to using them on Mariners personnel (and even his manager's 13-year-old son and the team owner's wife), manacling them in odd places in and around the ballpark, including a Nautilus machine. And when Caudill was a teammate of the 5-feet, 7-inch Joe Morgan, he teased Morgan by putting miniature doll furniture in his locker.

Stone continued, "One year they got a bullpen car—it was in the shape of a tugboat—and Caudill hated that thing. On Opening Day, he stole the key so they couldn't bring it in for the pre-game ceremony. They had to delay the start of the game. He was also famous for getting in prank wars, even with his manager. One time Rene Lachemann came back to the hotel, and his bathtub had been filled with Jell-O."

Dan Quisenberry (1979–1990)

When Quisenberry and catcher Jamie Quirk teamed up on April 13, 1980, they became the first battery mates whose surnames began with "Q."

Author Bill Deane shared a classic Quisenberry line that "kind of gives a window to his sense of humor: 'I've seen the future and it's like the present, only longer.'" Another time, upset with the poor defense by his outfielders, Quisenberry commented, "Our fielders have to catch a lot of balls—or at least deflect them to someone who can."[2] A reporter once asked him what he liked best about baseball and he said, "There is no homework." He also made fun of his own less-than-stellar ability to strike out batters, saying he chalked up more saves than strikeouts "though recently I had a couple of 0–2 counts."[3]

Infielder Greg Pryor wrote a book, *The Day the Yankees Made Me Shave,* and devoted a chapter to Quisenberry because "that's how much he means to me. He was probably the nicest major leaguer that I ever met and even though he was a Rolaids Relief Man award winner, he didn't get the respect that he deserved because he didn't have long hair, a mustache, and he wasn't frothing at the mouth. He just got the job done. He was the strong glue that held the Royals together for several years. You need pitchers that are leaders, and he was certainly a leader. Everybody loved Dan Quisenberry. I even have a book of his poetry. His funniest line was when he said, 'I found a delivery in my flaw.'"

Mark Grace said pitchers such as Kent Tekulve and Quisenberry put "sink on the ball, trying to get you to hit the ball on the ground. They're not trying to strike you out—they want you swinging." Well, not always. Quisenberry knew what occurred when his sinker wasn't working. "The batter still hits a grounder. But in this case the first bounce is 360 feet away."

One of his teammates had teeth that jutted out, so Quisenberry tapped on them, pretending to play a xylophone. He detested giving clichéd answers to reporters. He defined a good response as, "How do I feel? I feel like I need to go poop."[4]

At season's end one year, Quisenberry was asked what his plans were. He answered, "I'm looking forward to putting on my glasses with the fake nose so I can walk around and be a normal person."

Dennis "Oil Can" Boyd (1982–1991)

Boyd, a Red Sox pitcher, got his nickname because in Mississippi where he grew up, "oil" was slang for beer, a drink he savored and favored. It follows that the phrase oil can meant a can of beer. Boyd is said to have started games having already downed three or four cans of high-grade oil—not exactly the same as Dock Ellis, who claimed to have thrown a no-hitter while on LSD, but still colorfully controversial. After a game thrown by Boyd, who sometimes called himself "the Can," it was time for him to kill off a six-pack, ensuring his nickname would stick.

Author Dan Schlossberg said he was taken with "how thin [Boyd] was. He was incredibly thin for a guy who threw as well as he did and was as successful. He was a very wiry guy. He kind of looked like an oil can, he was that thin." He was listed at 6 feet, 1 inch and weighed between 144 and 155 pounds.

Nolan Ryan once joked that Boyd owned a Doberman that had "acquired a taste for beer. They both cut down, but how would you like to encounter a Doberman kicking a six-pack-a-day beer habit?"

Boyd was once asked about a bomb threat that had been made on a flight his team had taken. In all seriousness he said, "They keep me pretty much in the dark about these things. Even if it had blown up, I wouldn't have known anything about it."

Baseball writer Bill Deane said, "I remember his facial expressions on the mound—he really wore his heart on his sleeve. He was an average pitcher with a good team behind him."

The eccentric, troubled Boyd was inconsolable when he learned he hadn't been selected to the All-Star Game one year. He became so infuriated his behavior led the Red Sox to suspend him, and he would up spending time in a hospital's psychiatric ward.

Boyd's problems with drinking and cocaine (which he sometimes used while pitching) provide yet another example of how substance abuse is a common motif among so many players covered in this book. Deane noted, "You see that with some professional comedians. Robin Williams and David Letterman. Behind the facade of the joking, the life of the party, [there are] some deep-seated issues."

Brad Lesley (1982–1985)

The 6-feet, 6-inch, 230-pound Lesley was given the nickname "the Animal" by teammates for his untamed ways. Lesley began his career with the Cincinnati Reds. As a fireman, Lesley was actually more of a walking four-alarm blaze, constantly raging.

He was even featured during the weekly closing credits of the television program *This Week in Baseball*. The film footage captured his almost maniacal facial expressions. He'd bellow after, say, finishing off a save; he'd pose his arms in front of himself in the style of the old Schwarzenegger-like *Saturday Night Live* weightlifters who proclaimed, "We want to pump you up!" Sometimes he'd even rip his jersey off his chest.

Then there was the Ryan incident, which took place when the all-time strikeout king, who had often observed Lesley in bemusement, mocked him. The venerable Nolan Ryan was on the mound facing Lesley's Reds. Art Howe, a former Astro, recounted the scene. "I remember Lesley and his antics on the mound. It was funny one day when he was pitching against Ryan, and in the first inning Ryan struck out one of their hitters and he gave it the Lesley growl. Their whole bench fell out laughing. It was great." It was probably even greater because it was so out of character for the staid Ryan to do such a thing. Houston's Denny Walling was there that day, too, and said that such moments are great when done in good taste. Ryan, apparently, had flawless taste.

Goose Gossage was a standout reliever who racked up 310 saves, ranking him sixth all time upon his retirement. He believes some pitchers who act wild are doing just that, acting. When it comes to Lesley, however, Gossage admits that, while he's not a mind reader, he truly believes Lesley's wild ways were not just an act.

As Hall of Famer Tom Glavine tolerantly put it, "I think anybody who plays this game, at some time or another their emotions get the best of them, and they do something a little off the wall. Just some guys do it more often and in front of more people."

Jim Lefebvre didn't care if Lesley was emoting as a diehard competitor or doing so theatrically. Like many men who have been around baseball for an eon, Lefebvre is conservative and has an abiding respect for the game and how it should be played. So his views on Lesley's behavior were quite direct: "It cost him his job. There are guys who have very unusual mannerisms, but when you start doing a circus act, it backfires. He used to come off the mound and go, 'Raar-hh.' He tried to show you up. My feeling is it was all an act." After recording a key out, Lesley would sometimes imitate a man wielding a chainsaw, pretending to mow down a batter like a lumberjack.

Lefebvre believes opponents got fed up with his histrionics and then got fired up. "Hitters just said, 'This guy's not going to get me out.'" Lefebvre may be right; Lesley lasted for only 54 big league appearances, but he did leave an impression on those who saw him.

Charlie Kerfeld (1985–1990)

One of Kerfeld's most provocative comments came when he stated, "People in New York have black teeth and their breath smells of beer. And the men are even worse."

He got caught by a television camera while standing in line at a concession stand in Shea Stadium during a game.

One of Kerfeld's baseball cards listed him as 5 feet, 11 inches, and 175 pounds instead of the correct figures of 6 feet, 6 inches, and 245 pounds. Asked about it, he joked that his mother must have sent the card company his baby picture because that was the last time he weighed 175.

Kerfeld was so proud of his jersey number, 37, that when he negotiated a contract in 1987, he asked for $110,037.37 along with 37 boxes of Jell-O.

Norm Charlton (1988–2001)

When Charlton was with the Phillies in 1995, he was facing San Diego's Steve Finley when a scalding line drive struck Charlton on his forehead—causing it to resemble a geyser, with blood spurting freely from a gaping wound. People wondered if they had just witnessed the end of his career, but Charlton was back with his team the next day. He dismissed the injury by saying, "I've had worse headaches than this."

On May 2, 1996, he went through a more harrowing experience when his Seattle Mariners were playing the Indians. During the game an earthquake, jolting seismographs with a 5.4 reading, rattled the Kingdome. Charlton was able to find humor even in this situation. The following day he told reporters, "When I got home, my clothes were strewn all over the place and the pictures were off the wall." He then smiled, adding, "But that's the way it was when I left."

The Cincinnati organization produced Rob Dibble, who, along with Randy Myers and Charlton, comprised the Reds' Nasty Boys. Charlton and Dibble once threw water glasses out of their hotel window 19 floors above street level. Their goal was to shatter the glasses in a nearby river. Ironically, wild man Dibble says Charlton is crazy, but at least he concedes that Charlton is also quite smart—he holds three degrees from Rice.

When Mike Timlin was with the Mariners, he experienced one of Charlton's zany acts. He recalled, "There are two phones in the Baltimore bullpen. Charlton was with the Orioles and he called us in our locker room from their bullpen and gave us the play-by-play from his game."

Ken Griffey Sr. said of the Nasty Boys, "They were serious. I mean, the seventh, eighth, and ninth inning, they knew that was their time. The toughest one was actually Charlton. He was the only one out of the three of them who threw a forkball. It was more of a spitter than anything. He was the nastiest one. Charlton was tough because he had that split finger—well, it was actually a spitter, but he called it a split finger."

Injured, Charlton sat out the 1994 season. "I'm the ugliest cheerleader in history," he judged.

Rob Dibble (1988–1995)

A person would have to go no further than All-Star reliever Rob Dibble to prove that flakes were still in abundance during his days in the majors, and not just in breakfast cereals. Author Dan Schlossberg said, "In 1990, the Nasty Boys helped the Reds win the World Series. I remember Dibble throwing a ball in the stands and hit a schoolteacher." After a poor outing, he fired the baseball about 400 feet into the second-deck center field seats in Cincinnati, accidentally striking the first-grade teacher. That action earned him about the same punishment a schoolboy might receive for outrageous behavior, a four-day suspension.

Dibble gained notoriety for his volatile temper. He dramatically ripped his jersey off his chest at times. Then there was the time he intentionally hit an opposing base runner with the ball. Cubs outfielder Doug Dascenzo had laid down a successful squeeze bunt late in a one-sided game against Dibble, who resented that tactic. He fielded the ball, then nailed Dascenzo in his leg with the baseball.

In a minor league season finale, Dibble was called on to perform mop-up duty with his team down by 10 runs. Furious, he aimed several pitches into his own dugout, targeting his manager. After he hurled an opponent's bat up the screen behind home plate, he told the media that he wasn't as crazy as he seemed to be.

Dibble said Giants fans were rude and rowdy, comparing them to people who grew up near a nuclear plant. He once dyed his hair white and styled it to resemble a rock star. When told by his manager he wouldn't pitch again until he got rid of that look, he stomped off to the clubhouse, shaved his head, then demanded the ball.

He also claimed he didn't like to shake hands because he feared that could result in an injury. Plus, he once said he was cutting down on signing autographs in order to watch out for his arm.

Hot-tempered, he could nevertheless be a cool customer. In a high school game, the bases were loaded with two outs and two strikes on the batter in the final inning. Dibble called time-out, strolled to his dugout, casually took a drink of water, returned to the hill and whiffed the batter.

Bill Deane observed, "He was painted as a whack job—had a lot of talent, but didn't have a very high IQ. That was the impression that maybe the media painted of him. When I saw him as a commentator, he seemed like an intelligent, thoughtful guy. Maybe that tells us that sometimes the flakes are something of a media creation."

Denny Neagle (1991–2003)

Neagle called himself a straightforward kind of guy, yet a colorful one. "I guess," he said, "when you're left-handed and a pitcher in the big leagues, you've got to have some sort of goofy side to you. I think I fit that mold pretty much." When told some righties are goofy, Neagle joked, "It's true, but I always say those guys who are goofy and crazy are left-handers dying to get out of a right-hander's body."

Chipper Jones said, "Denny Neagle was a hoot; always kept the clubhouse mood light. He was the prankster, he was the guy who could do a [spot-on] train whistle imitation."

A confessed former class clown who spent quite some time in the principal's office, Neagle also did a great impersonation of Cosmo Kramer and the crazy laugh of Jim Carrey. Neagle's talent may have rubbed off on another Brave pitcher, as Jeff Blauser said Steve Bedrosian had such ability: "Every time a batter would get a fastball that broke his bat, you'd hear Bedrosian doing a chainsaw noise."

Reliever Mark Wohlers said, "Bedrosian and Neagle were all business when they're between the lines." Their humor kept the Braves loose, though, and that's something big leaguers "absolutely better do—it's a long season. We look up to those guys because sometimes it's tough to do and you wish you could do those [funny] things."

Jose Lima (1994–2006)

Only 21 years old when he broke into the majors, Lima was doomed to live a short life—he would be dead just 16 years later. He reportedly had at least six children with six different women, so his motto may have been one lifted from a Humphrey Bogart movie: Live fast, die young, and leave a good-looking corpse. As a baseball "hot dog," he definitely lived life with a carpe diem philosophy.

When Lima had a 1–13 record in early July of 2000, his manager was Larry Dierker, who said that Lima, "is the most animated player on this team not only when he pitches, which is a little disturbing because a lot of times he makes the other team mad, but he doesn't really care. He says, 'If you're mad at me, hit a home run off me.' A lot of them have been doing that lately." Lima went on to serve up 48 home runs, still a National League record and just two shy of the season record set by Bert Blyleven. Dierker continued, "He's a nut—he's always got his hat on sideways and he's just loud. He has a recording contract and he's as full of life and of himself as any player I've ever been around."

His demonstrative habits upset many hitters. He said, "Baseball is a short career, and I'm going to enjoy every single day. Everybody should. If you don't like what I do, take me deep. You can dance around every base if you want, I don't mind. I'm not going to stop being who I am."[5] And he didn't.

Sitting in the dugout, Lima once spied a camera trained on him, so he wiggled his fingers voodoo style at his audience as if doing a "booga booga" incantation for no apparent reason.

Pitcher Doug Henry said, "You watch him from across the field, you hate him and the stuff he does." But as a fellow Astro, Henry found Lima to be something special. "When you see him in the clubhouse, you realize he's just a character having fun. He throws his music on and just starts dancing in the clubhouse the days he pitches—it's how he gets himself all wired up. He's actually a pretty good guy."

Carlos Perez (1995–2000)

Jim Leyritz, a Yankee hero after he launched a memorable shot off Atlanta's ace reliever Mark Wohlers in the 1996 World Series, was no fan of Perez and his flamboyant ways. "Carlos Perez goes a little beyond the norm. It's his style, though, and if he does it, he's got to be ready for people to style against him." Larry Bowa took it further as he sneered and tersely stated, "He's a little goofy."

Former manager Terry Collins said that eccentric players eventually learn not to show off too much. "Even Carlos Perez [learned what's acceptable]. When I was with Houston, we would play the Expos, and when he would pitch all he did was fire up the other team. He got them angry. We had pretty good success against him because our guys wanted to beat him." Back then, somebody such as a veteran leader would take an all-too-colorful guy aside and school him in the baseball facts of life. As Collins put it, "When your teammates start saying, 'Hey, a little of that [clowning] is okay, but . . .'" an ultimatum is implied, and usually clearly understood.

Chipper Jones singled out Perez as the game's most colorful player during a 1997 interview. "He dances around the mound much like his brother Pascual did with the Braves a while back. He makes a lot of people mad, but he puts butts in the seats, and that's what people like nowadays."

But did that make Carlos merely colorful, or was he a full-blown flake? "Oh, he's flaky," said Jones. "Definitely flaky, but I know Carlos on a personal level and he's very colorful, too, happy-go-lucky, and he enjoys playing the game. I don't think he does [his gyrations] to show anybody up, he's just out there to have fun."

Will Clark disagreed. He feels that Perez is, in the worst possible definition of the word, flaky, and he doesn't equate Perez's behavior with good old-fashioned wholesome fun, the kind of fun that eases teams' tension. Furthermore, while Clark was not averse to taking part in club-house humor, on the field he was an intense professional. As such, he said he didn't appreciate on-the-field antics. He believes there is a clearly etched line between keeping loose and Perez-like shenanigans on the diamond. For instance, when asked for his thoughts about Carlos and Pascual, Clark candidly stated, "Oh, I don't care about those guys. I'm not a big fan of those guys."

J. T. Snow apparently felt the same way. In 1999, he victimized Carlos, who had just beat out an infield hit. Predictably, after he ran through the bag and down the line, he celebrated his single by making self-satisfied gestures. That's when Snow let his pitcher know he wanted to keep the baseball in order to try to pull off the hidden ball trick. As soon as the oblivious Perez stepped off the bag, Snow tagged him.

Tony Muser, Kansas City's manager that year, said, "When players do things on the field with antics, they draw attention to themselves. And what Perez did is draw attention to himself, and there is what you call subtle intimidation in this game, or payback. No doubt about it." Meanwhile, another major league skipper, Phil Garner, added, "You just figure, if a guy's out there celebrating who doesn't appear like he's in the game, he's not paying attention to what he's doing on the field, so you take a chance on a guy like that—those are the guys you try to make the hidden ball play work on."

Larry Bowa contributed one last anecdote about Perez: "The big thing I know about him is when he was playing against Philly, he struck Mariano Duncan out. After that, he gestured with his hand." Bowa demonstrated Perez's motion by waving the fingers of his right hand, a la voodoo doctors. "The next time Duncan gets up, he hits a double off the wall, and as Perez is getting the ball back, Duncan made the same hand motion back at him." Take that, showboat.

Mike James (1995–2002)

Right before the turn of the century, Terry Collins was the manager of the Angels, and had a rather peculiar relief pitcher to deal with. "I got a guy, Mike James, who's got a tongue pierced," Collins said, in an era in which such behavior was still startling. Some say James was the first big leaguer with a pierced tongue and a nose ring. "He's a big-time surfer, so he lives on the edge all the time. One thing about him, he has no fear. Those guys are like that, that's the way Mike is—when he comes in a game, he has no fear. He's not intimidated by anything. You look at him on the mound, and he's got the long sideburns, he's got the pierced tongue, and you have to say to yourself, 'He's not afraid to pitch inside, for sure.'" The impression opposing hitters got was self-evident: this guy is loose, so, in turn, you had better stay loose in the batter's box.

Thus, James's unique ways don't bother Collins. In fact, his demeanor and style, Collins said, were "the things that make him good. He's got his own mind. He does what he wants to do.

"You can say to him, 'You're crazy,' and nothing fazes him. That's why I think those kind of [free-spirited] guys can be special. When it comes to crunch time, they're not afraid."

Before James made it to the majors, Von Joshua managed him in Double and Triple A ball. He said, "Mike James was flaky, goofy. He took it to the next level when he went to the majors. We wouldn't allow him to be [in the minors]." Unfettered in the majors, James may have been a goofball, but he did his job with a lifetime ERA of 3.67.

In 1998, James sported pierced ears adorned with earrings, additional piercings, and a bleached head of platinum-blonde hair. When he transacted business in his bank, it took the tellers quite some time before they quit looking at him as if he was about to rob them.

Tim Hudson (1999–2015)

If Hudson had done only one prank in his career, he'd still qualify as a colorful character. Fellow pitcher Chris Reitsma said, "He was a trip. He was hiding in Eddie Perez's closet on the road one time and when Eddie came in, Hudson jumped out of the closet and scared him." Chipper Jones added more details: "He hid with the Scream mask on, and Eddie is scared of anything—any quick movements, a little spider, whatever—he's scared of anything, so he flipped it."

Former Brave Jeff Francoeur said Hudson, a man he calls one of the two funniest guys he ever played with, and John Smoltz "got me good. In DC one time in 2006 we got there the second week of the season and it was really cold. We went to Morton's Steakhouse and after that there was a huge pond with a fountain, not far from the Capitol. They were going to give $3,000 to anybody who would jump in the pond. Well, you know, I was in my second year, so I was like, 'Heck, yeah,' so I jumped in. I swam around and they gave me $3,000.

"Now, two days later two cops show up at the locker room and told me they found out a Braves group did it. They sat by my locker and told me I was going to pay a fine or they were going to put me in handcuffs." Ticked off and suspecting something was up, Francoeur glanced around the locker room but nobody said anything. "Finally, after about 20 minutes they almost turned me around and put me in handcuffs. I looked over and saw that it was Huddy and Smoltzy who had played this huge prank on me."

Jonathan Papelbon (2005–2016)

Papelbon's jig was much more famous and elaborate than Fernando Rodney's. After nailing down the 2007 American League Championship Series, as promised, he uninhibitedly did a wild Riverdance-like dance, prancing about with hands on hips, which was captured on national television.

When Francoeur heard the name Papelbon, he chuckled, "He's by far the most colorful and the funniest person you have mentioned. By far. He really was a character. He should have been on the '86 Mets, put it that way." That team, of course, was infamous for their wild ways.

"When I was with Philly with the man, he would get a save and he'd come in and he'd put on a Ric Flair robe. He would do his interviews by his locker sometimes with the robe and with that hair sticking up. He beat to his own drum, I'll give him that. You remember when he kind of tugged [his privates] at the fans in Philly. They booed him every time he came in to pitch in 2015, and all he did was tip his hat up and wave to the crowd.

"And I'll never forget in 2016 when he was with Washington and I was with the Braves. That off-season I saw him in Florida and he told me, 'You were one of my favorite teammates. Next year, the first time I face you, I'm going to pump heaters right down the middle to you, your whole first at bat.' So we're at home opening day of the season and I'm facing Papelbon in the tenth of a tie ball game. So I got a chance to hit a walk-off home run, and this guy literally pumped me four fastballs at probably 92 [mph], right down the middle. I popped up to center field. In the back of my mind I thought, 'Is he going to mess with me?' But he's the only guy I ever faced that was a man of his word and said, 'Here you go. I'm giving you fastballs right down the middle,' especially in a tie ball game in the tenth inning. It's one of the only at bats I ever regret because if I had got ready I could have hit a walk-off homer on opening day."

QUICK-PITCH ITEMS FOR POSITION PLAYERS

Charlie Grimm (1916–1936; managed 1932–1960)

A great quickie from Grimm: he once perused a scouting report critiquing a minor league pitcher who had thrown a perfect game. Only one opposing batter hit a ball out of the infield, and that one went foul. Grimm commented on the prospect, "Forget the pitcher— send [me] the guy who hit the foul."

Known as Jolly Cholly, Grimm sometimes strummed his banjo and sang for fans prior to games. Other times when he was in the on-deck circle, he would rub two bats together as if he were sharpening knives. He began one season as the Cubs manager, then switched jobs with the team's radio announcer, Lou Boudreau.

Fresco Thompson (1925–1934; also a longtime baseball executive)

Thompson was the quarterback on the same freshman team at Columbia University as halfback Lou Gehrig. Thompson was a second baseman before gaining much more recognition with Brooklyn's scouting and player development. His Dodgers won eight pennants and four World Series from 1952 to 1966, tops in the majors aside from the Yankees. He helped develop five Rookies of the Year, best in baseball, and his scouts discovered Sandy Koufax, Don Drysdale, and Don Sutton. Thompson evaluated a minor league prospect who was of French Canadian roots by saying he couldn't hit a lick because, "He's thinking in French and they're pitching to him in English."

Once in the Brooklyn Dodgers locker room, Babe Herman, a horrible defensive outfielder, kidded his teammate Thompson by lamenting, "It's a helluva note to dress with a .250 hitter." Thompson shot back, "How do you think I feel dressing with a .250 fielder."

His take on a terrible Phillies team was, "On a clear day they could see seventh place." He deprecated a fellow Dodger, saying, "We don't have a guy who can hit a sacrifice fly far enough to score Jesse Owens from third base." On another occasion he tried to sign a player his Dodgers coveted, but who was also being pursued by the NFL. He asked the player, "What do you want, a bonus or a limp?"

Carl Erskine said, "Fresco was more clever than he was funny. For instance, he turned in a scouting report one time on a player. His report said this guy is a good lowball hitter and he has good power, but he's slower than he looks."

Thompson gave advice to a player who griped that he was swinging just a tad under the baseball, saying he should put insoles in his cleats to lift himself up a bit.

Jackie Price (1946)

Including shortstop and pinch hitter Price here is a bit of a stretch because he played just one season, 1946, and went to the plate a mere 14 times, collecting three major league singles in his career. However, the man Bill Veeck called the greatest entertainer in the game stuck around until 1959 and appeared in more big league parks than many of the younger players who saw him perform. That's because Price was a clown in a line of baseball entertainers that included Al Schacht and Max Patkin.

Price was famous for hanging by his ankles from a bar about 12 feet off the ground for more than 15 minutes, spraying baseballs pitched to him all over the field, sometimes for distances of 150+ feet—and he could do that while batting either lefty or righty. He could hit two baseballs with one swing and have one ball travel into fair territory and the other one into foul grounds.

He amused crowds with his ability to throw three baseballs at the same time and with uncanny accuracy, cleanly firing them to three different players. One report stated he could make all three baseballs curve and that he could also throw two balls, with one going straight and the other curving. He simultaneously fired three baseballs to three different catchers for strikes. He threw two balls with one motion, with one traveling to a pitcher standing on the mound and the other one sailing all the way to a player at second base. He also caught balls in his shirt or pants while he stood on his head.

Erskine said, "In my era they used to stage some entertainment. An infielder from Cleveland, Jackie Price, used to do a pre-game show, clever. He had a bazooka and he'd shoot [baseballs out of] it from back of home plate. The ball would look like a pea. I mean, it was up there, way high. None of the outfielders would ever even attempt to catch it, but Price would be in a Jeep down the right-field line, and he'd give the signal to shoot and he would tool around the outfield and eventually catch the ball one-handed in the Jeep. All of that entertaining beforehand was a big part of baseball. Now that's all disappeared." Price even caught baseballs dropped from blimps high overhead.

Like Drabowsky, Price had an affinity for snakes. He was kicked off a train, though, when he let two of his 20 snakes loose, causing a panic.

Johnny O'Brien (1953–1959)

O'Brien is colorful in that he is a great storyteller. He began by relating a tale of Ted Williams. O'Brien said one day he was talking baseball with Williams in the outfield before the start of a spring training game. "I'll tell you a story. You know, Williams didn't like the media, but he sure liked players, and he would spend all kinds of time with you.

"He would really punish the ball. I mean you would get to feel sorry for the ball. He's got a bat and he's moving his hips and showing me [a hitting tip]. And these two guys show up and they start taking pictures. Williams says, 'Watch this.' He turns to them and says, 'What the [fudge, only he didn't say fudge] are you guys doing?' They said they were taking pictures. He said, 'John and I are having a private conversation. Get your ass outta here.' So they left and Williams looked at me and said, 'Did you see what I just did?' I said that I sure did. He said, 'You can only do that when you're hitting .340.'"

O'Brien went on with a Gene Freese story. "Someone got a base hit to win a ball game in extra innings. Gene was on first base but he failed to go down and touch second base. Richie Ashburn noticed it, got the ball in, they touched second base for a force out and the game went on and the Phillies won. [Pirate manager Fred] Haney got all over Freese. About a month later, the same situation existed and Freese went down to second base and not only tagged the base, he picked it out of the ground and brought it back and gave it to Haney. He said, 'I got it this time, didn't I?'"

O'Brien, who had a twin brother, Eddie, wasn't through. "Let me tell you another story. We got quite a bit of acclaim for playing college basketball. Now, on my first trip to the plate in the majors, Carl Erskine's pitching for the Dodgers. I go by Ralph Kiner and he says, 'Sneaky fastball.' I go by George Metkovich and he says, 'Best curveball in the league.' I go by Eddie Pellagrini and he says, 'Watch out for the change-up.' Christ, I don't want to get out of the dugout at this time.

"So I grab a bat and go up to the plate and Augie Donatelli's the umpire. I look down at third base and get the take sign. Erskine winds up and throws the first pitch—it's a dinky little curveball that comes over the plate. I stepped out and said, 'That's the best curveball in this league?' Then he threw the next one and the bottom dropped out of it and my mouth fell open. Donatelli said, 'That's his good curveball. Strike two.'

"I fouled off a pitch, then he threw that great curveball again and I swung and took half of the air out of the park. I stepped out and I'm crossing the plate and Roy Campanella says, 'Johnny, those basketballs don't curve, do they?'"

Jackie Brandt (1956–1967)

Author Marty Appel said he believes "the first time the word flake was used was with Brandt." They said things just seemed to "flake off his mind and disappear." It didn't faze Brandt—he was deserving of the title. He once pestered Orioles teammates into making a taxi trip of about an hour outside of New York City to get some ice cream. At the time, he said one could only buy a few basic flavors in the city's shops, but Brandt knew of a parlor that was like Baskin Robbins. It featured so many tantalizing flavors, it was, he said, worth the long trip. However, when they arrived there, the selections overwhelmed him and he wound up ordering a vanilla cone.

Brandt was once involved in a multi-player trade that included a flake for a flake when he was dealt for Billy Loes in 1959. Brandt sometimes slid into each base after homering, and he even turned a backflip trying to evade a tag when caught in a rundown.

Some of his Baltimore teammates called him Moon Man. He once alibied that he lost a fly ball in the jet stream. At a party he announced he was going to take his alligator shoes for a swim, so he walked into a swimming pool, emerged, then acted as if everything was normal. He came up with the line, "This year I'm going to play with harder nonchalance." Once, when told he had just said something bizarre, he explained, "My lips must have been sunburned."[6]

Brandt later became an electrician, which prompted people to joke that a house that he wired was as flaky as he was, that when someone rang the doorbell, the toilets inside flushed and the garage door opened as if by magic.

Whitey Herzog (1956–1963; managed 1973–1990)

Herzog's teams won three pennants and the 1982 World Series. Recognized as a stupendous manager, Herzog freely admitted his playing ability had not been anywhere nearly as good as his managerial machinations. He put it this way: "Baseball has been good to me since I quit trying to play it."[7]

When he was managing the Cardinals, he was going through contract negotiations with team owner August Busch, then 85 years old. Busch valued Herzog and wanted so desperately to keep him, he offered him a lifetime contract. Herzog, no dummy, asked, "Whose lifetime, yours or mine?"

Herzog managed the Rangers in 1973 and watched what went on when the team held a Pantyhose Night. Team owner Bob Short had purchased 75,000 pairs of panty hose and wound up having to get rid of them by giving them away at a ton of home games. The giveaway promotion didn't help at the gates, and it certainly didn't help Short turn a profit, because he paid $3.75 per pair of stockings and women who paid as little as $1.25 for a bleacher seat were given a free pair. Herzog said, "Lots of women came in one gate, got their panty hose, and went right out another gate." He added with a grin, "They were gone before we played the national anthem."[8]

When asked if he thought trading pitchers Chuck Finley and Jim Abbott made sense, he replied, "I might trade them if I was offered Sandy Koufax and Babe Ruth, but they're dead. Well, Sandy isn't dead, but his arm is." And when he was told his Cardinals had poor team chemistry, he responded, "Yeah and we're missing a little geography and arithmetic around here, too."

Norm Cash (1959–1974)

At his small college, halfback Cash set a record with his 1,255 yards rushing, and he was drafted by the Chicago Bears in the 13th round. Cash was the first man to win the Comeback Player of the Year Award twice. He also won the 1961 American League batting crown when he hit a lusty

.361. The following season he plummeted to .243, a 118-point deficit, the largest one-year plunge by a reigning batting king, and he would never again hit higher than .283. Take away his '61 season and his lifetime batting average works out to .264, not his actual .271. He said, "The only mistake I made in my whole baseball career was hitting .361 that one year, because ever since then people have expected me to keep on doing it."

Another mistake he made was using corked bats, ones he had operated on in a wood shop he had in his house. He confessed later that he had used the illegal bat in 1961 (and in subsequent seasons) when he starched a career high 41 of his 377 lifetime round-trippers. He would go on to quip about his baseball sin, "I owe my success to expansion pitching, a short right field fence and my hollow bats."

In Baltimore, a pre-game show featured a drum-and-bugle group. When they marched by the Detroit dugout, Cash joined them, high-stepping all the way while brandishing a bat as a makeshift baton. When he went after a pop-up, he would yell, "I got it," hesitate, then add, "I hope."

Long before Willie Stargell jokingly tried to call a time-out when he was about to be tagged several feet shy of second base on an ill-fated stolen base attempt, Cash asked for a time-out when trapped in a run-down. Once, he was on second base when rain caused a stoppage of play. When the game was about to resume, Cash took a berth on third, but an umpire was on to him. Cash joked he had stolen third during the rain delay.

Detroit signed Ron LeFlore out of prison, where he had served time for armed robbery. Several observers were impressed by LeFlore's flaming speed, but Cash commented wryly, "He can't be too fast, the cops caught him."[9]

Cash was not immune from striking out, doing so 1,091 times over his 6,705 big league at bats. He observed, "Prorated at 500 at bats a year, that means for two years out of the fourteen I played, I never even touched the ball."

Speaking of futility, baseball historian Morris Eckhouse recalled Nolan Ryan pitching his second no-hitter of the 1973 season against Cash's Tigers. "He was basically unhittable, and Cash went up there to hit with a [table leg]. I think Cash was one of the last players to not wear a batting helmet." Of course, against a Ryan, being helmetless would be as perilous as playing long toss with a vial of nitroglycerin. Cash had struck out twice in his first three at bats. With two outs in the ninth inning, Cash trudged to the plate lugging the table leg instead of a bat—not exactly a corked bat, but an illegal item nevertheless. Umpire Ron Luciano told him he could not use the table leg. Cash shot back, "Why not? I won't hit him anyway." He later stated, "I had as much chance with that as with a bat." He was correct. He popped up to end the game.

Dick Allen (1963–1977)

Allen, out of Wampum, Pennsylvania, was a formidable slugger. He also played at least one game at six different positions. Author Rich Westcott said, "One time he hit a home run over the roof and the sign on top of the roof at Connie Mack Stadium." Two men tried to locate where the ball landed when they saw a little boy playing with a baseball. He said the ball had soared over the roof of these houses. "So it went over a little street behind the park and over the rooftops of a row of houses. They figured it went 529 feet, one of the longest hits in Philadelphia."

During games Allen, somewhat like lyrics from the old song, "Love Letters in the Sand," would carve messages in the dirt by first base with his spikes. He wrote "BOO" to show his displeasure with the Philly fans jeering him. When instructed to cease writing messages, he carved "NO" in the dirt. Allen, a Rookie of the Year who also won an MVP award, was, in effect, his own fan message board, rather like a scoreboard Fan-O-Gram. Resenting authority figures, he "printed" the word "MOM" to indicate only his mother could tell him how to behave.

Westcott remembered a funny Allen line: "When the Phillies went into Veterans Stadium, which had Astroturf, he said, 'If a horse can't eat it, I don't want to play on it.'"

When he was with the Cardinals, Allen was asked what position he'd most like to play. He stated, "I'll play first, third, left. I'll play any-where—except Philadelphia." Ironically, he later did return to the Phillies. When his Philadelphia manager, Gene Mauch, was asked if Allen had trouble with the high fastball, he supposedly said, "No, the fast high-ball."

Alex Johnson (1964–1976)

Dan Schlossberg said Johnson was "a colorful and controversial guy who won a batting crown with the Angels. He had some bad moments." Most people found him boorish, and he famously waged a running war with the media.

Steve Foucault, a teammate of Johnson, said that he was one of the most colorful characters he ever saw. "He would hardly say boo to anybody. He was kind of within his own world." The brother of NFL two-time 1,000-yard runner Ron Johnson, Alex was, according to Foucault, "a great teammate. He was an outstanding player—the only thing he couldn't do was throw, but he could hit, he could run, he could drive runs in, he hit home runs. He just couldn't throw and everybody knew that—they took advantage of him when he was playing left field, but other than that he was an awesome teammate.

"He just didn't say much to anybody, even to his teammates he didn't say a lot. That was just his personality. He kept to himself and he'd always read his electronics books in his locker and he'd have shirts in front of him so you couldn't see him. It seemed like he never changed pages, but I'm sure he did." Foucault's opinion of Johnson was not shared by the majority of his teammates, who found him combative.

Anticipating many kangaroo court fines, he began one season by giving a $500 check to the court's tribunal. He said when that ran out they should let him know. If it didn't run out, they could keep the change.

When Johnson got off to a hot start one year, a writer interviewed him. "Alex, you hit only two homers all last year, and now you already have seven. What's the difference?" He answered concisely, "Five,"[10] qualifying him as a one-hit wonder.

Rick Dempsey (1969–1992)

Dempsey, who lasted 24 grueling seasons behind the plate spanning four decades (something only three catchers ever did), caught 10 different 20-game winners. He could clown around, but he was also capable of being very thoughtful. Fred Claire said, "When the '88 World Series ended, I went into the Dodgers clubhouse. Dempsey had caught the final pitch and put it in his pocket. When I went up to Dempsey, we hugged, and he reached in his back pocket for the final ball, and said, 'Fred, this belongs to you.' It was a wonderful gesture." Claire said that Mickey Hatcher and Dempsey had "great, outgoing personalities, but Dempsey was as competitive and as serious as anybody who ever played the game. Both he and Hatcher were instrumental [in our success]."

Mike Gibbons said, "One of the most beloved Orioles, Dempsey, is famous for being named MVP of the '83 World Series, but also for his rain-delay entertainment, when he would mimic Babe Ruth's 'Called Shot' at bat, taking and swinging at pretend pitches from a pretend Charlie Root pitcher, then pointing, and then clobbering the final pitch far into the rainy night. He then rounded the tarp-covered base paths, pointing and gesturing, just like Ruth had done in 1932, before scrambling home. The crowd, as they say, went crazy with delight."

At times Dempsey, who borrowed the pantomime idea from Sparky Lyle, stuffed his jersey to give the appearance of a Ruthian pot belly. Other times he did his act pretending to be Robin Yount, and he sometimes wore underpants on the outside of his uniform to make fun of teammate Jim Palmer, who endorsed underwear.

Claire recounted Dempsey's dramatic finale to his act. "With the Orioles he did that belly slide across home plate." His floppy headfirst slide created a miniature tsunami on the soggy tarp. The son of a vaudevillian father and a mother who acted on Broadway, Dempsey was a natural performer.

Former pitcher Alan Mills said Dempsey was certainly entertaining when he and Glenn Davis "put a hamster in a player's jockstrap between his cup and supporter as he was putting it on. At first he didn't even know it was in there, for 15 minutes before stretching pre-game. When he found out, he kinda freaked out."

A more elaborate prank came when Dempsey hid in a closet near the room where three Orioles teammates were playing poker. Dempsey, still in hiding, then bellowed an ominous demand for the men to leave their money on the table and walk away. He threatened to kill them if they disobeyed. Tippy Martinez dashed to the kitchen and grabbed a knife. "Now get out," Martinez shouted to the still unseen thief. "I have a knife." Dempsey one-upped him, yelling, "I've got a gun." "OK. Take the money," said Martinez meekly.

John Lowenstein (1970–1985)

Lowenstein was an unusual character who, by an uncanny coincidence, hit exactly .242 in 1974, 1975, and 1977, but this oddity didn't impress him—not much did. In fact, he started his own Lowenstein Apathy Club, saying a fan automatically became a member of the group if they showed absolutely no interest in him. Often the cavernous park Lowenstein played his home games in for the Indians had the vast majority of its 78,000 seats empty. He claimed each empty seat represented one of his apathetic, as opposed to athletic, supporters.

Most fans went along with his joke, and sent letters vowing not to care about his career. There was even facetious talk of holding a special day for him—when his Indians were on the road. Asked what type of banner he'd like his fans to display to show their support for him, his choice was blank ones. He honored fans' requests for autographs by apologizing, saying he had left his autograph back in the clubhouse. And when a fan letter came with a request for a photo of Lowenstein, he'd send back a picture of an Indian, but it wouldn't be him.

He joked about things such as bang bang plays, contending, "They should move first base back a step to eliminate all the close plays." He also said, "If you act like you know what you're doing, you can do anything you want—except maybe perform neural surgery."

Mike Gibbons recalled, "He was also a character. In his seven years in Baltimore from 1979 to 1985, he helped the Orioles to a remarkable .580 winning percentage, with two World Series appearances and one world title in 1983. On June 19, 1980, with the Orioles on their way to a 100 victory, second-place finish, Lowenstein was hit by an outfield throw while racing for second. It knocked him unconscious. With an almost packed Memorial Stadium frozen with fear looking on, Lowenstein was placed on a stretcher and carried from the field by his teammates. As the stretcher moved near the Orioles dugout, John rose up, thrusting his arms in a 'V' for victory expression, and the crowd went crazy."

Lowenstein taught his parrot to say naughty things, and he liked to go up to strangers in airports, peek at their luggage name tags to learn their names, then strike up conversations as if he knew them, saying things like, "How's your family?" At times his victims fell for it, and they would engage in long talks with him.

Dave Engle (1981–1989)

John Massarelli, who once managed in the Frontier League, remembers Engle's ways. "He was my hitting coach for a couple of years in Triple-A in Tucson. He was from San Diego, West Coast. I called him a West Coast flake. He would do goofy stuff just to keep the guys loose. He was kind of [manager] Bob Skinner's right-hand man—we used to call him Skinner's Funny Man and the Dean and Jerry Show. He'd come out, showing up in the park in an Elvis wig and glasses, a pink leotard suit one day."

One day at an airport, Engle and Mickey Hatcher dressed up like construction workers. They asked a man to help out by holding an end of a string against a wall. Then they walked around a corner and asked another man to please hold the other end. At that point, they vanished to a location where they could observe the men.

During an interview conducted in 2000, Brad Ausmus said one of the best stories he heard was "when Dave Engle was a catcher in Minnesota and he was being harassed by a rookie pitcher whose name escapes me right now. This pitcher would keep throwing firecrackers in the bathroom while Engle was in the stall, so to get back at him one day he put Ex-Lax in his coffee while the guy was in the bullpen, just before he had to come in. Late in the game the Ex-Lax started working, then Dave went in and put superglue on the toilet rim just as he heard the pitcher was running in. He runs in, pulls his pants down, sits down on the toilet, and now he's superglued to the toilet. To this day, Dave still doesn't know how he got off."

Mel Hall (1981–1996)

Sportswriter Ralph Wimbish said, "Hall was an interesting character. He tried to pull everything down the right-field line. I've never seen anybody with a more deliberate batting style. If anybody deserved to be shifted on, it was Mel Hall, and this was before everybody did the shift." The short porch at Yankee Stadium was his target.

Jim Lefebvre was miffed at Hall, who, like Jeffrey Leonard, theatrically cruised around the bases after homering. Hall sauntered around the bases as if on a leisurely tour. His home run trot was timed once at 33 laborious seconds. It featured three batting gloves tucked loosely into his two back pockets. The gloves bobbed up and down as he ran. He explained that was his way of tauntingly waving goodbye to his opponents.

Lefebvre was livid about that. "That [kind of posturing] upset a lot of people. Everybody said, 'What's that all about?' He was trying to make a statement, but this game is too big for an individual to go out there and isolate himself like that. He was trying to bring attention to himself."

Hall was fined for owning two unusual pets—mountain lions—but laughed it off, saying he was considering getting a grizzly bear.

Hall's story has an ironic and tragic ending. After being traded to the Yankees, he was asked if he ever thought he would wind up wearing pinstripes. He joked, "Yeah. In prison."[11] Well, after being found guilty of aggravated sexual assault of a young girl in 2009, that prophecy came true; he was sentenced to 45 years in prison.

Glenn Wilson (1982–1993)

Wilson, a veteran of five teams, came to the plate with two men out in the bottom half of the ninth inning, faced with the possibility of coming through with a game-winning hit. Instead, he whiffed to end the game. He sadly said, "It's what you dream of right there . . . either you're Billy the Kid or Billy the Goat."

Steve Blass said Wilson "used to talk about Nolan Ryan. He said if you were on deck when Nolan gave up a home run, you would pretend you were a dog and roll over and show your belly. You were subservient so he wouldn't hit you with the next pitch."

Wilson owned a gas station which employed two auto repairmen. One day as he took batting practice, someone told him they noticed he had a flaw, that he had to improve his mechanics. Wilson replied, "I can't afford it. I just gave them a raise."

5

THE ROYAL JESTERS

Honorary Mentions

The men discussed in this chapter are not among the legends of colorful character. Furthermore, by and large, they didn't earn a spot in baseball's register of humor as often as the men covered previously. Nevertheless, like some recording artists who produced only one song—but a memorable one—these men did, through one (or a few) incidents/quotes, ensure a place in baseball lore. They are listed chronologically with no regard to positions played.

FLINT RHEM (1924–1936)

Rhem topped his league in wins in 1926 with 20, but his biggest flake event came in 1930. He was slated to start a key game, but was a no-show. A few days later he showed up and explained his disappearing act, claiming he had been kidnapped in New York City by several armed gamblers and then, get this, whisked away to New Jersey, where he was forced to swallow whiskey all day long. Many years later he changed his story, saying he missed the game because he must have gotten hold of some bad meat. Of course the truth was he had gone on a bender—no coercion was ever needed to make him drink.

CHAPTER 5

Baseball clown Nick Altrock began joking that he planned on strolling around town, hoping to be mistaken for Rhem and forced to drink free whiskey.

JOE MEDWICK (1932–1948)

Medwick's greatest witty observation came after a 1934 World Series contest, where he had streaked into third with a triple, sliding into Marv Owen who firmly put his foot into Medwick's leg. In turn, Medwick kicked Owen in the stomach. When order was restored, Medwick scored, then later trotted out to his left-field position where he was pelted with grapefruit, oranges, apples, assorted vegetables, and eggs by enraged Tiger fans. Medwick, who was removed from the game for his own protection, later observed, "I knew why they threw all that garbage at me. What I could never figure out is why they brought it to the park in the first place."

KIRBY HIGBE (1937–1950)

Higbe had a strong fear of flying. On one flight, Brooklyn teammate Pee Wee Reese tried to console him, saying there was no need to fret because when a person's number is up, it doesn't matter if you're in the air or on the ground. Higbe refused to be placated: "Suppose I'm up here with a pilot and my number isn't up, but his is."

One day a letter from a female admirer arrived at Higbe's house. His wife opened it, read it, then demanded to know what it was all about. Higbe verbally fumbled, then said that it must have been meant for another Kirby Higbe.

He said he knew of a third baseman with an arm so weak he had to make his throws to first by way of the pitcher as his relay man.

LOU NOVIKOFF (1941–1946)

Nicknamed the Mad Russian, long before Al Hrabosky acquired a similar nickname, Novikoff once stole third base when the bases were already loaded. He later explained, "I had such a good jump on the pitcher, I couldn't resist."

CURLY WILLIAMS (1945–1951)

Robert Williams, a veteran of the Negro Leagues, said of Curly, "He was a shortstop who could really hit the ball. When he'd hit a line drive, he'd walk to first base, and sometimes he'd get thrown out from the outfield. Then he'd just laugh. If he made an error, he'd just say, 'Boot,' and laugh. Our owner would curse him out, but he didn't care about anything." In a 1999 interview, Williams said, "I still see him, and he's still crazy."

RYNE DUREN (1954–1965)

Duren was one of the hardest throwing and wildest throwing pitchers ever. To make matters worse, he had a serious drinking problem. Once when Jimmy Piersall was scrutinizing Duren's warmup pitches from the on-deck circle, Duren took exception and fired the ball at him, knocking Piersall on his can.

Former big league catcher Bob Oldis was a teammate of Duren. "We played together in Denver in '57 and he could throw hard. Hitters didn't want to come up and hit against him because Duren changed the color of his glasses when the sun set. They were tinted and thick—he couldn't see, that's why they were so thick. It would be no fun to be the hitter against a guy who could throw as hard as Ryne Duren, a guy who can't see. I think he's the only guy I ever played baseball with that took a shower with glasses on."

Yogi Berra once said Duren had several pairs of glasses, but he didn't appear to see well with any of them. Duren helped his legend grow by intentionally letting some of his warmup pitches fly, often sailing over his catcher's head to the backstop. Casey Stengel remarked, "I would not admire hitting against Duren because if he ever hit you in the head, you might be in the past tense."[1]

LEW KRAUSSE (1961–1974)

Krausse loved to play around with fire extinguishers, the same way a child loves to wield a squirt gun. However, Krausse also liked to shoot a real pistol out of his bedroom window nightly, firing off a two-shot salvo at bedtime. Usually he did that from his 12th-floor room, but one night he was moved to a new room on the third floor and, at about 2:00 a.m., he capped off the night with his ritual shooting. The following morning police came to his hotel questioning him about shots which had been fired into—not over—a building across the way.

Krausse was let off with a warning, but his team owner Charlie Finley had a private eye follow him through the end of the season. That's when Finley called Krausse into his office and told him that the detective observed him and his friend Catfish Hunter going out on the town, but doing nothing untoward. But, he added, the detective did say that he was sad his assignment was through because he was having a ball.

GAYLORD PERRY (1962–1983)

Big league coach Mike Cubbage said, "When the Texas Rangers traded for Perry, Jim Fregosi walked up to Gaylord to greet him. He handed Gaylord a small tube of Vaseline and asked him, 'What's this?' Gaylord looked at him for a moment then said, 'That? That's a two-hit shutout.'"

Actually, said Cubbage, "Gaylord was more of a K-Y Jelly guy." Perry said playfully, "I'd always have that in at least two places, in case the umpires would ask me to wipe off one. I never wanted to be caught out there without anything." He added ironically, "It wouldn't be professional."

DICK RADATZ (1962–1969)

Call him "the Monster." That's precisely what Mickey Mantle called him one day, and the moniker stuck. Radatz weighed 230 pounds, stood 6 feet, 6 inches, and was about as strong as Godzilla. In 1964, he won 16 to set an American League record for bullpen wins, up one win from 1963.

When he pitched for the Montreal Expos in 1969, he got involved in a donnybrook after throwing a brushback pitch. In the skirmish Radatz came across the 5-feet, 5-inch Freddie Patek, who gave away about 80 pounds to Radatz. Peering down at the diminutive infielder with disdain, Radatz growled, "I'll take you and a player to be named later."

A man who had a perverted craving that could only be satisfied by having someone pelt him on his derriere sought out a professional pitcher to perform this task, offering $100. Radatz accepted. The man stripped, stood against a wall, and had Radatz heave his supply of several crates of oranges at his buttocks. Hard. Imagine this: What if Radatz had run out of oranges and suggested an alternative to the man—"How about if we use grapefruit now?"—would the man have said in disgust, "Grapefruit?! Are you sick?!"

Radatz wanted revenge on Bert Campaneris, who had bunted for a hit when his team was winning handily. So he called his iron-handed first baseman, Dick Stuart, over and said he was going to blister a pick-off throw his way and he wanted to hit Campaneris with it. He later joked that after he told Stuart not to catch the throw, he was thinking, "Not that he would catch it anyway."

KEN HARRELSON (1963–1971)

The Hawk insisted on having that nickname on his jersey instead of his surname. A nonconformist playing in a conservative era, he wore his hair long, claiming that gave him Samson-like power, and he favored the "mod" fashion of his era, wearing Nehru jackets and sporting gold medallion necklaces.

Harrelson has taken a ride on Charlie Finley's mascot mule, and he's dressed up as McDonald's Hamburglar. He's believed to be the first player to don batting gloves in a regular season contest, supposedly wearing them after playing 36 blister-inducing holes of golf one game day.

Author David Nathan said of Harrelson's on-air persona, "He wasn't my favorite, but Hawk Harrelson was colorful." He coined so many sayings, such as, "Put it on the board. YES," for home runs. After an opponent struck out, he gloated, either saying, "He gone," or telling the batter to "grab some bench," which basically meant, "Sit down, ya bum."

He commuted to work via helicopter when he was with the Indians. The pilot picked him up from the rooftop of an apartment building and dropped him off in Cleveland Municipal Stadium's center field before home games.

LUIS TIANT (1964–1982)

Tiant, who smoked cigars while showering, once served up a pitch that was blasted deep to dead center. He shouted, "Go foul! Go foul!" He loved to tease Tommy Harper. While flushing the toilet in the clubhouse, he would speak loud enough for teammates to hear him say, "Bye Tommy," as the water and waste swirled away.

CHICO SALMON (1964–1972)

This is a man (manchild?) who slept with the lights on in his hotel rooms, saying he was afraid of ghosts. After being picked off first base, Salmon reportedly used his phobia as an excuse. He claimed his attention was diverted from the action on the field due to a ghost sighting. He placed a wad of gum over his hotel room keyholes and towels under doors to prevent spirits from getting in.

The rap on Salmon was his bad hands. A Baltimore teammate joked that if his hands got any worse, they'd have to be amputated. When Salmon was asked what his best position was, he said at bat.

As a utility player, the Panama-born Salmon seldom saw action. Former Baltimore teammate Merv Rettenmund said, "He was a smart player. He was there the whole year [1972] and only got a few at bats [16]. Every year our team was loaded, so every year they would only make about one change in the roster and that would be the utility man—Chico's job." Yet Salmon managed to stick with the Orioles four seasons, hitting as low as .179 and .063 but manning five positions.

DARREL CHANEY (1969–1979)

Chaney finished his career with Atlanta where he was asked the best way to keep the Braves on their toes. He responded, "Raise the urinals." Rettenmund said, "He was clever, a very smart man."

MICKEY RIVERS (1970–1984)

Author David Nathan said of Rivers, "He was not the brightest guy in the world. He said, 'Pitching is 80 percent of the game, and the other half is hitting and fielding,' and 'When you get out to center field, the first thing you do is stick your finger up to check the wind chill.' And, 'We'll do all right if we can capitalize on our mistakes.'" He also said, "My goals are to hit .300, score 100 runs, and stay injury-prone." A walking thesaurus he was not.

TERRY FORSTER (1971–1986)

Author Dan Schlossberg noted that Forster is the answer to a tricky trivia question: "What man who played in at least 500 games has the highest batting average in baseball history? The answer is Forster because he was a relief pitcher who had a .397 batting average. He was often used as a pinch hitter by the White Sox, even for position players. One year he went 10-for-19. And, don't forget, David Letterman called him a fat tub of goo on national television." Forster's reaction was, "I'd probably sue him if it wasn't a fact." He also joked that when he started cooking at home, his dog stopped begging for food at the table.

Forster once obtained Davey Lopes's credit card number, ordered $400 in porno magazines, and had them delivered to Lopes at Dodger Stadium, causing him repeated humiliation.

ROSS GRIMSLEY (1971–1982)

When he was pitching well, Grimsley wouldn't wash, earning his nickname, "Skuz." Fans mailed him pictures of wolfmen and bearded ladies and they'd write on the photos, "Grimsley's brother and sister."

He said he met the girl he married by running her car off the road, the only way he could conceive to make her acquaintance.

DON STANHOUSE (1972–1982)

Nicknamed "Stan the Man Unusual" (a pun on the nickname "Stan the Man" for Hall of Famer Stan Musial), Stanhouse kept some stuffed animals in his locker. Not wanting to celebrate or drink alone, after victories he poured beer into their mouths. He drove a black Cadillac, and once drove along in a funeral procession just for fun.

GEORGE BRETT (1973–1993)

The man who threatened to hit .400 in 1980, when he wound up at .390, Brett said, "If a tie is like kissing your sister, then losing is like kissing your grandmother with her teeth out."

Brett underwent minor surgery for a hemorrhoid issue after Game 2 of the 1980 World Series. He homered the next game and joked, "My problems are behind me."

BOB LACEY (1977–1984)

Yet another lefty hurler, Lacey was a teammate of Mike Hargrove, who said, "Bullet Bob was a little off-center at times. One time he was trying to lose weight so he wore one of those rubber suits, rolled the windows up in his car, and turned the heater on high as he drove back and forth to the ballpark. That was his idea of a sauna. They called him 'Spacey' Lacey."

LARRY BOWA (1970–1985)

Bowa came up with one classic line. He and his rival, Dave Concepcion, were two of the slickest fielding shortstops in the game. A story has it Bowa ran into Concepcion and asked him if his first name was Elmer. A perplexed Concepcion said, "Why do you ask that? You know my name is Dave." Bowa teased, "Every time I look at the box score I see E Concepcion."

JEFFREY LEONARD (1977–1990)

Traditionalists were not enamored of Leonard's stylings after homering. He ran the bases with his left arm virtually immobile, dangling it dramatically and limply alongside his thigh. Ken Griffey Sr. said, "He called it his 'one flap down' style." As he rounded each base he also made a slight dip of his left shoulder.

Sportswriter Larry Stone said, "One of the all-time great nicknames is Penitentiary Face, which is what Mike Krukow called Leonard." Leonard objected to that, so some began calling him Correctional Institute Face. Leonard, by the way, attended the same Philadelphia high school, Overbrook, as Wilt Chamberlain.

SAMMY STEWART (1978–1987)

Stewart's best prank was played on Baltimore teammate Tippy Martinez. Knowing he wasn't due back in his room for some time, Stewart got in the room, placed a chair atop Martinez's bed, stripped, and sat on the chair. When Martinez entered his room he spotted Stewart sitting there with a glazed expression. Fearing that Stewart had taken drugs and might harm him, Martinez elected to sleep outside on his veranda.

DAVE SMITH (1980–1992)

One great line from Smith came after he said a fan hovered over him when he was in the bullpen and urinated on him at Shea Stadium. Smith managed to joke about it: "That's the first time I've ever been used for long relief."[2]

In a blowout, the Cubs used the 5-feet, 8-inch outfielder Doug Dascenzo in a relief role, causing Smith to say, "We've finally found the perfect short man."

DAVE BRESNAHAN (MINORS, 1984–1987)

There has never been a hidden ball trick like the one performed by Bresnahan, the great-nephew of Roger Bresnahan, one of the greatest catchers of all time. The Williamsport Bills catcher was in the middle of a meaningless minor league contest on August 31, 1987, when he pulled off his unconventional scheme.

He knew the moment was right to unveil his plan when a runner from the opposing Reading team had steamed home, and another runner, Rick Lundblade, pulled up at third. Bresnahan had been waiting for just such a situation.

So, he asked the umpire to call time-out, claiming he needed a new mitt. What the runner on third did not realize was the new glove had, of all things, a peeled potato hidden inside. As the next pitch came in to Bresnahan, he held the potato in his bare hand. He then intentionally threw the vegetable wildly, like a hot potato, past third base and into left field.

Lundblade saw the white blur streak by and naturally assumed it was the ball being thrown his way to pick him off—after all, how many potatoes does a guy see whizzing around a baseball diamond? So at that point he raced to the plate. Bresnahan, of course, was waiting there for him, ball in hand, in a scene straight out of a Warner Brothers cartoon. It was a sort of now-you-see-it, now-you-see-it-again bit of prestidigitation.

However, the ump ruled Lundblade safe, calling the play a balk (or an error depending on another version of his misadventure). Not only that, the creative catcher was ejected from the game, fined $50 by the Williamsport manager, Orlando Gomez, and labeled unprofessional. He even was released from the team by the Cleveland Indians, the parent major league club of the Bills. His .149 average at the time didn't help his cause, either.

Ironically, two nights later this seventh-place team ran a promotion for its last game of the year. Any fan bringing a potato to the game got in for one dollar. Bresnahan even returned to the park and autographed potatoes with the inscription, "This spud's for you."

He also made appearances on David Letterman's television show and on an NBC pre-game show. He once joked of his fame, "I could run for governor of Idaho." In 1988 he again visited Bowman Field, the site of his infamy, where the team that had vilified him now honored him by painting his uniform number of the outfield fence. A team spokesperson quipped, "He's probably the only .149 hitter to ever have his jersey retired."

As if to prove the cliché, "There's nothing new under the sun," it should be noted that the same potato play had already been performed a few years earlier by a high school team who regularly practiced it.

TOM BROWNING (1984–1991)

In 1988, southpaw Browning achieved something many greats never managed, something only a tiny slice of the pitching population ever did—he threw a perfect game. Three years prior to that he became the first rookie to win 20 games since Bob Grim in 1954.

During a 1993 game at Wrigley Field between his Cincinnati Reds and the Cubs, Browning became the most unusual spectator ever at a big league game. Bored, and on a whim, he decided to watch the game not from, say, the bullpen or dugout, but from a rooftop across the street from the ballpark. Originally, he wanted to go inside the scoreboard, but when that plan was thwarted, he had the visiting clubhouse attendant contact the owner of a nearby three-story brownstone. Arrangements were made to sneak Browning out of Wrigley and on to the rooftop of the apartment building. Wearing a sweatsuit over his uniform, the incognito Browning joined a party there. Peeling off his sweatsuit, he cheered his Reds on, doing so in full uniform.

Some time later while circling the bases on a homer, teammate Kevin Mitchell spied a fan on the distant roof rooting exuberantly for him. Out of curiosity, Mitchell asked a cameraman to zoom in on the fan. He was astonished to discover it was Browning.

When Browning returned to the bullpen a few innings later, he waved to his party pals behind right field. He was fined $500 for his actions but expressed the same basic sentiment as Mt. Everest explorer Sir Edmund Hillary: "I just wanted to say I could do it."[3]

Ken Griffey Sr. was with the Reds that day. "Everybody looked up and saw him and said, 'What the hell is Browning doing up on that roof.' He got fined by Marge [Schott, team owner] and the league fined him, too. It was strange—nobody noticed he was gone. Well, being a starting pitcher, they're not going to notice that. Most of the starting pitchers were up in the clubhouse anyway. But he went out of the ballpark in uniform and sat with that crowd. He didn't have any beers or anything, but he was on top of that roof."

Browning's caper was much like the time pitcher Will McEnaney switched places with his identical twin, having his brother dress in his uniform and spend the game in the bullpen while Will watched a football game on television in the clubhouse.

RANDY MYERS (1985–1998)

Yet another lefty reliever, Myers ended his career with a laudatory total of 347 saves. In 1993, his 53 saves set a National League record, since broken. Bill Deane said, "He was a very intense player." After his Reds won the 1990 World Series, everyone was celebrating. "They're looking for Myers, and he was in the weight room, working out to stay in shape. He didn't even take time to celebrate what they played all year for. He was marching to his own drum."

Myers was into military memorabilia, and housed disarmed hand grenades, cartridge bands of ammo, and swords in his locker. He tazed his manager Lou Piniella, causing him to collapse after Piniella had boasted that he felt he could handle a jolt from a stun gun.

When pitcher Bob Ojeda was asked if he'd like to have Randy Myers's fastball, he responded, "Not if I had to have his brains too."

DAN PLESAC (1986–2003)

Reliever Plesac was shellacked one outing, surrendering seven hits and as many runs in 1⅓ innings. After the game, reporters asked him if he could remember the last time he had been hit so hard. He responded, "Yeah, when I was 12 years old and stole $20 out of my father's wallet."

JIM WALEWANDER (1987–1993)

When Walewander was in the minors playing for Toledo, he had just a few possessions in his apartment—a blanket, a pillow, and a dog dish he used for his breakfast cereal. He used tinfoil for curtains. He did own a television set, but it was far from a huge modern one—it was a nine-inch model with bad tubes, so he could only watch it for five minutes at a time.

He played 18 holes of golf using only two clubs and while wearing combat boots. When asked to produce some identification, he would whip out his baseball card. He backed up Lou Whitaker for Detroit, which led to him joking that fans bothered him for autographs, asking Walewander, "Can you get Whitaker's autograph for me?"

He got two hits in his big league debut off a tough pitcher, Mark Langston. When asked how he found Langston, Walewander joked, "I took a left at the on-deck circle and there he was, on the mound." He also said the only difference between the minors and the majors was that the apartment he stayed at as a big leaguer had fewer bugs. Trivia item: he attended the same high school as Hillary Clinton.

MIKE MAKSUDIAN (1992–1994)

Maksudian lasted three seasons in the majors, hitting .220 lifetime. In all, he only got into 34 games, but he belongs in the Flakes' Hall of Fame for his rather repugnant eating habits. On a dare he has been known to eat a locust, a cockroach, a cricket, and a three-inch long lizard. He calmly stated that he had never refused a dare and would do virtually anything other than suicide.

Reliever Mike Timlin said that when he and Maksudian were with Toronto, "We were in Kansas City and he ate bugs. He found large locusts and we took up a collection— $1,500 for him [if he'd eat them]. It was nasty. He took five good chews. It was one of the grossest things I ever saw. He was well known for eating bugs—it was worth it. For $1,500 I even thought of doing it."

Along similar lines, minor leaguer Todd Welborn chewed dirt. He said it didn't cause disease like chewing tobacco, it was free, and nobody bummed any of it off him.

JIM DEDRICK (1995)

Minor league manager Paul Carey said Dedrick and Jimmy Rosso were in the Northwest League around the time the movie *Bull Durham* came out. It must have inspired them to perform a life-imitating-art act. Carey remembered, "They returned to the hotel after a game, tired. They decided they didn't want to play the next day so they took a taxi to the stadium that night around two in the morning and turned on the sprinkler system. It flooded the field and the game was cancelled, but they got caught and sent home. It ended their season, but Russo went on to play with Baltimore."

RYAN DEMPSTER (1998–2013)

A Dempster standard was leaning a large garbage can full of water precariously on a teammates' hotel door. Then he would knock on the door and take off. Naturally, when the door was opened, a cascade of water gushed into the room and onto Dempster's target.

When teammate Will Ohman superglued the zipper open on Dempster's uniform pants before he went to the mound, Dempster sought revenge. The following day Ohman stumbled across a tire from his SUV in the bullpen. The other three tires purloined from his vehicle, which was now sitting atop blocks, were hidden around the ballpark, forcing Ohman to go on a lengthy treasure hunt.

Dempster once threatened to rent a billboard near Wrigley Field and plaster the name of a player on it complete with his cell phone number and the words, "Call Me Anytime."

He loves to perform magic tricks, like turning a $100 bill belonging to, say, a patron at a bar, into a $1 bill. He shows the trick, then when the man asks him to change it back to his $100 bill, Dempster teases, "If I could do that, I'd get in a lot fewer bar fights." Then Dempster enjoys seeing how long the victim follows him around, puppy-like, until he relents and returns the bill.[4]

CHAD PARONTO (2001–2009)

"Right now," Chipper Jones said in a 2007 interview, "Chad Paronto is probably the funniest man on the planet as far as our little world is concerned here in Braves' nation." Paronto may not have made a big splash in the majors, but when he was in the minors with the Pawtucket Red Sox, he was voted by his peers as the funniest player on the team, the best dancer, and the best teammate.

Braves teammate Jeff Francoeur said, "He's built like a defensive end or an offensive guard," which tied in directly with how he kept teammates loose and laughing with his wild ways. For instance, in a YouTube video, Paronto is the Hulkster, amusing teammates with an imitation of Hulk Hogan, exhorting his audience by preening and flexing around the clubhouse, and dancing to "I Am a Real American."

DIDI GREGORIUS (2012–)

Marty Appel said Gregorius, who was born in Amsterdam and whose real first name is Mariekson, "seems to be colorful with his tweets. He's the team barber, giving players haircuts in the clubhouse. He seems like the kind of guy you'd want to be around. He's got a lot going for him."

Another New York writer, Mike Vaccaro, said that Gregorius, aka Sir Didi, is the kind of guy who loves to play the game, one "who is not afraid to show he's having fun, that he's enjoying himself and his teammates. He's a reminder that while you're playing for pretty serious stakes, you don't always have to take yourself all that seriously in order to succeed."

Just as Satchel Paige had nicknames for his pitches, Gregorius created names for his celebratory handshakes. Some were "Turning the Wheel,"

"Salt Shake," "the Explosion," and "the Salsa," which is much more of a shuffling dance move than a handshake.

Vaccaro said, "He's a real good go-to guy for quotes. If you need a great take on the game that was just played, he's the guy you want to talk to. I find him a very pleasant person to talk to. He's a guy who loves to play as much as anybody I've ever been around."

Gregorius once did a Candid Camera–like gag, capturing on video his portrayal of a men's clothing salesman. His only disguise was wearing glasses, which he said was sufficient deception for Clark Kent.

YOLMER SANCHEZ (2014–)

In May of 2018, the White Sox resiliently came back from losing 5–1 to the Twins to winning on a walk-off homer by Trayce Thompson (the brother of NBA star Klay and the son of former NBA star Mychal). When Thompson neared home plate, teammates got ready to drench him by pouring the contents of water coolers on him. One Chicago player, Yolmer Sanchez, who had driven in two runs, decided to celebrate by pouring his cooler over his own head. Quite unorthodox.

CODY DECKER (2015) AND JORGE REYES (MINORS, 2009–)

Appel called Decker "kind of a career minor leaguer. He's sort of Crash Davis with all the home runs he's hit. He's what they call a 4A player, good for Triple-A ball, not quite good enough for the majors. He is a guy like Fritz Peterson, who would go to great lengths to set up a really good practical joke. He's kind of a throwback with his elaborate schemes. He's really an interesting character."

One such joke took place in 2014 when Jeff Francoeur was the victim of an amazing, and stunningly interminable practical joke. He related some background first. He signed late in spring training with the Padres, and reported to their El Paso minor league team. Pat Murphy was a coach there. He was the man who Francoeur credits "for getting me back to the big leagues for my last two-and-a-half years. If it wasn't for him, I probably would have quit. He kept me going at Triple-A saying, 'You gotta keep getting better.' Anyway, I show up the first day we're taking batting practice and the pitchers are in left field. I smoke a ball there and every-body scattered except this one guy. And I look at Murph and say, 'What the hell's wrong with that guy?' He goes, 'Oh, you didn't know? He's deaf.'" At that point, Francoeur had swallowed the bait.

"So the next morning, we opened up in Tucson and practiced there. Murph tells everybody we had a meeting at 9:30, but then he tells every-body except me that they're going to meet at 8:30." At the meeting they hatched the plan to have Jorge Reyes pretend he was deaf. "They carried it out for 16 days on me," said Francoeur incredulously. "That's a long time. I got to give them credit. I ended up buying the whole team a spread from Longhorn when I found out about it because to do that for 16 days! Everybody played it great.

"Reyes was unbelievable. He would sit on the airplane and just sit there—he'd read and that was it, he didn't have earphones on, nothing. It was hilarious." When Francoeur wanted to communicate with him, "I literally patted him on the chest and yelled at him, 'Great job,' and all these people around me—nobody laughs. The whole crew was in on this. They all played it off."

Why did they finally break character and tell Francoeur the truth? "I think it was because my dad flew up to see me in Tacoma. They were like, 'This is how stupid your son is.'"

Teammate Cody Decker, who is also an actor, was instrumental in the joke. He also produced a short film focusing on the elaborate prank. He titled it "On Jeff Ears," and it can seen it on YouTube. The film's credits include Reyes playing "The Deaf Kid," other players as "Backstabbing Teammates," and the good-natured Francoeur playing "The Idiot."

"It was Murph's idea and then Cody ran with it—he filmed the whole thing." Decker is a card-holding member of the Screen Actors Guild and appeared in an NBC show, *State of Affairs*, playing a mall security guard who is blown up. He also has held charity events to raise money for deaf people.

BRENT SUTER (2016–)

Suter, a Brewers pitcher, went to Cincinnati's Moeller High School, which also produced Barry Larkin, Ken Griffey Jr., and Buddy Bell as well as Bell's sons, Mike and David. Suter's father played safety for Penn

State's national championship team of 1982, while his mother won four letters as a swimmer there and was also on a championship squad.

Suter spent Game 1 of the 2018 National League Championship Series in the dugout despite not being on the roster, something not permitted. Suter tweeted and promised that if he would be allowed to continue to watch future games from the dugout he would behave and be just a bit weird.

An internet video shows Suter playing catch before a game with a fan behind the right-field wall. That type of interaction with fans is extremely rare. Not unlike Roger McDowell, Suter even ran deep pass patterns, hauling in the ball the rifle-armed fan threw.

The genial and articulate Suter—he attended Harvard—sees himself as "the left-handed guy that's goofy. Not a prankster. More like a high-energy goofy guy." His peak moment of silliness may be the viral video parody he did of the Jim Carrey movie *Dumb and Dumber*. "The marketing department asked me to be Lloyd Christmas in the video, and I love doing Jim Carrey. It blew up and before you know it, Carrey tweeted me saying, 'You either have some comedy chops or a severe behavioral disorder.' I came back, 'It's the latter.'"

CONCLUSION

That's it. We've come to the end of a long cast of colorful characters even though, inevitably, the game will continue to churn out more wits, flakes, and clowns. A 1979 magazine article lamented the state of baseball, calling players colorless. Men such as Suter, Puig, and Bauer prove such hasty appraisals to be incorrect.

Plus, to those who say there's no place in the game for the clowns and colorful characters, a rebuttal could come from a character in the movie *Stripes*. An army sergeant was listening to one of his men belligerently saying things like if anyone touches him, he'd kill him, or if anyone calls him by his real first name, Francis, which he loathes, he'd kill him. The sergeant silences him with a terse, "Lighten up, Francis."

It sounds like the kid who dashed off a unique fan letter to Moe Drabowsky had it right years ago when he wrote, "Baseball needs more nuts like you."

NOTES

1. BACKGROUND

1. Al Drooz, "But Memories of Hack Wilson Fade Away," *Baseball Digest*, October 1974, 56.

2. Bob Chieger, *Voices of Baseball* (New York: Atheneum, 1983), 47–48.

3. John Kuenster, ed., *The Best of Baseball Digest* (Chicago: Ivan R. Dee, 2006), 211.

4. Vernona Gomez and Lawrence Goldstone, *Lefty* (New York: Ballantine Books, 2012), 303.

5. Ibid., 370.

6. Jack Murphy, "Frenchy Bordagaray—Just Too Zany, Even for Casey," *Sporting News*, January 24, 1970, 46.

2. KINGS OF THE HILL

1. *Baseball Digest*, November 1978, 96.

2. Lee Allen, *Cooperstown Corner* (Cleveland: SABR, 1990), 14.

3. Bill James, *The New Bill James Historical Baseball Abstract* (New York: Free Press, 2001), 493.

4. Derek Zumsteg, *The Cheater's Guide to Baseball* (Boston: Houghton Mifflin, 2007), 103.

5. Curt Smith, *The Storytellers* (New York: Macmillan, 1995), 60.

6. John P. Carmichael, "They'll Never Forget Dizzy Dean," *Baseball Digest*, October 1974, 48.

7. Bill Lee and Jim Prime, *Baseball Eccentrics* (Chicago: Triumph Books, 2007), 7.

8. Smith, *The Storytellers*, 60.

9. Lew Freedman, *Baseball's Funnymen* (Jefferson, NC: McFarland, 2017), 56.

10. Myron Cope, *Broken Cigars* (Englewood Cliffs, NJ: Prentice-Hall, 1968), 15.

11. Ibid.

12. Myron Cope, "A Dialogue between Baseball's Big Mouths," *True*, August 1965, 31.

13. Lee and Prime, *Baseball Eccentrics*, 102.

14. John Thorn and John Holway, *The Pitcher* (London: Simon & Schuster, 1987), 107.

15. Frank Dolson, "Sparky Lyle: The Yankees' Life Saver," *Baseball Digest*, October 1973, 43.

16. Bill Lee, with Dick Lally, *The Wrong Stuff* (New York: Viking Press, 1984), 26.

17. Thorn and Holway, *The Pitcher*, 31.

18. Bill Shlain, *Oddballs* (New York: Penguin Books, 1989), 195.

19. Mike Blake, *Baseball Chronicles* (Cincinnati: Betterway Books, 1994), 273.

20. Wayne Stewart, "Gotcha," *Beckett Focus on Future Stars*, August 1992, 57–59.

21. Thorn and Holway, *The Pitcher*, 33.

22. Rick Sorci, "Baseball Profile," *Baseball Digest*, June 1992, 37.

23. Deron Snyder, "Inside Pitch," *USA Today Baseball Weekly*, October 13–19, 1999, 3.

24. Jake Mintz, "Fernando Rodney Makes the Exceptionally Fun Oakland A's Even More Exciting," August 20, 2018, https://www.mlb.com/cut4/get-to-know-fernando-rodney-the-newest-oakland-athletic/c-289713912.

3. KINGS OF THE DIAMOND

1. Bill Bishop, "Casey Stengel," n.d., https://sabr.org/bioproj/person/bd6a83d8.

2. Paul Dickson, *Baseball's Greatest Quotations* (New York: Harper Perennial, 1991), 421.

3. Bob McCoy, "Brew Crew's Mr. Malaprop," *Sporting News*, April 11, 1988, 10.

4. "Insiders Say," *Sporting News*, April 11, 1970, 4.

5. Bill Lee and Jim Prime, *Baseball Eccentrics* (Chicago: Triumph Books, 2007), 137.

6. John Thorn and John Holway, *The Pitcher* (London: Simon & Schuster, 1987), 24.

7. Leonard Shecter, "Steve Barber, Pitcher," *Sport*, May 1964, 60.

8. Roy Blount Jr., "Yogi: What Did Berra Say, When Did He Say It and What Does It All Mean?" September 16, 2014, https://www.si.com/mlb/2014/09/16/yogi-berra-si-60-rou-blount-jr.

9. Dan Schlossberg, "Berra Became American Treasure," *USA Today Sports Weekly*, September 30–October 6, 2015, 28.

10. "Insiders Say," *Sporting News*, July 11, 1970, 4.

11. Harvey Araton, *Driving Mr. Yogi* (New York: Houghton Mifflin Harcourt, 2012), 120–121.

12. Joe Garagiola and Martin Quigley, *Baseball Is a Funny Game* (New York: J. P. Lippincott, 1960), 44.

13. Bill James, *The New Bill James Historical Baseball Abstract* (New York: Free Press, 2001), 527.

14. Dave Brown, *Baseball Bafflers* (New York: Black Dog & Leventhal Publishers, 2001), 75.

15. Mike Puma, "A Hall of Fame Personality," n.d., http://www.espn.com/classic/biography/s/Piersall_Jim.html.

16. Julie Cart, "Jimmy Piersall: A Bit Too Colorful," June, 29, 1986, http://articles.latimes.com/1986-06-29/sports/sp-130_1_jimmy-piersall/2.

17. Bob Dolgan, "Piersall More Than a Little Rascal," *Cleveland Plain Dealer*, June 6, 2001, 8-D.

18. John Kuenster, ed., *The Best of Baseball Digest* (Chicago: Ivan R. Dee, 2006), 293.

19. Ross Newhan, "Big Stu Talks of Angel-Like Quality in Glove," *Sporting News*, March 22, 1969, 16.

20. Bruce Shlain, *Oddballs* (New York: Penguin Books, 1989), 122.

21. Dick Mackey, *Baseball Digest*, August 1973, 73.

22. Jim Bouton, *Ball Four* (New York: Dell Publishing, 1970), 313.

23. "Class A Notes," *Sporting News*, August 6, 1984, 56.

24. Lew Freedman, *Baseball's Funnymen* (Jefferson, NC: McFarland, 2017), 148.

25. Roy Blount Jr., "How Did This Mild-Mannered Outfielder on a Sane Metropolitan Team Become the Flakiest Man in Baseball?" *Inside Sports*, July 1981, 80.

26. Jason Turbow, with Michael Duda, *The Baseball Codes* (New York: Pantheon Books, 2010), 18.

27. Kevin Kerrane, *Dollar Sign on the Muscle* (New York: Fireside, 1984), 70.

28. Rory Costello, "Kevin Rhomberg," n.d., https://sabr.org/bioproj/person/b9fc86d.

29. Bruce Anderson, "A Most Unlikely Slugger," May 23, 1988, https://www.si.com/vault/1988/05/23/117702/a-most-unlikely-slugger.

30. John Kruk, with Paul Hagen, *I Ain't an Athlete, Lady* (New York: Simon & Schuster, 1994), 97.

31. Seamus Kearney, "John Kruk," n.d., https://sabr.org/bioproj/person/6afcbd09.

32. Ibid.

33. Nick Underhill, "The 10 Best Manny Being Manny Moments," April 9, 2011, https://www.masslive.com/sports/2011/04/the_10_best_manny_being_manny.html.

34. James Wagner, "Dodgers' Yasiel Puig Is an Object of Affection Once More," October 17, 2017, https://www.nytimes.com/2017/10/17/sports/baseball/dodgers-yasiel-puig-nlcs.html.

35. Ibid.

4. QUICK TAKES ON THE PRINCES OF PRANKS AND ZANINESS

1. Joseph Wancho, "Jim Kern," n.d., https://sabr.org/bioproj/person/c0f238d6.

2. Glenn Liebman, "Some Major Leaguers Were Disasters on Defense!" *Baseball Digest*, November 1992, 42.

3. John Thorn and John Holway, *The Pitcher* (London: Simon & Schuster, 1987), 32.

4. Mike McKenzie, "The Inside Track," *Inside Sports*, September 30, 1981, 11.

5. Kostya Kennedy, "The Mambo King," *Sports Illustrated*, June 14, 1999, 38.

6. Mike Klingaman, "Orioles Outfielder Jackie Brandt's Goofy Inconsistency Was Consistent, July 30, 2015, https://www.baltimoresun.com/sports/orioles/bs-sp-daffy-dozen-jackie-brandt-0730-20150729-story.html.

7. Glenn Liebman, "Here Are Some New Names for Humor Hall of Fame," *Baseball Digest*, March 1992, 23.

8. Sam Blair, *Baseball Digest*, March 1992, 17.

9. Maxwell Kates, "Norm Cash," n.d., https://sabr.org/bioproj/person/b683238c.

10. "A Matter of Simple Arithmetic," *Baseball Digest*, June 1992, 67.

11. Deanna Boyd, "Hall: 'Guilty of Lifestyle,'" *Chronicle Telegram*, June 21, 2009, F3.

5. THE ROYAL JESTERS

1. J. Ronald Oakley, *Baseball's Last Golden Age, 1946–1960* (Jefferson, NC: McFarland, 1994), 277.

2. John Thorn and John Holway, *The Pitcher* (London: Simon & Schuster, 1987), 33.

3. Wayne Stewart, "Here's Recap of a Few Zany Moments from Last Season," *Baseball Digest*, April 1994, 73.

4. Kostya Kennedy, "Ryan Dempster," *Sports Illustrated*, July 4, 2005, 31.

BIBLIOGRAPHY

BOOKS

Allen, Lee. *Cooperstown Corner*. Cleveland: SABR, 1990.
Alvarez, Mark. *Baseball for the Fun of It*. Cleveland: SABR, 1997.
Araton, Harvey. *Driving Mr. Yogi*. New York: Houghton Mifflin Harcourt, 2012.
Barthel, Thomas. *Pepper Martin: A Baseball Biography*. Jefferson, NC: McFarland, 2003.
Berney, Louis. *Tales from the Orioles Dugout*. New York: Sports Publishing, 2016.
Blake, Mike. *Baseball Chronicles*. Cincinnati: Betterway Books, 1994.
———. *Baseball's Bad Hops and Lucky Bounces*. Cincinnati: Betterway Books, 1995.
Bouton, Jim. *Ball Four*. New York: Dell Publishing, 1970.
———. *I'm Glad You Didn't Take It Personally*. New York: William Morrow, 1971.
Brown, Dave. *Baseball Bafflers*. New York: Black Dog & Leventhal Publishers, 2001.
Cairns, Bob. *Pen Men*. New York: St. Martin's Press, 1992.
Chieger, Bob. *Voices of Baseball*. New York: Atheneum, 1983.
Connor, Anthony J. *Voices from Cooperstown*. New York: Galahad Books, 1982.
Connor, Floyd. *Baseball's Most Wanted*. Dulles, VA: Brassey's, 2000.
Cope, Myron. *Broken Cigars*. Englewood Cliffs, NJ: Prentice-Hall, 1968.
Dickson, Paul. *Baseball's Greatest Quotations*. New York: Harper Perennial, 1991.
Einstein, Charles, ed. *The Fireside Book of Baseball*. New York: Simon and Schuster, 1956.
Engle, Brad, and Wayne Stewart. *Tales from First Base*. Washington, DC: Potomac Books, 2013.
Erskine, Carl. *Tales from the Dodgers Dugout*. New York: Sports Publishing, 2014.
Freedman, Lew. *Baseball's Funnymen*. Jefferson, NC: McFarland, 2017.
Garagiola, Joe. *It's Anybody's Ballgame*. Chicago: Contemporary Books, 1988.
Garagiola, Joe, and Martin Quigley. *Baseball Is a Funny Game*. New York: J. P. Lippincott, 1960.
Gomez, Vernona, and Lawrence Goldstone. *Lefty*. New York: Ballantine Books, 2012.
Hunter, Jim "Catfish," and Armen Keteyian. *Catfish: My Life in Baseball*. New York: McGraw-Hill, 1988.
James, Bill. *The New Bill James Historical Baseball Abstract*. New York: Free Press, 2001.
Kerrane, Kevin. *Dollar Sign on the Muscle*. New York: Fireside, 1984.
Kruk, John, with Paul Hagen. *I Ain't an Athlete, Lady*. New York: Simon & Schuster, 1994.
Kuenster, John, ed. *The Best of Baseball Digest*. Chicago: Ivan R. Dee, 2006.
Lee, Bill, with Dick Lally. *The Wrong Stuff*. New York: Viking, 1984.
Lee, Bill, and Jim Prime. *Baseball Eccentrics*. Chicago: Triumph Books, 2007.

Lyons, Steve, and Rick Talley. *Some of My Best Friends Are Crazy*. New York: Macmillan, 1990.

Moffi, Larry. *This Side of Cooperstown*. Iowa City: University of Iowa Press, 1996.

Nash, Bruce, and Allan Zullo. *The Baseball Hall of Shame 3*. New York: Pocket Books. 1987.

Nathan, David H., ed. *Baseball Quotations*. New York: Ballantine Books, 1993.

Oakley, J. Ronald. *Baseball's Last Golden Age, 1946–1960*. Jefferson, NC: McFarland, 1994.

Pepe, Phil. *Catfish, Yaz, and Hammerin' Hank*. Chicago: Triumph Books, 2005.

Peterson, Fritz. *Mickey Mantle Is Going to Heaven*. Denver: Outskirts Press, 2009.

Pluto, Terry, and Burt Graeff. *Super Joe*. New York: Stein and Day, 1981.

Ritter, Lawrence S. *The Glory of Their Times*. New York: Macmillan, 1966.

Shannon, Mike. *Tales from the Dugout*. Lincolnwood, IL: Contemporary Publishing, 1997.

Shlain, Bruce. *Oddballs*. New York: Penguin Books, 1989.

Smith, Curt. *The Storytellers*. New York: Macmillan, 1995.

Stewart, Wayne. *Baseball Bafflers*. New York: Sterling Publishing, 1999.

———. *Baseball Oddities*. New York: Sterling Publishing, 1998.

———. *Baseball Puzzlers*. New York: Sterling Publishing, 2000.

———. *Fathers, Sons, and Baseball*. Guilford, CT: Globe Pequot, 2002.

———. *The Gigantic Book of Baseball Quotations*. New York: Skyhorse Publishing, 2007.

———. *Hitting Secrets of the Pros*. New York: McGraw-Hill, 2004.

———. *Indians on the Game*. Cleveland: Gray & Company, 2001.

———. *Match Wits with Baseball Experts*. New York: Sterling Publishing, 2006.

———. *Pitching Secrets of the Pros*. New York: McGraw-Hill, 2004.

Sullivan, George. *Baseball's Wacky Players*. New York: Dodd, Mead, 1984.

Thorn, John, and John B. Holway. *The Pitcher*. London: Simon & Schuster, 1987.

Turbow, Jason, with Michael Duda. *The Baseball Codes*. New York: Pantheon Books, 2010.

Williams, Billy, with Fred Mitchell. *Billy Williams*. Chicago: Triumph Books, 2008.

Zumsteg, Derek. *The Cheater's Guide to Baseball*. Boston: Houghton Mifflin, 2007.

MAGAZINES

Blount, Roy, Jr. "How Did This Mild-Mannered Outfielder on a Sane Metropolitan Team Become the Flakiest Man in Baseball?" *Inside Sports*, July 1981.

Carmichael, John P. "They'll Never Forget Dizzy Dean." *Baseball Digest*, October 1974.

Cope, Myron. "A Dialogue between Baseball's Big Mouths." *True*, August 1965.

Dolson, Frank. "Sparky Lyle: The Yankees' Life Saver." *Baseball Digest*, October 1973.

Downey, Mike. "Life in the Bullpen Often Provides Comic Relief." *Baseball Digest*, October 1981.

Drooz, Al. "But Memories of Hack Wilson Fade Away." *Baseball Digest*, October 1974.

Kennedy, Kostya. "Ryan Dempster." *Sports Illustrated*, July 4, 2005.

———. "The Mambo King." *Sports Illustrated*, June 14, 1999.

King, Peter. "Joe Charboneau: A New Star Shines in Cleveland." *Baseball Digest*, November 1980.

Kuenster, John. "Here's a Personal List of the Best and Worst over the Last 50 Years." *Baseball Digest*, June 2007.

Liebman, Glenn. "Here Are Some New Names for Humor Hall of Fame." *Baseball Digest*, March 1992.

———. "Some Major Leaguers Were Disasters on Defense!" *Baseball Digest*, November 1992.

Lyon, Bill. "Whatever Happened to All Those Bullpen Pranksters?" *Baseball Digest*, November 1977.

McCoy, Bob. "Brew Crew's Mr. Malaprop." *Sporting News*, April 11, 1988.

McKenzie, Mike. "The Inside Track." *Inside Sports*, September 30, 1981.

Murphy, Jack. "Frenchy Bordagaray—Just Too Zany, Even for Casey." *Sporting News*, January 24, 1970.

Newhan, Ross. "Big Stu Talks of Angel-Like Quality in Glove." *Sporting News*, March 22, 1969.

Ribowsky, Mark. "Baseball's Unheralded Wild and Crazy Guys." *Sport*, June 1979.

Schlossberg, Dan. "Berra Became American Treasure." *USA Today Sports Weekly*, September 30–October 6, 2015.

Shecter, Leonard. "Steve Barber, Pitcher." *Sport*, May 1964.

Snyder, Deron. "Inside Pitch." *USA Today Baseball Weekly*, October 13–19, 1999.

Sorci, Rick. "Baseball Profile." *Baseball Digest*, June 1992.

Stewart, Wayne. "Gotcha." *Beckett Focus on Future Stars*, August 1992.

———. "Here's Recap of a Few Zany Moments from Last Season." *Baseball Digest*, April 1994.

———. "Humorous Side Remarks Enliven the Baseball Scene." *Baseball Digest*, June 1993.

NOTE: In addition to the above sources, various issues of the *Sporting News* and *Baseball Digest* were used throughout my research. Those directly quoted in this book have been fully cited in the endnotes.

NEWSPAPERS

Boyd, Deanna. "Hall: 'Guilty of Lifestyle.'" *Chronicle Telegram*, June 21, 2009.

Dolgan, Bob. "Piersall More Than a Little Rascal." *Cleveland Plain Dealer*, June 6, 2001.

Stone, Larry. "The Art of Baseball: A Tradition of Superstition." *Seattle Times*, September 26, 2005.

WEBSITES

Websites for the following newspapers and organizations were consulted. Specific articles used for this book have been fully cited in the endnotes.

Baltimore Sun: https://www.baltimoresun.com/
Banished to the Pen: http://www.banishedtothepen.com/
Baseball Reference: https://www.baseball-reference.com/
Bleacher Report: https://bleacherreport.com/
ESPN: http://www.espn.com/
Fox Sports: https://www.foxsports.com/
Los Angeles Times: https://www.latimes.com/
Major League Baseball: https://www.mlb.com/
New York Times: https://www.nytimes.com/
SBNation: https://www.truebluela.com/
Society for American Baseball Research: https://sabr.org/
Sports Illustrated: https://www.si.com/

INDEX

ABOUT THE AUTHOR

Wayne Stewart was born in Pittsburgh and raised in Donora, Pennsylvania, a town that produced four big league baseball players, including Stan Musial and the father–son Griffeys. Stewart was on the same Donora High School baseball team as classmate Ken Griffey Sr.

Stewart began covering sports in 1978, freelancing for publications such as *Baseball Digest*, *Beckett Baseball Card Monthly*, *Baseball Bulletin*, *Boys' Life*, and for official team publications of 10 major league clubs, including the Braves, Orioles, Red Sox, Yankees, and Dodgers.

He has interviewed sports immortals such as Joe Montana, Mike Ditka, Don Maynard, Larry Bird, George Gervin, Robert Parish, Nolan Ryan, Bob Gibson, Rickey Henderson, and Ken Griffey Jr. and has written biographies of Babe Ruth, Stan Musial, and Alex Rodriguez. In addition, he has written books ranging from *Fathers, Sons, and Baseball* to *All the Moves I Had*, the autobiography he cowrote with Hall of Fame wide receiver Raymond Berry.

This is his 34th book. Stewart has appeared as a baseball expert/historian on numerous radio and television shows, including an ESPN Classic program, on ESPN radio, and on the Pat Williams radio program. He also hosted radio shows for a Lorain, Ohio, station including pregame reports prior to Notre Dame football games and Cleveland Indians baseball games, and a call-in talk show. He has written for several newspapers, and some of his works have been used in eight anthologies.

A teacher for 31 years, Stewart now lives in Amherst, Ohio. For more information about Stewart and his books, go to https://waynestewartonsports.blog/.